IRISH TEXTS SOCIETY

comann na sзríbeann зaeòilзe

VOL. XII

[1910]

buiLe suibne

(THE FRENZY OF SUIBHNE)

BEING

The Adventures of Suibhne Geilt

A MIDDLE-IRISH ROMANCE

EDITED

With Translation, Introduction, Notes, and Glossary

BY

J. G. O'KEEFFE

WITH A NEW INTRODUCTION (1996)

BY

JOSEPH FALAKY NAGY

LONDON

IRISH TEXTS SOCIETY

1913/1996

First Published 1913

Reprinted 1996
with a New Introduction
by Joseph Falaky Nagy

Irish Texts Society
c/o Royal Bank of Scotland
Drummonds Branch
49 Charing Cross
Admiraly Arch
London SW 1A 2DX

ISBN 1 870 16612 4

Reprinted in Ireland, 1996
at the Elo Press Ltd.,
Dublin 8, Ireland
and bound by Duffy Bookbinders Ltd.
Dublin, Ireland

CONTENTS

INTRODUCTION TO 1996 EDITION
BY JOSEPH FALAKY NAGY
OF BUILE SUIBHNE: THE FRENZY OF SUIBHNE

The images of the poet as hunter and as warrior are well-established themes in medieval Celtic literatures, as exemplified for instance in the Irish traditions about the *rígfhénnid* Finn mac Cumaill, who is champion, tracker, and poet (*éices*) in one.[1] The poet's mastery over words and meters, the power of his metered words in the service, or to the detriment, of his poetic subjects, and the intense professional competitiveness among poets: all form a milieu that corresponds strikingly to the world of heroic warriors, an analogy sustained and cultivated in the idiom of praise poetry as well as in the repertoire of tales of which the poets of medieval Ireland and Wales were supposed to be in control. Hence, in so many of the poems that have survived from medieval Celtic traditions we are witness to a subtle merger between the vaunted heroic acts commemorated in the verse and the vaunting poetic act itself that memorializes them.[2] Moreover, in the rhetoric and legendry of poets, the poet as one whose aim is true, who finds his 'mark', can be figured as a hunter in pursuit of game that has left a trail of signs. The poet, in both a literary and pre-literary sense, is a 'reader', who can find his way both to the truth and to the proper and necessary form his poem should take. This talent, sensitive enough to context to generate advantageous misreadings as well as readings, is evident in the quick response of the Continental bard described in a classical source, who, upon being rewarded with gold flung by his departing patron out of his chariot and falling onto the tracks left in the vehicle's wake, compounds his original praise with the observation that even the patron's trail produces a miraculous sign of his wealth and magnanimity.[3] On a less spectacular, more intimate, and yet no less

1. The synergistic relationship among these roles in the narrative tradition centered on Finn is the topic of the author's The Wisdom of the Outlaw: The Boyhood Deeds of Finn in Gaelic Narrative Tradition (Berkeley, Los Angeles, and London, 1985), especially pp. 124-92.
2. This merger is by no means unique to the poetics of Celtic traditions. See Richard Martin's study of heroism as speech act in Homeric epic, *The Language of Heroes: Speech and Performance in the Iliad* (Ithaca and London, 1989).
3. Athenaeus 4.37 (following Posidonius), as quoted by J. J. Tierney, 'The Celtic Ethnography of Posidonius', *Proceedings of the Royal Irish Academy*, 60 C (1960), 225-26. Appropriately enough, the patron leaving the conspicuous trail is called Louernios 'Fox'.

[1]

profound level, the author of the famous ninth-century Irish poem addressed to his cat compares his own human acts of scholarship, including the composition of the poem itself, to the feline's activity of tracking down mice.[4] The poet is a man of action and a predator, while the poem he produces and the vision the poem communicates are his captured prey, proudly put on display.

And yet there is another side to the poetic craft, an aspect that threatens the poet's controlling stance as viewer, as speaker, as reader of signs. The force of poetry can dislodge the occupants of the roles of 'subject' and 'object' in the poetic utterance: he who sheds light upon others is illuminated himself; the bringer of fame invents his own conspicuousness; the reader of signs becomes a sign himself in a play of mirrors; and the wielder of poetic power can become a victim of the poetic institution. The moment that a person receives the inspiration to see and speak like a poet can also be the moment that he is robbed of his identity, his autonomy, and his freedom from the tyranny of words, both his and those of others. This is precisely the moment undergone by the figure of Suibne in the late Middle Irish text edited and translated here by J. G. O'Keeffe. And so Suibne's 'frenzy' (*buile*), flowing as it does out of this moment, is more than a wrenching personal experience. It constitutes a remarkable adventure in the inner workings of the persona of the poet as he vacillates between power and powerlessness.[5]

As befits a figure whose adventures and fame are predicated on his outsider status, much of the scholarly explorations of Suibne and

---

4. Edited and translated in the Thesaurus Palaeohibernicus: A Collection of Old-Irish Glosses, Scholia Prose and Verse, ed. Whitley Stokes and John Strachan, Vol. 2 (Cambridge, 1903; repr. 1975), pp. 293-94. This famous poem is from the same miscellany of Irish verse included in a ninth-century manuscript (Codex Sancti Pauli) that contains the poem attributed to Suibne discussed below (pp. 29-30).

5. The plight of Suibne has been an inspiration to some of his modern colleagues in the crafts of storytelling and poetry, such as Flann O'Brien (*At Swim-Two-Birds* [London, 1939]) and Seamus Heaney (*Sweeney Astray* [Derry, 1983]). On Heaney's rendering of the *Buile Shuibne*, see H. A. Kelly, 'Heaney's Sweeney: The Poet as Version-Maker', *Philological Quarterly*, 65 (1986), 293-310. Ms. Annette Pehnt of the University of Freiburg is currently working on a Ph.D. dissertation examining the appropriation of the Suibhne legend by nineteenth- and twentieth-century authors.

the *Buile Shuibhne* have centred on the question of whether the affinities among Suibne, the celebrated Welsh figure of Myrddin Wyllt ('Wild Man Myrddin [Merlin]'),[6] and the legendary northern British madman Lailoken[7] constitute a shared Celtic 'type' or are to be explained by means of a theory of intercultural borrowings taking place in the seventh century (see O'Keeffe's introduction, p. xxxv). The features common to the three narrative traditions were neatly summarized by Kenneth Jackson in his 1940 article 'The Motive of the Threefold Death in the Story of Suibhne Geilt':

> A man goes mad in a battle (Mag Rath, A.D. 637, Suibhne; Arfderydd in Cumberland A.D. 574, Myrddin – Lailoken – Merlin) because of the curse of a saint (Suibhne) or a horrible vision in the sky (Lailoken; traces of it in Suibhne) or fear of the battle (traces in Suibhne) and grief for the slain (Merlin). He takes to a life in the woods

---

6. The origins and development of the Myrddin/Merlin legend are the subjects of A. O. H. Jarman, The Legend of Merlin (Cardiff, 1960); 'Early Stages in the Development of the Myrddin Legend', Astudiaethau ar yr Hengerdd / Studies in Old Welsh Poetry, ed. Rachel Bromwich and R. Brinley Jones (Cardiff, 1978), pp. 326-49; and 'The Merlin Legend and the Welsh Tradition of Prophecy', in The Arthur of the Welsh: The Arthurian Legend in Medieval Welsh Literature, ed. Rachel Bromwich, Jarman, and Brynley F. Roberts (Cardiff, 1991), pp. 117-45; Jenny Rowland, Early Welsh Saga Poetry: A Study and Edition of the Englynion (Cambridge, 1990), pp. 200-202; and Jan Ziolkowski, 'The Nature of Prophecy in Geoffrey of Monmouth's Vita Merlini', Poetry and Prophecy: The Beginnings of a Literary Tradition, ed. James L. Kugel (Ithaca and London, 1990), pp. 151-62. More general studies of the figure of the wild man in literature and art beyond the Celtic world are Ronald M. Smith, 'King Lear and the Merlin Tradition', Modern Language Quarterly, 7 (1946), 153-74; Richard Bernheimer, Wild Men in the Middle Ages: A Study in Art, Sentiment, and Demonology (Cambridge, MA, 1952); Edward Dudley and Maximillian Novak, eds., The Wild Man Within: An Image in Western Thought from the Renaissance to Romanticism (Pittsburgh, 1972); David A. Wells, The Wild Man from the Epic of Gilgamesh to Hartman von Aue's Iwein: Reflections on the Development of a Theme in World Literature (Belfast, 1975); and Timothy Husband, The Wild Man: Medieval Myth and Symbolism, with the assistance of Gloria Gilmore-House (New York, 1988).
7. The Lailoken legend and its intimate connection with traditions centered on the sixth-century Saint Kentigern of Glasgow are discussed by Kenneth H. Jackson in 'The Sources for the Life of St Kentigern', *Studies in the Early British Church*, Nora K. Chadwick and others (Cambridge, 1958), pp. 328-30, 355.

(all), where he lives on berries, roots, or apples, etc. (all). Being mad, he is a prophet, and has dealings with various visitors (all) to whom he prophesies (Myrddin, Lailoken, Merlin). Finally, he makes friends with a saint (Suibhne with Moling; Lailoken with Kentigern) and dies.[8]

Capping off this basically biographical pattern in the Welsh and Northern British tradition is the motif of the 'threefold death'. The wild man predicts three different scenarios for his death, all of which, much to the surprise of those to whom the prediction was made, take place simultaneously or in rapid succession. As Jackson noted, this motif is missing from the *Buile Shuibhne*, at least in a fully developed form, but is to be found in connection with the outcome of the story of Suibne's tragic death as we can reconstruct it from a Middle Irish poem concerning Moling and Suibne.[9] However, the prophecy is issued not by the (by then dead) wild man but by the saint who takes Suibne under his wing, Moling, and the bizarre death serves as the punishment of Suibne's slayer (here called Grácc, not Mongán, as in the *Buile Shuibhne*).

Keenly aware that definite conclusions are beyond any scholar's reach in this matter, Jackson proposed that the 'wild man' story, consisting of the elements listed above, may have developed among the Dál Riata, a people of east Ulster who during the early middle ages expanded their domain into what are now the Highlands and islands of Scotland. From the Dál Riata, who in Scotland were located at a 'crossroads' of Goidelic and Brythonic cultures, the story entered Irish tradition in association with the figure of Suibne, while it also spread into Strathclyde and ultimately to Wales. Jackson's reasons for positing diffusion instead of a common Celtic heritage as the explanation of the affinities among the three 'wild men', and for

---

8. In *Féil-Sgríbhinn Eóin mhic Néill: Essays and Studies Presented to Professor Eoin MacNeill*, ed. John Ryan (Dublin, 1940), p. 546.
9. Ed. Whitley Stokes, 'Poems Ascribed to S. Moling', *Anecdota from Irish Manuscripts*, Vol. 2, ed. O. J. Bergin and others (Halle and Dublin, 1908), pp. 26-28. This is one of twenty Middle Irish poetic texts having to do with Moling that are preserved in a seventeenth century manuscript. The contents of the poem in question and of others from this set that feature Suibne as well as Moling are summarized in Jackson 1940, 539-40. These verses are not to be found in the *Buile Shuibhne*. An edition and translation of the Suibne-Moling poems, along with commentary on them, are available in Bryan R. Frykenberg, 'Poetry of Suibne Geilt and St. Mo-Ling from Brussels MS. Bibliothèque Royale MS. 5100-04', Ph.D. dissertation (Harvard University, 1994).

positing the Dál Riata in particular as the source, included the fact
that literary evidence for the Suibne tradition (ninth-tenth centuries)
antedate the existing references to his two counterparts. Jackson also
argued, following O'Keeffe, that there is no mention of the Suibne
of the *Buile Shuibhne* in the extant genealogy/king-list for the Dál
nAraide,[10] the Ulster people over whom (according to the text) he
reigned. On the other hand, as O'Keeffe and Jackson noted, in the
Moling poems noted above – a seemingly independent cycle not
included in the *Buile Shuibhne* – Suibne is characterized as an
Albanach 'Briton' or 'Scot'.[11] Moreover, playing a major role in the
Battle of Mag Rath, the occasion on which Suibne supposedly
became a *geilt*, were the 'Scottish' Dál Riata, who fought unsuc-
cessfully alongside their erstwhile neighbors, the Dál nAraide,
against the Uí Néill high-king Domnall mac Áeda.

In his earlier publication *Studies in Early Celtic Nature Poetry*
(1935), Jackson, in addition to noting the Myrddin/'wild man of the
woods' analogy,[12] initiated what was arguably a more productive
search for the origins of the Suibne legend, by way of a comparison
between the stance reflected in the poetry of the *geilt*, and that to be
found in poetry attributed to the figure of the early Irish Christian
hermit: 'In some ways the life of the hermit and that of the exile or
madman lurking in the wilds must have been alike; and though the
essential characters of the two groups of poetry... can be easily distinguished, sometimes the distinctions are blurred.'[13] This connection
was taken up in Nora K. Chadwick's 1942 article 'Geilt', which in
its wide-ranging roamings – worthy of Suibne himself – made some
valuable innovative observations concerning the mediating function
performed by the figure of the *geilt*, not just in the *Buile Shuibhne*
but in other texts where *gelta* or similarly 'marginal' figures appear:

> On the whole the gelta seem to represent an intermediate stage
> between the old heathen world and the Irish Church. They are not

---

10. M. A. O'Brien, ed. *Corpus Genealogiarum Hiberniae* (Dublin, 1962, repr.
    1976), p. 323.
11. Stokes, 'Poems Ascribed to S. Moling', p. 22.
12. (Cambridge, 1935), p. 111.
13. *Ibid.*, p. 121.

actually outside the pale of the Church; they are its 'back numbers.' They represent those who do not conform, who do not come under an authorised discipline.[14]

It was in regard to Suibne's connection with the 'old heathen world' that Chadwick, the first scholar to do so, conjured the notion of Suibne as shaman, of the *geilt* as both possessed by and possessor of supernatural inspiration and power, a practitioner of 'archaic techniques of ecstasy', to use Mircea Eliade's phrase, comparable to similar practitioners both in and well beyond the Celtic world.[15] Chadwick also adumbrated for future study a subtext to the Suibne saga involving the tensions between the oral and written elements in medieval Irish culture with her observation that Suibne is not the only productive casualty of the Battle of Mag Rath. He is in the company of Cenn Fáelad mac Ailella, a noted scribe who supposedly lost his 'brain of forgetfulness' in that battle and proceeded to become a virtuosic recorder of the legal and poetic traditions of his time:

> It would seem that Cennfaelad bridges the two extremes of oral and book learning represented in the story of the Battle of Moyra [Mag Rath] by Suibhne and St Ronan. The importance of Suibhne's contribution to the former is recognized by the Book of Achill, for it speaks of the wealth of poetry and stories which he left behind.[16]

Also building upon evidence marshalled by Jackson, but leading it in a rather different direction, is James Carney's theory of the British (specifically, Strathclyde) origins of the Suibne legend, presented in a study that first appeared in print in 1950 in the journal *Éigse*.[17] Carney too noted the designation of Suibne as an *Albanach*

---

14. *Scottish Gaelic Studies*, 5 (1942), 151.
15. On shamanism as a widespread cultural phenomenon, see Eliade's *Shamanism: Archaic Techniques of Ecstasy*, trans. Willard R. Trask (Princeton, 1964). Later explorations of the shamanic aspects of Suibne include Brigit Beneš, 'Spuren von Schamanismus in der Sage "Buile Suibhne"', *Zeitschrift für celtische Philologie*, 28 (1961), 309-34, and Joseph Falaky Nagy, 'The Wisdom of the Geilt', *Éigse*, 19 (1982), 44-60.
16. 'Geilt', p. 148.
17. '"Suibne Geilt" and the "Children of Lir"', *Éigse*, 6, pt. 2 (1950), 83-110; reprinted, with additional material, in Carney's *Studies in Irish Literature and History* (Dublin, 1955), pp. 129-64.

in the Middle Irish poem, but he pointed out that the term as used in Middle Irish could have referred as easily to the British as to the Scottish.[18] Given what Carney assessed as a paucity of references to Suibne and to *geltacht* in general outside the *Buile Shuibhne*, and the seeming intrusion of the figure of the phantom Dál nAraide king Suibne into the otherwise attested and 'native' cast of characters featured in the saga surrounding the Battle of Mag Rath, Carney saw the epochal conflict and the background figure of Suibne, son of Eochaid Buide and brother of the Domnall Brecc who reigned over the Dál Riata at the time of the battle, as the pegs onto which the British story of the battle-scarred 'wild man of the woods' was attached, soon to develop into a modest story-cycle of its own. Like Jackson before him, Carney found a reflexive reference to the origins of the *geilt* legend in the episode of the *Buile Shuibhne* featuring the *Albanach* madman (E)alladán (see below). Suibne's confrontation with this figure in *Albu* becomes, in Carney's understanding of the origins of the legend, a virtual return to the *geilt*'s British roots. These are linguistically demonstrated, Carney claimed, in Irish *geilt*'s being a borrowing from Welsh *gwyllt* 'wild, rustic person', a notion first suggested by Pedersen in his magisterial *Vergleichende Grammatik der keltischen Sprachen*.[19] The 'oicotypification' of the wild man legend in Ireland proceeded beyond the Mag Rath tradition, by way of the 'wild man/hermit' analogy. Specifically, Suibne grew attached to the figure of Saint Moling, a figure whose narrative repertoire of motifs already included, according to Carney's reconstruction, a story of the death of an enemy that was susceptible to refashioning along the lines of the 'threefold death' model, which

---

18. *Ibid.*, p. 150.
19. Vol. 1 (Göttingen, 1909), p. 96. Another pioneering effort to link *geilt* and *gwyllt*, as well as the poetic repertoires attributed to Suibne and Myrddin, is Ifor Williams, 'Gwyllon, Geilt, Wyll', *Bulletin of the Board of Celtic Studies*, 1 (1923), 228-34, cited in Jackson, *Studies*, p. 111, n. 4. See also Williams, 'The Poems of Llywarch Hen' (orig. pub. 1933), *The Beginnings of Welsh Poetry: Studies by Sir Ifor Williams*, ed. Rachel Bromwich (Cardiff, 1972), p. 123, and Margaret Enid Griffiths, *Early Vaticination in Welsh with English Parallels* (Cardiff, 1937), pp. 86-87, 104-105. Julius Pokorny in his *Indogermanisches Wörterbuch* supported the derivation of Irish *geilt* from Welsh (Vol. 1 [Bern and Stuttgart, 1959], p. 1139). See also John Carey, 'Suibne Geilt and Tuán mac Cairill', *Éigse*, 20 (1984), 95-99.

came as part of the British 'wild man of the woods' complex.[20] A further process of fusion took place, with Moling's hagiographically celebrated propensity for leaping, as well as various native concepts of supernaturally provoked levitation, informing the story of Suibne. Clearly, Carney saw Irish tradition as not altogether unfamiliar with the elements that went into what he saw as a British story pattern. Still, according to his reconstruction of its history, the saga of the *geilt*, as expressed in the *Buile Shuibhne*, was primarily if not exclusively a literary innovation, one that in turn provided many of the key elements in the story, and even elements of the prosimetric style, of the famous Early Modern Irish romance about the Children of Lir (*Oidheadh Cloinne Lir*).

In the following volume of *Éigse* (1953), Jackson issued a rejoinder to Carney's arguments. He pointed out that Carney's assertion of an eighth-century borrowing of the Myrddin-Lailoken story into Irish tradition is based on the rather adventurous assumption of the existence of this story at least two centuries before any of its elements are attested in surviving Welsh literature. (Carney's dating was predicated to a significant degree on the need to explain the ninth-century Irish attestation[s] of Suibne and the word *geilt*.) Moreover, while Jackson noted that tracing Irish *geilt* to Welsh *gwyllt* may allow for the satisfying derivation of both words from the same Indo-European root that gives us 'wild' in English, the *g-* of

---

20. The most recent discussion of the 'threefold death', its appearances in medieval Irish literature, and the various interpretations of the motif that scholars have proposed, is Tomás Ó Cathasaigh's 'The Threefold Death in Early Irish Sources', *Studia Celtica Japonica*, 6 (1994), 53-74. See also Donald J. Ward, 'The Threefold Death: An Indo-European Trifunctional Sacrifice?' in *Myth and Law Among the Indo-Europeans*, ed. Jaan Puhvel (Berkeley and Los Angeles, 1970), pp. 123-46; Joan Newlon Radner, 'The Significance of the Threefold Death in Celtic Tradition', *Celtic Folklore and Christianity: Studies in Memory of William W. Heist*, ed. Patrick K. Ford (Santa Barbara/Los Angeles, 1983), pp. 180-200; Jean-Michel Picard, 'The Strange Death of Guaire Mac Áedáin', *Sages, Saints and Storytellers: Celtic Studies in Honour of Professor James Carney*, ed. Donnchadh Ó Corráin, Liam Breatnach, and Kim McCone (Maynooth, 1989), pp. 367-75; and William Sayers, '*Guin & Crochad & Gólad*: The Earliest Irish Threefold Death', *Celtic Languages and Celtic Peoples: Proceedings of the Second North American Congress of Celtic Studies*, ed. Cyril J. Byrne, Margaret Harry, and Pádraig Ó Siadhail (Halifax, 1992), pp. 64-82.

Welsh *gwyllt* would only have developed in the later eighth century.[21] Even more important, *gwyllt* introduced into Irish would probably produce *guilt*. Whence, asked Jackson, comes *geilt*?

Carney, in an appendix to his *Studies in Irish Literature and History* (1955),[22] which included a slightly revised version of his *Éigse* article, picked up the gauntlet. Pointing out that Jackson did not appear to have any alternative 'native' etymology of *geilt* to offer, he defended the eighth-century dating, insisting that the time allotted by his theory was more than sufficient for Welsh *gwyllt* to be acclimatized and transformed into an Irish word. *Gwyllt*, as tracked by Carney, is more likely to have been analyzed by Irish speakers as *gw-* (unfamiliar to them and hence assimilated to *g-*) plus vowel *-i-*, rather than as *g-* followed by *-ui-*, which would have suggested a nominative singular *golt*. *Gilt* (or the less likely **golt*) then became *gelt* (as Carney insisted the nominative singular would have been spelled originally) under the influence of the semantically related *ge(i)nit* 'sprite', and possibly also under the influence of *geilt* 'grazing'.

Of course, definitive proof of a 'Scottish' or 'British connection' for the Suibne legend would illuminate the history of its development. However, even were the issue to be settled, the connection would not explain why the concept of *geltacht* and specifically the figure of Suibne left the traces that they did in the medieval literary record. As both Jackson and Carney freely admitted, there was clearly a cultural receptivity to the elements (whether domestic or imported) that came to constitute the story of Suibne – even perhaps a native mold or story pattern that underlay it. It was precisely this pattern that a contemporary scholar, Pádraig Ó Riain, set out to explore in his 1972 article fittingly titled 'A Study of the Irish Legend of the Wild Man':

> The repetitious nature of Irish literature in thematic terms is not necessarily indicative of a widespread literary course of derivation. Rather should it be taken as a reflection of the perennial Irish concern with a limited group of themes, and with the less limited, though by no means extensive, area of possible manoeuvre in the introduction of thematic variables. Rather than interpret thematic parallels in terms of literary

21.   *Language and History in Early Britain: A Chronological Survey of the Brittonic Languages First to Twelfth Century A.D.* (Edinburgh, 1953), p. 390.
22.   'The Origin of *Suibne Gelt*', pp. 385-93.

origins, I take them to reflect particular societal attitudes or patterns of behaviour, each with its share of identificatory characteristics.[23]

In a range of medieval Irish texts, from the *Buile Shuibhne* to the *Serglige Con Culainn* ('Wasting Sickness of Cú Chulainn'), from the Ulster cycle to stories from the Fenian tradition, Ó Riain located a repertoire of narrative situations pertaining to various degrees and manifestations of madness including *geltacht*. Certain circumstances almost demand that the narrative figure embroiled in them lose his or her sanity, a condition defined here as a temporary loss of social recognizability and accountability. Examples of these 'maddening' circumstances are the curse of a holy man, a battle, and the loss of a lover. There are, moreover, recurring characteristics associated with this state of madness, such as nakedness, levitation, and a preference for the wilderness. And just as the onset of this madness in its various manifestations (such as *geltacht*) is predicated on certain situations, so too its passing away depends upon a particular set of circumstances, such as the wild man's finding the favor of a holy man. The importance of this latter figure, the *sacerdos* as dubbed by Ó Riain so as to allow the 'wild man' pattern a life before the Christian milieu, indicates the ritual dimensions of the madness/wildness experienced by the narrative protagonist, who is characterized by Ó Riain as a liminal figure, experiencing a change in social identity by way of a bout of madness. In Suibne's case his transformation involves both loss and gain. He loses his status as king but he wins a reputation as a poet.[24]

That poetry is at the heart of Suibne's significance as a figure of

---

23. *Éigse*, 14 (1972), 181.
24. Following Ó Riain's lead, contemporary scholars have paid more attention to the possible meanings of *geltacht* within medieval Irish literature and culture, and to the affinities between Suibne and other bewildered, mad, or cursed figures in medieval Irish and Indo-European story: see Angela Partridge (now Angela Bourke), 'Wild Men and Wailing Women', *Éigse*, 18 (1980-81), 25-37, and David J. Cohen, 'Suibhne Geilt', *Celtica*, 12 (1977), 114-24. Other studies that have helped to map out *geltacht* on the cultural terrain of medieval Ireland include Gearóid S. Mac Eoin, 'Gleann Bolcáin agus Gleann na nGealt', *Béaloideas*, 30 (1962), 105-20, which traces the more recent traditions concerning the haunts of *gelta*; James Stewart, 'Gleann na nGealt: A Twelfth-Century Latin Account', *Celtica*, 17 (1985), 105-111, which focuses on a hitherto-unnoticed reference to one such haunt in medieval literature; and Thomas Owen Clancy, 'Mac Steléne and the Eight in Armagh: Identity and Context', *Éigse*, 26 (1992), 80-91, which provides an inventory of wild men in medieval Irish literary tradition.

story is not only indicated in the prosimetric design of our text but also in an unambiguous statement made in a Middle Irish legal text:

> Three virtues of that battle [the Battle of Mag Rath, 637 A.D.]: the defeat of Congal Claen in his untruth at the hands of Domnall in his truth; Suibne Geilt's becoming a geilt; and the excision of his brain of forgetfulness out of Cenn Fáelad's head. Suibne's becoming a geilt is not counted a virtue per se, but on account of the stories and poems he left behind in Ireland as a result of it.[25]

We should note that 'becoming a *geilt*' does not simply give Suibne a voice by which to be known to posterity. It creates situations that are memorable, the stuff of stories *about* Suibne. These stories, like Suibne's poetic accounts of his life and experiences, are transmitted by the protagonist himself. Here then are the poetic and storytelling functions turned inward upon themselves, with the poetic voice stripped of its illusion of impartial perspective. It is precisely this kind of voice and this merger of poet and topic that characterize the discourse of the great survivor figures of medieval Irish literary tradition, such as the Caílte and Oisín of the epochal twelfth-or thirteenth-century text *Acallam na Senórach*,[26] and bearers of even more

---

25. *Teora buada in catha-sin: maidm ar congal claen in anfir re domnall ina fírinne, 7 suibne geilt do dul ar geltacht, 7 a incinn dermait do buain a cind cind faelad; nocan ed-sin is buaid ann suibni do dul ar geltacht, is ar facaib do scelaib 7 do laidib dia eis i neirind . . .* (*Corpus Iuris Hibernici*, ed. D. A. Binchy, Vol. 1 [Dublin, 1978], p. 250, lines 36-39). This passage comes from a preface describing the historical milieu of a text often mistakenly referred to as the *Lebor Aicle* 'Book of Aicill'. The law tract is in fact called *Bretha Étgid* 'Judgments of Inadvertence' (see Fergus Kelly, *A Guide to Early Irish Law* [Dublin, 1988], p. 272) and, as it survives, consists of 'a few disjointed citations from the tract itself, which are simply used as pegs on which to hang voluminous commentaries written in Late Middle or Early Modern Irish' (Binchy, 'The Linguistic and Historical Value of the Irish Law Tracts', *Proceedings of the British Academy*, 29 [1943], 220).

26. Pádraig Ó Riain has noted a basic affinity between the *Acallam* and the *Buile Shuibhne*, roughly contemporaneous texts: 'The author of each brought together a number of floating traditions to form a coherent and highly artistic composition. In each the interplay between saint and outcast emerges as a linking theme, and bears implicit witness to monastic provenance as well as to the willingness of the Irish church in general to preserve and transmit what were basically secular literary remains' ('The Materials and Provenance of "Buile Shuibhne"', *Éigse*, 15 [1974], 173). And yet—as Ó Riain, following James Carney, goes on to point out—the Fenian tradition memorialized in the *Acallam* leaves a profound impression on Irish literary tradition, while the story of Suibne is barely attested in the later literature (*ibid.*, p. 174; see Carney, *Studies*, p. 160).

ancient history such as the venerable flood-survivors Fintan mac Bóchra[27] and Tuán mac Cairill,[28] and the holy woman-trout Líbán, also known as Muirgein or Muirgeilt ('Sea-*Geilt*').[29]

Suibne's fame is based on his living a life that alternates between nightmarish and ecstatic variations on a penitential model.[30] Reigning as the king of Dál nAraide in northeastern Ulster at the

---

27. Fintan is featured in the Middle Irish text *Do Suidigud Tellaig Temra* ('Of the Settling of the Manor of Tara'), edited and translated by R.I. Best, *Ériu*, 4 (1910), 124-61. On Fintan in the 'pseudo-historical' tradition, see Alwyn and Brinley Rees, *Celtic Heritage: Ancient Tradition in Ireland and Wales* (London, 1961), pp. 113-15, 119-21, and Kim McCone, *Pagan Past and Christian Present* (Maynooth, 1990), pp. 75-77.

    In the *Suidigud* text the figure of Cenn Fáelad, another survivor of the Battle of Mag Rath (see above, pp. 6 and 11), is also presented as a knowledgeable elder, albeit of a considerably younger generation than Fintan. In contrast to oral performers such as Suibne and Fintan, whose words happen to be recorded by fortuitously present amanuenses, Cenn Fáelad takes the matter of surviving and making himself known to posterity into his own hands. He is known in the tradition as a paradigmatic scribe. The extant references to Cenn Fáelad mac Ailella, his story, and his purported literary accomplishments are detailed by Proinsias Mac Cana in 'The Three Languages and the Three Law', *Studia Celtica* 5 [1970], 62-66; see also Edgar M. Slotkin, 'Medieval Irish Scribes and Fixed Texts', *Éigse* 17 (1977-79), 437-40, 450. The 'historical' Cenn Fáelad, designated *sapiens* in the Annals of Ulster (679 A.D.), is the subject of Robin Flower's *The Irish Tradition* (Oxford, 1947), pp. 10-13, and McCone's *Pagan Past and Christian Present*, pp. 23-24. See now also Hildegard Tristram, 'Warum Cenn Faelad sein "Gehirn des Vergessens" Verlor—Wort und Schrift in der älteren irischen Literatur', *Deutschen, Kelten und Iren: 150 Jahre deutsche Keltologie (Gearóid Mac Eoin zum 60. Geburtstag gewidmet)*, ed. Tristram (Hamburg, 1990), pp. 207-48.

28. The resemblance between Tuán, who survives through the ages by changing into various wild creatures, and the bestial *geilt* Suibne has been noted in Nikolai Tolstoy, '"Merlinus Redivivus"', *Studia Celtica*, 28-29 (1983-84), 25 (see also Tolstoy, *The Quest for Merlin* [London, 1985], pp. 77-78), and John Carey, 'Suibne Geilt and Tuán mac Cairill', *Éigse*, 20 (1984), 93-105.

29. Featured in *Aided Echach meic Maireda*, a text preserved in the Lebor na hUidre (ed. R. I. Best and Osborn Bergin [Dublin, 1929], lines 2926-3135). Ó Riain has speculated that the name Muirgil given to the pivotal character of the wife of Suibne's slayer in the *Buile Shuibhne* is perhaps borrowed from the Líbán/Muirgein/ Muirgeilt legend ('Study of the Irish Legend', p. 185, n. 54).

30. Suibne has been compared to other penitents and hermits from both Celtic and Old English traditions by Jackson and Chadwick (see above), and also in Carney, *Studies*, p. 180, and P. L. Henry, *The Early English and Celtic Lyric* (London, 1966), pp. 25-29, 198-202.

beginning of the story,[31] he subsequently runs away from his people and his kingship, and is reduced to the status of a beast in the wilderness, albeit a remarkably eloquent, poetic beast.[32] This dramatic reversal of fortune comes about as a result of Suibne's exhibiting his contempt for the signs of a saint's authority. In the course of a whole series of confrontations between him and Saint Rónán, Suibne throws the saint's psalter in water, thus showing what he thinks of

---

31. As noted by O'Keeffe and others (see above), Suibne does not figure in any more historically reliable sources in the regnal succession of the Dál nAraide. In this regard he resembles Mongán mac Fiachna, another figure associated with this kingdom, who is said in narrative to have been their king but is not so described in the annals. Moreover, like Suibne, the Mongán of story is known for having experienced a *baile* 'vision, frenzy', and he has a nearly disastrous encounter with a mill hag (see Nagy, 'In Defense of Rómánsaíocht', *Ériu*, 38 [1987], 13-24). The slayer of Suibne in the *Buile Shuibhne* is called Mongán, a name that differs from that assigned to his slayer in the above-mentioned Middle Irish poem concerning the death of Suibne and its aftermath (Stokes, 'Poems', 26-28). 'The change in names was dictated, perhaps, by a desire to provide the episode with something like an Ulster flavour, Mongán, at least, being more at home in the nomenclature of that part of the country' (Ó Riain, 'Materials and Provenance', p. 185). Other textual indications of an Ulster background to the *Buile Shuibhne* are identified in Ó Riain's article.

32. The most recent discussion of the parallel between the experience of Suibne and the enlightening stint of bestiality/madness undergone by Nebuchadnezzar in the Book of Daniel is William Sayers, 'Varia VII. The deficient ruler as avian exile; Nebuchadnezzar as Suibhne Geilt', *Ériu*, 43 (1992), 217-20.

[13]

writing as well as of the holy man.[33] Suibne also slays Rónán's fos-
ter son, damages the saint's bell, which can be as powerful an
expression of a saint's authority as is his actual voice, and violates
the truce arranged by Rónán between the sides in the impending
Battle of Mag Rath.

As the text makes clear, this monarch on an anticlerical rampage
calls down the fate of a *geilt* upon himself not only by abusing ecclesiastical signs but also by making a spectacle of himself. In order to
stop Rónán from building his church in Dál nAraide territory, Suibne
storms forth unmindful of his nakedness which, understandably,
offends the cleric. And, in the Battle of Mag Rath, which comes
about despite Rónán's efforts at peacemaking, Suibne is dressed
ostentatiously, the text tells us (p. 10). Later, during his *geltacht*
days, Suibne even refers to his cultivation of battlefield splendor as
one of the reasons why he deserved to be reduced to his deplorable
condition (pp. 66, 68). Being a *geilt*, as prescribed in Rónán's curse
and fleshed out in the story, presents an ironic counterpoint to the
extremes of appearance, from undressed to overdressed, in which
Suibne in his monarchical arrogance indulges. For the *geilt* is
stripped of human clothing but grows animal 'raiment', feathers,
which, on a human body, are even more conspicuous than the finery
worn by Suibne on the day of battle. Thus Suibne, in punishment for

---

33.   Chadwick views the scene in broader cultural terms: 'It is not impossible that the
      jealousy of the bards, the professional repositories of oral tradition with strong
      vested interests in both countries [Ireland and Wales], may have held back the
      development of a written tradition in some measure. It is easy to recall stories of
      the hostility of the poets to book learning—in Irish saga Suibhne Geilt throwing
      St Ronan's sacred book into the water; in Welsh poetry Yscolan doing the same;
      in the Welsh poem *Armes Prydein* the poet himself pours out a malediction on
      the *llyfrawr*, which is surely a cut at the 'book-learned man''' ('Early Culture and
      Learning in North Wales', in *Studies in the Early British Church*, ed. Chadwick,
      Kathleen Hughes, and others [Cambridge, 1958], pp. 6-7). I am grateful to Ms.
      Kyri Freeman for this reference. On the centrality of the act of book-bashing to
      the plot of the long-lived legend of the ill-fated Welsh Yscolan/Breton Skolan,
      see Donatien Laurent, 'La gwerz de Skolan et la légende de Merlin', *Ethnologie
      française*, 1 (1971), 36, and 'Breton Orally Transmitted Folk Poetry', *The
      European Folk Ballad: A Symposium*, ed. Otto Holzapfel and others (Odense,
      1978), pp. 20-24. Mr. Lawrence Eson of the UCLA Folklore and Mythology
      Program is writing a Ph.D. dissertation on the figure of Yscolan and the con-
      nections among the Breton, British, and Irish 'wild man' traditions.

his exhibitionism and other sins, is rendered a spectacle, as conspicuous as Rónán's bell was audible.

Paradoxically, the *geilt* as spectacle avoids public view as much as possible, although Suibne keeps coming within the peripheral vision of his former subjects and other interested parties, including clerics. In a process that is much in evidence in the realm of medieval Irish hagiography, the saint renders the challenger to the saint's authority and his sign of defiance signs of the very values that the challenger opposes. Usually, the converted opponent is kept by the saint for display and edification, or in some form stays available for public demonstration.

There are exceptions to this trend, such as the case of the impudent king Coroticus or Corictic, featured in Muirchú's seventh-century Latin *Life* of Patrick. In his dramatic demise and disappearance Corictic serves as a demonstration of what happens to those who do not heed Patrick's word. After he publicly rebuffs the saint's warning and is rebuffed in turn by his own poet, the evil Corictic is transformed into a fox in the sight of his entire court, and he runs away into the wilderness, never to be seen or heard again.[34] It is significant, however, that Muirchú's story of this silenced victim of saintly rage, like the story of the analogous figure of Suibne, features the demise of a king, and centers on the power of poetry as much as it does on the power of the saint. Corictic is not deposed and transformed by means of any direct face-to-face contact with Patrick, whose chiding letter the king blatantly ignores. Rather, the king loses his position in society as a result of a devastating performance and critique given by a poet in the presence of Corictic, who, almost in response to the performance, turns into a fox. While no poet plays a role in Suibne's public humiliation, the 'curse' of poetry looms at the other end of the king's term of wild exile. In his derangement and obscurity, Suibne waxes poetic, and his verses actually threaten the obscurity to which he is condemned, but which he comes to crave. They make him valuable to society at large so that the forces attempting to locate and retrieve him extend beyond the circle of the Dál nAraide, who simply, and understandably, want their king back.

---

34. Ludwig Bieler, ed. and trans., *The Patrician Texts in the Book of Armagh* (Dublin, 1910), p. 100 (Book 1, Chapter 29, in Muirchú's text). To the best of my knowledge, this important analogue to the Suibne tale has never been noted as such.

A cursory reading of the *Buile Shuibhne* might give us the impression that Suibne's poetry, the glorious outcome of his *geltacht*, consists of soliloquies, of the deranged poet talking primarily to himself about himself, his condition, and his natural environment. In fact, much if not most of this verse is cast within the framework of exchange between Suibne and the diverse characters whom he engages, and by whom he is engaged, in dialogue. Words form a mesh with which the *geilt* can be ensnared, or with which Suibne can draw closer to the few kindred souls who can appreciate his pain and his art.

Suibne, an ever-receding but tantalizingly productive sign of impiety, is no mean reader of the tracks upon which he stumbles in the course of his wanderings. In one of the few moments of rest and intimacy the story affords him, he makes the acquaintance of a British *geilt* named Alladán, with whom he exchanges information about how they came to be in their present condition (pp. 100, 102). Alladán's 'sin' is revealed to be comparable to Suibne's. Out of overzealous devotion to his lord Alladán made his fellow warriors dress up in showy finery for the battle in which they were about to fight (p. 102). For this display of conspicuous consumption he was roundly cursed by all the participants. Having shared their personal stories Suibne and Alladán form a pact according to which they will warn each other about the slightest sign of intrusion into their sylvan privacy:

> 'O Suibhne', said Alladhán, 'let each of us keep good watch over the other since we have placed trust in each other; that is, he who shall soonest hear the cry of a heron from a blue-watered, green-watered lough or the clear note of a cormorant, or the flight of a woodcock from a branch, the whistle or sound of a plover on being woke from its sleep, or the sound of withered branches being broken, or shall see the shadow of a bird above the wood, let him who shall first hear warn and tell the other; let there be the distance of two trees between us; and if one of us should hear any of the before-mentioned things or anything resembling them, let us fly quickly away thereafter'. They do so, and they were a whole year together. (pp. 103, 105)

Here is striking proof of the extent to which the *geilt*, rendered a stranger to society and vulnerable to its manipulative attempts at communication, compensatorily develops a knowledge of, and a mastery over, 'natural' modes of communication such as the songs

[16]

of birds and the rustlings of the forest, and all that these sounds can mean. In the life of a *geilt* weakness and deprivation are continually relative states, balanced out by special aptitudes and gifts. The talk of two *gelta* in the wilderness is immeasurably enriched by their sensitivity to the voices of the many other potential participants in the dialogue.

There are two partially successful attempts in the course of the story to recapture Suibne by means of talk and to put him back into the ongoing dialogues of everyday life. In both instances the goal of luring the *geilt* into conversation is clearly to capture what he knows or has learned as well as Suibne himself. As we shall see, however, in the case of the first, less successful attempt, Suibne's value to his captors is primarily as a king, not as a source of memories or a memorial himself, although these aspects are still important to his captors and even prove fatal to their plans. The second attempt, unlike the first, is launched under clerical auspices, and with an eye to Suibne's value as a poet. Yet, although this salvage mission seems to succeed, in the end Suibne is once again lost to the world, as he is at the conclusion of the first attempt to claim him. The difference, however, is that, as a result of the second rescue, Suibne's poems are captured in written form. Furthermore, the first attempt is undertaken deliberately and involves a concerted plan. The second attempt happens by accident, in a way reminiscent of the legendary poet Muirgein's stumbling upon the method for recovering the lost story of the *Táin Bó Cúailnge.*[35] Even more important, the first attempt is spearheaded by a character marked by name as marginal, while the second depends on a cleric, whose own brand of marginality is tempered by his ecclesiastical and literary authority.

When the Dál nAraide decide to find Suibne and restore him to his sanity and kingship, they entrust the task to one of their number named Loingsechán (meaning 'Exile'), a kinsman of Suibne's. He seems to have no difficulty in tracking down and identifying Suibne in his characteristic kind of lair, the foliage of a yew tree (p. 50).

Standing at its base, Loingsechán proceeds to engage the *geilt* above in dialogue, deviously reminding Suibne of how gloriously he lived in the good old days. Stirred by nostalgia, the *geilt* asks for news (*scéla*) about his people, and his fellow countrymen.

---

35. The variant accounts of how the *Táin* was recovered are arrayed and studied in Carney, *Studies,* pp. 165-79.

Loingsechán, untruthfully, tells him of the deaths of various members of his family, including his father and wife. Suibne responds to all of these with pithily formulated expressions of perfunctory grief, until he is told of the death of his son, information that unbeknownst to the gullible Suibne is as false as the rest. With the communication of this last piece of news the *geilt* drops like a corpse out of the tree into Loingsechán's arms but he is soon revived with his interlocutor's admission that he lied for Suibne's own good. Loingsechán then takes the captured *geilt* back to his kingdom where he is to be nursed back to normalcy (pp. 58, 60).

The scene in which Loingsechán contacts and tames the *geilt* clearly belongs to a type, examples of which are also to be found in the story of the *rígfhénnid* Finn and Derg Corra (a victim of the machinations of Finn's mistress)[36] and in the episode from the saga of the Munster anti-hero Lugaid Mac Con in which he and his fosterbrothers find the magical yew tree with the otherworldly musician in it.[37] What typically happens is that the marginal explorer in the wilderness (Finn, Lugaid, or Loingsechán) finds, intentionally or unintentionally, a stranger or estranged acquaintance in a tree. This arboreal figure proves a conspicuous sign-bearer, accoutered with traditional symbols that connote the possession of wisdom from outside the human realm: fish, musical instruments, nakedness, the tree itself. Once communication is commenced between explorer and epiphanic stranger, information flows from the man in the tree to his earthbound audience. With this information the signifying treedweller establishes his authority and numinous identity, and can even gain control over the situation at hand. The musician Fer Í, for example, puts his contending auditors to sleep by means of his performance and leaves them in thorough and lasting disarray. Derg Corra, on the other hand, never says anything from his perch in the tree, and Finn is allowed the last word in the tale. Nevertheless, it is the maligned *gilla* who makes the point of the story, constituting as

---

36. This tale is told in the brief text edited and translated by Kuno Meyer, 'Finn and the Man in the Tree', *Revue Celtique*, 25 (1904), 346, 348.
37. The ill-fated career of Lugaid Mac Con is recounted in the text *Cath Maige Mucrama*, edited and translated by Máirín Ó Daly (Irish Texts Society 50 [Dublin, 1975]) along with other pertinent texts. For the story of the encounter with the musician in the tree, see *ibid.*, pp. 40, 80, and also the poem from the Book of Leinster edited and translated by Myles Dillon in *Ériu*, 14 (1946), 156-65.

he does a mute reminder of the dramatic impact made by another, hardly mute, dweller in a tree, namely, Finn himself during his own youth as narrated in medieval story.[38]

In the comparable episode from *Buile Shuibhne*, however, the stereotype is broken, in that Suibne, the speaker in the tree, is not the one imparting information. Loingsechán is both the framer of the conversation and the source of the news imparted. Suibne just asks questions or responds to what he learns, which, contrary to the stereotype, is not about nature, the otherworld, or the past, but about the domestic present. This reversal of roles and the change in informational venue make for a displacement of authority and control. The marginal seeker thus gains control over the sought-after possessor of knowledge, and that knowledge, which in Suibne's case is ineluctably intertwined with his madness, is lost or rendered irrelevant. Loingsechán's strategy for recovering Suibne defies the *geilt*'s reputation as someone to whom it is worth listening. The outcome of their encounter reverses traditional notions of who supplies whom with information in this kind of situation, as well as related notions of what kinds of information are more, or less, authoritative. In the most ironic twist, the 'news' with which Loingsechán gains control over the situation and his dialogic partner is patently false, and establishes a 'past', the demise of Suibne's kinfolk, that is yet to happen.

Had it proved completely successful Loingsechán's perversion of traditional expectations about the process of getting and assessing knowledge would have left us with no trace of Suibne's poetry. The latter would have been lost in the amnesia of his social recovery with no means left intact for its continuation since, as we may infer from the episode to be discussed next, the production and performance of this poetry were contingent upon Suibne's remaining a *geilt*. Fortunately for us – the latter-day audience of the *geilt*'s poetry – the memory-erasing innovations of the impressively efficient if philistine Loingsechán are undermined by the methods used to keep the normalized but still recuperating Suibne under observation. Curiously, these methods are those of Loingsechán's own wife, the 'hag of the mill' (*cailleach an mhuilinn*), who is entrusted with the care of Suibne (pp. 60-83).

---

38.   The arboreal ambience of Finn's youth is described in Nagy, *Wisdom of the Outlaw*, pp. 118-19.

JOSEPH FALAKY NAGY

Soon after Suibne's sense and memory return and he remembers that he is a king, harvest time approaches, and Loingsechán departs to join in the work, leaving Suibne at home. Once she is left alone with the erstwhile curiosity, Loingsechán's wife starts to probe Suibne's potential as a source of information about his remarkable past, asking him to tell something of his adventures in madness (pp. 60, 62). Suibne rebuffs the woman and her request harshly, claiming that it is hateful of her to be baiting him so deceptively. She responds that her motives are sincere and that it is the truth that she wants from him. Indeed, she insists, nothing she could do would send Suibne into the condition of *geltacht*. She reminds him (and us) that it was by the 'miracles' (*ferta*) of Rónán that he was rendered a *geilt*. In response Suibne, while still nominally holding out against her request, boasts in the proud, masochistic vein so typical of his old *geilt* stance, recounting the many strenuous leaps he had to make. He states in effect that it would be difficult if not impossible for someone who 'wasn't there' to understand what a *geilt* experiences: 'Great are the hardships I have encountered, if you but knew' (p. 63).

The reticent ex-madman senses an underhanded trap being set for him once again, this time by the wife of the man who hunted him down before. While the woman may be merely attempting to draw Suibne out and gauge his true feelings about his return to normality, he clearly reads her query as a strategy to draw him out literally, away from the social realm and back into the wild state in which Loingsechán found him.[39] Significantly, it is Suibne's fear of this same situation, a woman's depriving him of regained social status and social ties, that lurks behind the first of two dialogues that the *geilt* has with his wife Éorann. He chides her specifically for having taken up with another mate after his, Suibne's, demise (pp. 46, 48). This anxiety reappears fatefully in the episode of Suibne's death, the circumstances of which the *geilt* knows in advance (pp. 104, 105). For Suibne dies, tragically and ironically, at the hands of an enraged

---

39. Suibne says as much later on in the tale (pp. 122-23). 'If the mill-hag had not invoked Christ against me so that I might perform leaps for her awhile, I would not have gone again into madness' (p. 122; see also p. 129). Suibne elsewhere also declares that with the death of the hag he may no longer venture in Dál nAraide territory, lest he be slain in vengeance by the widowed Loingsechán (pp. 82-83).

[20]

swineherd, misled by his sister's false report of his wife's interest in the madman (pp. 142, 144).[40]

Given Suibne's past and still-to-come experiences with women, we are not surprised to detect a sexual subtext to his exchange with the mill-hag. It would also seem legitimate to compare this scenario of a helpless male left at the mercy of the persistent wife of a man who has gone off to engage in masculine collective pursuits (harvesting) with similar scenarios for seduction that we find elsewhere in medieval Irish literature.[41] In the case of the mill-hag, however, the husband attending to his chores has not gone off into the wilderness, his 'exile' status notwithstanding, but deeper into the social realm, as but one of many attending to the task of harvesting. This change in the pattern seems to correlate with what we shall see is the supernatural nature of this hag and the ease with which she and Suibne will leave the social realm altogether. Conceivably, the trespassing woman and the seemingly helpless man are left alone at a point further out from the social center than where the husband locates himself in order to fulfill his agricultural duty.

Seeming to corroborate this sense of a relocation of the stereotypical scene is a pivotal change in the way the story pattern is usually played out. The woman, instead of asking for sexual gratification or discretion from the male object of desire, requests the act of recollection. No ordinary storytelling event, this performance will transport the auditor(s) into a previously unknown realm, namely, the world of *geltacht*.

Within the context of the medieval Irish literary tradition, which continually claims that its foundations rest on empowering dialogues with representatives of the past, this is in fact a rather unusual instance where it is a woman who initiates a dialogue with the 'ancient' figure who brings information from beyond the normal

---

40. The bizarre circumstances of Suibne's death and its relation to the 'threefold death' pattern are discussed in Carney, *Studies*, pp. 136-42. Valuable insight into the distasteful juxtaposition of milk and manure that constitutes the mode of Suibne's feeding and that seems somehow connected to his death, is provided in Eric Hamp, '*imbolc, oímelc*', *Studia Celtica*, 14/15 (1979/80), 106-113.

41. Some stories featuring such situations are discussed in Nagy, *Wisdom of the Outlaw*, pp. 131-35.

social world of the present.[42] The Old Irish poem *Reicne Fothaid Chanainne*, uttered by the head of a dead warrior to his mistress after she finds it on the battlefield, does indeed constitute a communication of such information.[43] That communication, however, is punctuated by the head's protestations that it does *not* want to talk with the woman who in fact plays only a silent role as audience and bearer of the head and what it communicates. In the mill-hag episode from *Buile Shuibhne*, on the other hand, we note how aggressively, and yet with what seemingly little authority of her own, the hag pursues her goal of having Suibne reveal what he remembers of his experiences as a *geilt*. Indeed, this over-eager female inquirer soon presses Suibne for more than story and loses her interest in event as recalled. With the first hint of story from him, the mention of the difficult leaps that Suibne has made, the hag no longer demands narration but demonstration. And no sooner does she get her wish than she replaces demonstration with a breathtaking emulation, which boldly violates the clichés of distance and hierarchy among interlocutors that usually dominate such dialogues:

> 'For God's sake', said the hag, 'leap for us now one of the leaps you used to leap when you were mad'. Thereupon he bounded over the bed-rail so that he reached the end of the bench. 'My conscience!' said the hag, 'I could leap that myself', and in the same manner she did so. He took another leap out through the skylight of the hostel. 'I could leap that too', said the hag, and straightway she leaped. This, however, is a summary of it: Suibne travelled through five cantreds of Dal nAraidhe that day until he arrived at Glenn na nEachtach in Fiodh Gaibhle, and she followed him all that time. When Suibne rested there on the summit of a tall ivy-branch, the hag rested on another tree beside him. (p. 63)

This surprising turn of events poses a breathtaking threat to the traditional conceit of a dialogue with the past and with the other-

---

42. Another notable example of a woman playing the role of 'human' interlocutor in a dialogic encounter with the supernatural is to be found in the famous *Tochmarc Étaíne* (ed. and trans. by O. J. Bergin and R. I. Best in *Ériu* 12 [1938], 137-96). Of course what the otherworldly Midir has to say to Étaín is that she herself is of otherworldly origin.

43. See pp. 10-17 in Kuno Meyer, *Fianaigecht*, Todd Lectures Series 16 (Dublin, 1910). The poem is also edited and translated in David Greene and Frank O'Connor, *A Golden Treasury of Irish Poetry, A.D. 600 to 1200* (London, Melbourne, and Toronto, 1967), pp. 86-92.

world that underlies the tale of Suibne as well as many of our other medieval Irish texts. Such dialogue is supposed to render the knowledge that a figure such as Suibne has to impart intelligible within the latter-day world of texts. While such communication can take place between figures who mirror each other, only here in the *Buile Shuibhne* does the confrontation become an attempt on the part of the seeker to appropriate the characteristics and reputation of the one sought after and to emulate the pyrotechnics that mark the 'other' as other. 'Dost thou not deem my arts better, / thou noble, slender madman, / that I should be following thee / from the tops of the mountains?' brags the hag to Suibne (p. 75). What the *caillech* does to Suibne, we might add, is certainly no indication of saintly power. Her own display of power nearly replaces that of Saint Rónán as the primary catalyst for Suibne's ascent into madness. Further on in the text Suibne describes her soul as being taken away by demons, a fate that hardly betokens a holy character (p. 128).

This volatile exercise in one-upmanship also poses a personal challenge to Suibne, one that drives him again outside his social and epistemological ken. Pathetically, once he is reinstated in the element of the *geilt* by way of his bizarre contest with the *caillech*, he appears to display mental confusion as opposed to the keen insight with which we have come to associate the madman:

> It was then [that is, when Suibne, accompanied by the hag, had leapt back into the wilderness] the end of harvest-time precisely. Thereupon Suibhne heard a hunting-call of a multitude in the verge of the wood. 'This', he said, 'is the cry of a great host, and they are the Ui Faelain coming to kill me to avenge Oilill Cédach, king of the Ui Faelain, whom I slew in the battle of Mag Rath'. (p. 63)

The reader never finds out whether Suibne's understanding of his present situation as dangerous and evocative of his past is correct. Was it just a hunting party or returning harvesters, or was it an invading army? Despite the hag's insistence on the distinction between the two, deception and truth have now become interchangeable commodities in the confusing, post-stereotypical world into which Suibne and we have been propelled by this leaping woman. Suibne, obsessed with the past and capable of reading the data of the present only in terms of the past, is profoundly disturbed by the unrelenting 'attack' of the present upon his perennially hidden but ultimately disclosed person. At this point he is hemmed in although the attacks may be altogether illusory. On the one side is the eerie *caillech*, a fellow countryman, perched in the nearby tree waiting for his next move. On the other side is the mysterious but possibly quite mundane hunting party from a hostile tribe that he claims is on his trail. The temporal, tribal, sexual, and metaphysical convergences, the presence of which Suibne senses at this moment, are compounded by the confusion of the socio-economic activities of hunting, warring, and farming that appears in Suibne's conceptualization of what is happening around and to him. This confusion is already hinted in the glimpse we are given earlier of a seemingly undomestic type such as Loingsechán going off to help in the work of bringing in the sheaves.

The only way for Suibne to assert any kind of control over this bewildering pile-up of pressing data is to compose a poem. That is indeed what Suibne does, with a composition that is longer than any of the others included in the *Buile Shuibhne* (pp. 62-82).[44] It is as if, in his full-throated return to the life of a *geilt*, Suibne is displaying the full range of his poetic powers. In his *tour de force* the reborn *geilt* reaffirms his intimate familiarity with his environment (including the trees that he lists) and once again rebuffs the hag in person and her husband Loingsechán *in absentia*. Fleeing from the 'overload' is another sensible strategy, and that is Suibne's choice after he has finished performing the poem. With this twin reassertion of what Suibne the *geilt* is best known for, namely, his poetic production and his ability to flee and hide, the illusion of parity between *caillech* and *geilt* soon breaks down, much to our, and the story's, relief:

> After that poem Suibne came from Fid Gaible to Benn Boghaine . . . but he found no refuge from the hag until he reached Dun Sobairce in Ulster. Suibne leaped from the summit of the fort sheer down in front of the hag. She leaped quickly after him, but dropped on the cliff of Dun Sobairce, where she was broken to pieces, and fell into the sea. In that manner she found death in the wake of Suibne. Thereafter Suibne said: 'Henceforth I shall not be in Dál nAraide, for Loingseachán, to avenge his hag, would kill me if I were in his power'. (p. 83)

---

44. Ruth Lehmann in her study of the language of the poems in the *Buile Shuibhne* points out the remarkable length of this poem (sixty-five stanzas), as well as its miscellaneous character ('A Study of the *Buile Shuibhne*', *Études Celtiques*, 7 [1955], 130-31).

With the destruction of the hag, Suibne's remaining links to his people and previous life are totally severed. Even though what happened was the *caillech*'s doing, Loingsechán, according to Suibne, will from now on consider him an enemy to be tracked down and slain, as opposed to a fellow countryman and lord to be found and restored. Suibne is established once again as the ultimate exile. His banishment this time is self-imposed, being in effect a flight from a woman making unseemly proposals, in this case, however, involving stories and not sex.

In light of all that powerful females do and undo in medieval Irish story, we can see why the supreme challenge to Suibne's authority, and to the traditional course the events in the story of Suibne should take, would be posed by a woman. The hag proves to have a source of power all her own, by which she can subvert conventional expectations concerning what she, and the men around her, can or cannot do. As saints' lives indicate often enough, women can function as ideal mediators between seemingly antithetical principles and factions.[45] Yet surviving among competing power structures (the vantage of women as mediators), being marginal to those structures, and provoking an altogether different distribution of power are situations that tend to merge easily enough in medieval Irish narrative. Hence women can form alliances with saints representing a new order to replace the old, or with outlaws and exiles on the peripheries of society, as in the union of Loingsechán and the hag of the mill. Most revealing, however, are the narrative instances, such as the one we have just discussed, where women operate on their own, threatening to take over the very story itself, until they are artificially contained, and usually condemned, by the reassertion of generic specifications that return predictability to the story.

Further on in the *Buile Shuibhne*, the *geilt* is lured back to civilization once again. This time, as we shall see, the rapprochement seems stabler and provides a site for the establishment of the corpus of story and poetry concerning Suibne that will be transmitted to future generations. Significantly the second, more successful taming of the *geilt* takes place under the supervision of a saint. It does not

---

45. For instance, in Muirchú's *Life* of Patrick, it is the wife of Lóegaire, high king of Ireland, who mediates between her recalcitrant husband and the saint (Bieler, *Patrician Texts*, p. 90; Book 1, Chapter 18, in Muirchú's text). Suibne's wife Éorann, who attempts to dissuade him from sacrilege (p. 4), mirrors Lóegaire's queen in this regard.

involve the total reprogramming of the personality of the restless madman into that of a settled king, only the addition of a regularly visited social, monastic terminus to his wanderings. The therapeutic 'deal' struck between saint and *geilt* is founded upon a lively interest in, and respect for, what Suibne has experienced and has to say, and upon the assumption that for this knowledge to be preserved and transmitted it must be written down.

One day Suibne arrives at Tech Moling, the monastery of Saint Moling, and settles down nearby within visual range to have a meal of his favorite food, watercress. We have already learned in previous episodes of *Buile Shuibhne* that the *geilt* must compete for watercress with both women and eremetically inclined holy men who have a yen for this food of the wilderness (pp. 82-90, 94, 130, 132). Moling, when Suibne approaches, is reading from the psalter to his monastic students. He notices the wild man eating nearby and comments to him in verse that it is still early in the monastic day for repast. Suibne surprises him by responding that, while it may seem early to Moling, it is already terce in Rome. The poetic dialogue continues:

> [Moling:] How dost thou know, mad one,
> when terce comes in Rome?
> [Suibne:] Knowledge comes to me from my Lord
> each morn and each eve.
> [M:] Relate through the mystery of speech
> tidings (*scéla*) of the fair Lord.
> [S:] With thee is the (gift of) prophecy,
> if thou art Moling. (p. 139)

The saint is surprised and delighted at how much the stranger knows. On the basis of further conversation Moling is able to identify Suibne, and their dialogue, having established the objective facts of who is speaking to whom, shifts to a subjective comparison of the monastic life with that of a *geilt*:

> [M:] Delightful is the leaf of this book,
> the psalter of holy Kevin.
> [S:] More delightful is a leaf of my yew
> in happy Glenn Bolcáin. (p. 141)

The exchange of matching half-quatrains ends with Moling asking Suibne whether he knows how he will die, and with Suibne giving him the salient details: 'A herd of thine will slay me at early morn' (p. 141). Then the saint, while putting no restrictions on Suibne's activities during the day, binds the *geilt* to come to Tech Moling to have his 'news' and 'adventures' (*sgéla* and *imthechta*, p. 142) recorded in writing every evening.[46] Suibne accepts this condition without complaint and thus, presumably, the account of his adventures and the poems contained in the *Buile Shuibhne* are compiled.

Obviously, the difference between this encounter and those between Suibne and the team composed of the tracker Loingsechán and his wife is considerable. At Tech Moling Suibne is not the sought-after but the seeker, at least initially, even though the *geilt* and his conversation-partner do not have previous familiarity with one another on which to base their discourse, as do Suibne and his fellow countryman Loingsechán. Remarkably, however, Suibne and Moling share an affinity based on their possession of preternatural knowledge, an affinity that makes dialogue possible and mutually beneficial. Moreover, it is now Suibne who has news for the other speaker about matters of current and vital interest. The *geilt* informs the cleric about Rome and the sequence of canonical hours, topics as relevant to a monk as are developments in the family to the alienated Suibne. The knowledge that Loingsechán imparts to Suibne, however, is blatantly and admittedly false, while what the saint and the *geilt* have to say to one another, even though mutually contradictory, is valid within each character's particular context, the monastic versus the sylvan. Most important of all, as a result of this dialogue Suibne is not 'declawed' or rendered a prisoner. What is left behind in the possession of the representative of civilization is a manuscript containing the 'best' of Suibne, a metonymic sign that is not vulnerable to the instabilities that inform Suibne's existence and society's attitude toward him. Indeed, it is a sign that thrives on those very instabilities which make it the fascinating literary work that it is.

Also worth noting in our comparison of the two reconciliation episodes of *Buile Shuibhne* is the decisive difference between the

---

46. It is worth noting that the text ends with a characterization of itself as a synecdochic sampling of Suibne's 'news' and 'adventures' (p. 158).

contentions that provide impetus for the dialogues. In the Moling episode, the sequence of exposition, demonstration, and emulation or competition that proves so strangely digressive in the encounter between Suibne and the hag is not to be found. After all, Moling could have begrudged Suibne the watercress that he desires, and the saint, whose name is traditionally explained as referring to his remarkable leaping skills,[47] could presumably have given the volatile Suibne a run for his money, as did the hag. While Moling's initial comment to the *geilt* is mildly reproving and attempts to regulate his seemingly irregular eating habits, the dialogue reveals the mutual intelligibility of their separate claims to authority, which are thus allowed to complement, instead of compete with, each other. Moling and Suibne clearly do not do or think the same things, but since they both 'come from God', they must find a way to coexist. It is the mode of representation afforded by writing that provides the solution.

Sadly, Suibne's importance dwindles after he leaves behind a written heritage. He falls prey, as he intuited he would, to the same kind of danger that threatened him in the Loingsechán episode, namely the machinations of a woman. The sister of Moling's swineherd overhears a slighting comment made by another woman to the swineherd's wife and, as a result, misconstrues the latter's task of supplying the *geilt* with his food as evidence for Suibne's having an affair with her. The sister informs her brother the swineherd who, in a pique of jealous rage, slays the innocent *geilt* (pp. 142, 144).

In this instance, the interference of women in the ongoing dialogue among males, Moling and Suibne, does not raise disturbing questions about the hidden, barely tapped resources of knowledge and authority available to women. The unidentified female who makes the comment that starts the unravelling of Suibne's life at Tech Moling simply distorts the facts, intentionally or unintentionally, while the swineherd's sister misinterprets what she sees when she

---

47. Moling's and the *geilt*'s shared propensity for leaping is noted in Carney, *Studies*, pp. 143-44. The possible Indo-European mythological significance of the saint's leaping is the subject of Rees and Rees *Celtic Heritage*, pp. 76-80. Another useful study of the distinguishing features of the Moling tradition is Bryan R. Frykenberg, 'Suibne, Lailoken, and the *Taidiu*', *Proceedings of the Harvard Celtic Colloquium*, 4 (1984), 105-20. Ó Riain has pointed out the initiatory subtext to the story of the young Moling's wondrous leaps and his subsequent renaming ('Study of the Irish Legend', p. 198).

spies on her brother's wife. While they and their false reports have considerable impact, as did the report of Loingsechán, that other bearer of disturbing false news, women here display no unexpected talents or powers. Such pyrotechnics are limited to the episodes detailing Suibne's encounters with the wily team of Loingsechán and the hag who threaten to derail the course of events leading up to Suibne's sabbatical at Tech Moling.

And so, the *geilt* cannot find a safe berth anywhere, even in the protective custody of a saint. There is, however, one space in which Suibne survives and thrives, and in which false perceptions, attempts at manipulation, and the malevolent dialogues of others cannot harm him. That space is perhaps what is being described in an Irish poem preserved in a ninth-century manuscript housed in a monastery in Austria. This 'curious riddling poem' (p. xvii), as O'Keeffe and others after him described it, does not mention Suibne but is ascribed to *Suibne Geilt*:

> My little oratory in Tuaim Inbir,
> it is not a full house that is. . .
> with its stars last night,
> with its sun, with its moon.
>
> Gobban hath built that –
> that its story may be told to you –
> my heartlet, God from heaven,
> He is the thatcher who hath thatched it.
>
> A house wherein wet rain pours not,
> a place wherein thou fearest not spear-points,
> bright as though in a garden
> and it without a fence around it.[48]
> (trans. O'Keeffe, pp. xvii-xviii)

---

48. The Irish text is printed on p. xvii in O'Keeffe's introduction, from Stokes and Strachan, *Thesaurus*, p. 294; see also Jackson, *Studies*, p. 3. Another edition/translation can be found in Murphy, *Early Irish Lyrics*, pp. 112-13 (along with editions/translations of one of the Moling/Suibne Middle Irish poems mentioned above, and verses from the *Buile Shuibhne*). A valuable recent analysis of the Túaim Inbir poem, with commentary on earlier criticism, is included in Donnchadh Ó Corráin, 'Early Irish Hermit Poetry?' *Sages, Saints and Storytellers*, ed. Ó Corráin and others, pp. 251-67.

JOSEPH FALAKY NAGY

This site of meditation, impervious to the elements and to human violence, a place of enclosure and security where, however, there is no fence and only God's sky for a ceiling – the creation of a legendary craftsman, a replica of the natural world with its own sun, stars, and moon, wherein God can be addressed in terms of the utmost intimacy: is this not the poem itself, or more specifically the textual, written form of the poem that we share with its author, and even with the author of us all, 'so that its story may be told to you?' This is indeed a space in which to feel paradoxically free despite if not through its restrictions, in which engaged poet and equally engaged reader can obliterate the distinction between dialogue and monologue, and in which even a *geilt* – or, perhaps, especially a *geilt* – can obtain respect and everlasting fame.

Joseph Falaky Nagy
University of California,
Los Angeles

INTRODUCTION TO 1996 EDITION

SELECT BIBLIOGRAPHY OF WORKS CITED

Beneš, Brigit: 'Spuren von Schamanismus in der Sage "Buile Suibhne"', *Zeitschrift für celtische Philologie*, 28 (1961), 309-34.

Carey, John: 'Suibne Geilt and Tuán mac Cairill', *Éigse*, 20 (1984), 93-105.

Carney, James: *Studies in Irish Literature and History* (Dublin, 1955).

Chadwick, Nora K.: 'Geilt', *Scottish Gaelic Studies*, 5 (1942), 106-53.

Clancy, Thomas Owen: 'Mac Steléne and the Eight in Armagh: Identity and Context', *Éigse*, 26 (1992), 80-91.

Clancy, Thomas Owen: 'Fools and Adultery in Some Early Irish Texts', *Ériu*, 44 (1993), 105-24.

Clarke, Basil: *Mental Disorder in Earlier Britain: Exploratory Studies* (Cardiff, 1975).

Cohen, David J.: 'Suibhne Geilt', *Celtica*, 12 (1977), 114-24.

Frykenberg, Bryan R.: 'Suibhne, Lailoken, and the *Taídiu*'. *Proceedings of the Harvard Celtic Colloquium*, 4 (1984), 105- 20.

Frykenberg, Bryan R.: 'The Wild Man in Celtic Ecclesiastical Legend and Literary Tradition'. M. Litt. thesis (University of Edinburgh, 1984).

Frykenberg, Bryan R.: 'Poetry of Suibne Geilt and St. Mo-Ling from Brussels MS. Bibliothèque Royale MS. 5100-04'. Ph.D. dissertation (Harvard University, 1994).

Griffiths, Margaret Enid: *Early Vaticination in Welsh with English Parallels* (Cardiff, 1937).

Hamp, Eric P.: '*imbolc, óimelc*', *Studia Celtica*, 14/15 (1979/80), 106-113.

Heaney, Seamus: *Sweeney Astray* (Derry, 1983).

Henry, P. L.: *The Early English and Celtic Lyric* (London, 1966).

Jackson, Kenneth H.: *Studies in Early Celtic Nature Poetry* (Cambridge, 1935).

Jackson, Kenneth H.: 'The Motive of the Threefold Death in the Story of Suibhne Geilt', *Féil-Sgríbhinn Eóin mhic Néill: Essays and Studies Presented to Professor Eoin MacNeill*, ed. John Ryan (Dublin, 1940), pp. 535-50.

Jackson, Kenneth H.: *Language and History in Early Britain: A Chronological Survey of the Brittonic Languages First to Twelfth Century A.D.* (Edinburgh, 1953).

Jackson, Kenneth H.: 'A Further Note on Suibhne Geilt and Merlin', *Éigse*, 7 (1953), 112-16.

Jackson, Kenneth H.: 'The Sources for the Life of St Kentigern', *Studies in the Early British Church*, Nora K. Chadwick and others (Cambridge, 1958), pp. 273-357.

Jarman, A. O. H.: *The Legend of Merlin* (Cardiff, 1960).

Jarman, A. O. H.: 'Early Stages in the Development of the Myrddin Legend', *Astudiaethau ar yr Hengerdd / Studies in Old Welsh Poetry*, ed. Rachel Bromwich and R. Brinley Jones (Cardiff, 1978), pp. 326-49.

Jarman, A. O. H.: 'The Merlin Legend and the Welsh Tradition of Prophecy', *The Arthur of the Welsh: The Arthurian Legend in Medieval Welsh Literature*, ed. Rachel Bromwich, Jarman, and Brynley F. Roberts (Cardiff, 1991), pp. 117-45.

Kelly, H. A.: 'Heaney's Sweeney: The Poet as Version-Maker', *Philological Quarterly*, 65 (1986), 293-310.

Laurent, Donatien: 'La gwerz de Skolan et la légende de Merlin', *Ethnologie française*, 1 (1971), 19-47.

Laurent, Donatien: 'Breton Orally Transmitted Folk Poetry', *The European Folk Ballad: A Symposium*, ed. Otto Holzapfel and others (Odense, 1978), pp. 16-25.

Lehmann, Ruth Preston: 'A Study of the *Buile Shuibhne*', *Études Celtiques*, 6 (1953), 289-311; 7 (1955), 115-38.

[31]

JOSEPH FALAKY NAGY

Mac Eoin, Gearóid S.: 'Gleann Bolcáin agus Gleann na nGealt' *Béaloideas*, 30 (1962), 105-20.

Nagy, Joseph Falaky: 'The Wisdom of the *Geilt*', *Éigse*, 19 (1982), 44-60.

O'Brien, Flann [Brian Ó Nualláin]: *At Swim-Two-Birds* (London, 1939).

Ó Cathasaigh, Tomás: 'The Threefold Death in Early Irish Sources' *Studia Celtica Japonica*, 6 (1994), 53-74.

Ó Corráin, Donnchadh: 'Early Irish Hermit Poetry?', *Sages, Saints and Storytellers: Celtic Studies in Honour of Professor James Carney*, ed. Ó Corráin, Liam Breatnach, and Kim McCone (Maynooth, 1989).

O'Keeffe, J. G.: *Buile Shuibhne*. Mediaeval and Modern Irish Series, Vol. 1 (Dublin, 1931).

Ó Riain, Pádraig: 'A Study of the Irish Legend of the Wild Man', *Éigse*, 14 (1972), 179-206.

Ó Riain, Pádraig: 'The Materials and Provenance of "Buile Shuibhne"', *Éigse*, 15 (1974), 173-88.

Partridge, Angela [now Angela Bourke]: 'Wild Men and Wailing Women', *Éigse*, 18 (1980-81), 25-37.

Picard, Jean-Michel: 'The Strange Death of Guaire Mac Áedáin', *Sages, Saints and Storytellers: Celtic Studies in Honour of Professor James Carney*, ed. Donnchadh Ó Corráin, Liam Breatnach, and Kim McCone (Maynooth, 1989), pp. 367-75.

Radner, Joan Newlon: 'The Significance of the Threefold Death in Celtic Tradition', *Celtic Folklore and Christianity: Studies in Memory of William W. Heist*, ed. Patrick K. Ford (Santa Barbara/Los Angeles, 1983), pp. 180-200.

Rowland, Jenny: *Early Welsh Saga Poetry: A Study and Edition of the Englynion* (Cambridge, 1990).

Sayers, William: '*Guin & Crochad & Gólad*: The Earliest Irish Threefold Death', *Celtic Languages and Celtic Peoples: Proceedings of the Second North American Congress of Celtic Studies*, ed. Cyril J. Byrne, Margaret Harry, and Pádraig Ó Siadhail (Halifax, 1992), pp. 64-82.

Sayers, William: 'Varia VII. The deficient ruler as avian exile; Nebuchadnezzar as Suibhne Geilt', *Ériu*, 43 (1992), 217-20.

Stewart, James: 'Gleann na nGealt: A Twelfth-Century Latin Account', *Celtica*, 17 (1985), 105-111.

Stokes, Whitley: 'Poems Ascribed to S. Moling', *Anecdota from Irish Manuscripts*, ed. O. J. Bergin and others, Vol. 2 (Halle and Dublin, 1908), pp. 20-41.

Stokes, Whitley, and John Strachan: *Thesaurus Palaeohibernicus: A Collection of Old-Irish Glosses, Scholia Prose and Verse*. Vol. 2 (Cambridge, 1903; repr. 1975).

Tolstoy, Nikolai: '"Merlinus Redivivus"', *Studia Celtica*, 28-29 (1983-84), 11-29.

Tolstoy, Nikolai: *The Quest for Merlin* (London, 1985).

Ward, Donald J.: 'The Threefold Death: An Indo-European Trifunctional Sacrifice?', *Myth and Law Among the Indo-Europeans*, ed. Jaan Puhvel (Berkeley and Los Angeles, 1970), pp. 123-46.

Williams, Ifor: 'Gwyllon, Geilt, Wyll', *Bulletin of the Board of Celtic Studies*, 1 (1923), 228-34.

Williams, Ifor: *The Beginnings of Welsh Poetry: Studies by Sir Ifor Williams*, ed. Rachel Bromwich (Cardiff, 1972).

Ziolkowski, Jan: 'The Nature of Prophecy in Geoffrey of Monmouth's *Vita Merlini*', *Poetry and Prophecy: The Beginnings of a Literary Tradition*, ed. James L. Kugel (Ithaca and London, 1990), pp. 151-62.

INTRODUCTION

I.—SUMMARY

THE tale here edited and translated for the first time deals
with the adventures of Suibhne, surnamed Geilt, and described
as king of the Irish territory of Dal Araidhe, after his flight
from the battle of Magh Rath. Before proceeding to discuss
a number of important points arising out of this strange and
in many respects unique literary document, which has come
down to us from medieval Ireland, it will be convenient to
summarize it briefly.

§ 1-6.—St. Ronan Finn (the Fair), Abbot of Druim
Ineasclainn (Drumiskin, Co. Louth), proceeds to mark
out the site of a church in Dal Araidhe. Suibhne, the
king of the territory, is angry thereat, and despite the
efforts of his wife Eorann—who in trying to hold him
drags the cloak off him leaving him naked—he sets
off to expel the cleric. Ronan is discovered chanting
his psalms. Suibhne seizes the psalter and flings it
into a lake. Just as Suibhne is dragging the cleric
away, a messenger arrives from Congal Claen, described
as king of Ulaidh, bidding Suibhne join him at Magh
Rath. Leaving the cleric behind, Suibhne proceeds
to Magh Rath. In the meantime an otter brings the
psalter uninjured out of the lake to Ronan. The latter
curses Suibhne, praying that he be ever wandering and
flying stark-naked throughout the world, that his death

b

be from a spear, and that destruction be the lot of the race of Colman—Suibhne's race—the day they set eyes on Ronan's psalter.

§ **7-10.**—Ronan intervenes at Magh Rath to make peace between Domhnall, the High King, and Congal Claen, but Suibhne thwarts his efforts. Moreover, Suibhne slays one of Ronan's psalmists, and even attempts to slay the cleric himself. Ronan again curses Suibhne, praying that he ascend into the air, and that his manner of death be that which had been meted out to the psalmist.

§ **11-19.**—The battle of Magh Rath follows; so dreadful is the din that Suibhne literally flies, a stark madman, out of the battle-field. He wanders throughout Ireland and, after many adventures, arrives at Glen Bolcain, a place sacred to the madmen of Ireland. It is there—so the tale runs—the madmen of Ireland went 'when their year of madness was complete.' Glen Bolcain is described, also Suibhne's sufferings and privations during his first year of madness.

§ **20-34.**—He sets out again on his wanderings; he recounts his miseries, and tells how he lives on watercress and water, and sleeps in ivy-bushes. For seven years he wanders thus, and at the end of that time a kinsman named Loingseachan, a miller, goes in search of him. Loingseachan's care for Suibhne is exemplified by the fact that he had already rescued Suibhne three times from madness. Suibhne is angry at being discovered; he tells Loingseachan that it was Ronan's curses that drove him to madness. Suibhne promises to go to his wife. Eorann in the meantime appears to have taken another mate, namely Guaire, Suibhne's successor in the kingship of Dal Araidhe. Eorann receives Suibhne in a friendly way; she even longs to share his strange life; but their discourse is interrupted by the appearance of

Guaire's followers, and Suibhne flies off to Ros Ercain, where the erenagh's wife tries to tempt him.

§ **35-45.**—His hiding-place is discovered by the nobles of Dal Araidhe, who send Loingseachan to seize him. Suibhne asks for news of his country, whereupon Loingseachan tells him that his father, mother, brother, wife, son, and daughter are dead. So moved is Suibhne at the tidings that his senses come to him, and he consents to go with Loingseachan. The latter then tells him that his folk are still alive. Suibhne is taken in charge by the nobles of Dal Araidhe, and his senses are restored to him. He is entrusted to the care of Loingseachan, but one day when Loingseachan has to go out to reap, he is left in the charge of the woman who looks after Loingseachan's mill. She is warned that she must not speak to him, but speak she does, and she goads him into talking of his wild life ; he mentions his feats of flying, and she urges him to fly. He does so, and the woman flies after him, pursuing him from place to place. Then follows (§ 40) the longest and, in many respects, the most interesting poem in the story ; it opens with a description of the trees of Ireland, after which Suibhne recounts his own sorrows and sufferings. He resumes his flight, but the hag still clings to him ; she is killed, however, in trying to leap from the summit of Dun Sobairce (Dunseverick). Then he leaves Dal Araidhe, for he is afraid lest Loingseachan should kill him to avenge the mill-hag. He goes to Ros Comain, where he endures more hardships.

§ **46-58.**—After further wanderings in Ireland he proceeds to Britain, where he falls in with another madman, Ealadhan. They interchange their histories and enter into a compact of friendship. They spend a year together and then part. Suibhne returns to Ireland and goes to Magh Line, thence to Glen Bolcain, where he encounters a mad woman. Then he goes to his wife Eorann, who, seeing he is still mad, orders him away, whereupon he indulges in further melancholy reminiscences. He goes to Benn Boirche and describes his life there.

§ **59-67.**—He resolves to return to Dal Araidhe and entrust himself to his people. His reason is returning, but Ronan again curses him, with the result that Suibhne encounters goblins on Sliabh Fuaid at midnight. Madness seizes him once more and he flies away in terror. The pursuit of Suibhne by the goblins is described ; he escapes from them. Again he recounts his woes, harking back to the mill-hag and to the spectres on Sliabh Fuaid.

§**68-76.**—After further wanderings, Suibhne goes (§74) to Tech Moling, where he encounters Saint Moling, who was reading the psalter of Caoimhghin (St. Kevin) at the time to students. Moling welcomes Suibhne and tells him that not only was his coming there prophesied, but also the fact that he would die there. He binds Suibhne that, however much he may wander during the day, he is to return each night so that Moling may record his life-story.

§ **77-78.**—For a year Suibhne continues visiting Moling, who has given orders to his cook that she is to leave milk ready for him each evening. The cook was Muirghil, wife of Moling's swineherd Mongan. Muirghil used to dig her heel in the cowdung and leave the full of the hole of new milk for Suibhne to drink. Muirghil and another woman have a dispute ; the latter charges Muirghil with preferring Suibhne to her husband. The herd's sister, who was listening, tells Mongan, who promptly thrusts a spear in Suibhne.

§ **79-83.**—One of Moling's community, who witnessed the deed and prophesied that evil would ensue from it, reports the news to Moling. Moling gives Suibhne the sacraments and both of them remonstrate with the herd. Moling promises Suibhne that he will be in heaven as long as himself.

§ **84-86.**—A death-swoon comes on Suibhne. Moling and his clerics each place a stone on Suibhne's tomb. Moling delivers a funeral oration in prose and verse. Suibhne rises out of the swoon, and Moling takes him to church, where he dies. The tale ends : ' so far some of the adventures of Suibhne son of Colman Cuar king of Dal Araidhe.'

II.—THE MANUSCRIPTS

The *Buile Suibhne* occurs in one form or another, so far as I am aware, in three manuscripts, viz. : —

B—B IV I. fo. 82a to 95b.
K—23 K 44, p. 131 to 180.
L—Brussels, 3410, fo. 59a to 61b.[1]

B.—This is one of the most valuable MSS. of the famous Stowe collection in the Royal Irish Academy. It is a paper folio, and was written between the years 1671 and 1674 at Sean Cua, Co. Sligo, by Daniel O'Duigenan,[2] who was one of the best of the later Irish scribes. The MS. contains, in addition to the present text, the *Banquet of Dun na nGedh*, the *Battle of Magh Rath*, the *Adventures of the Two Idiot Saints*, and a considerable number of other pieces in prose and verse. The whole is written in a clear flowing hand. I have made this MS. the basis of my text ; I have but rarely

---

1 See Vol. v. of Rev. J. Van Den Gheyn's Catalogue of MSS. in the Royal Library, Brussels. This MS. was formerly numbered 2324-2340.

2 The dates are given in footnotes at folios 97a, 192a, and 197b.

departed from its readings, and where I have done so the fact
will be found indicated in the footnotes.[1]

K.—This is a quarto paper MS., also in the Royal Irish
Academy. It contains only the *Banquet of Dun na nGedh*,
the *Battle of Magh Rath*, and the present text. It was
written in 1721-2 by Tomaltach Mac Muirghiosa for Seumas
Tiriall. This MS. was used by O'Donovan in his edition
of the *Banquet of Dun na nGedh* and *Battle of Magh Rath*,
published for the Irish Archæological Society in 1842 ;
he refers to it throughout as Mac Morisey's copy. On the
whole, I consider that the readings of **K** are better than those
of **B**, and I would have made it the basis of my text were it
not that in the poems many stanzas which occur in **B** are
absent from **K**. The stanzas which have been omitted will be
found enumerated in the Notes.[2]

L.—This MS. is in the Royal Library, Brussels. I have
worked on it partly from a photograph and partly from a
partial transcript for which I am indebted to Professor Kuno
Meyer. The MS. was written by Michael O'Clery, one of the
Four Masters, in 1629. Michael O'Clery seems to have
handled the material before him very freely. Assuming that
he worked from an original as full as **B** or **K**, he condensed
the prose narratives very much and he omitted all the poetry
except occasional first lines. In fact he has omitted everything

---

1 The scribe has employed contractions very freely ; some of these I have
expanded silently, but wherever there appeared to me to be any doubt I have
indicated the expansions in italics.

2 I do not think that these omissions point to any special significance,
although it is somewhat curious that, except for a passage near the beginning,
there are no omissions from the prose. Some of the stanzas were possibly
omitted accidentally, some may have been omitted because they appeared obscure
to the scribe ; but I should say that most of them are traceable to a MS. in
which the particular stanzas were illegible. The omission of some final stanzas
and half stanzas seems to point clearly to an illegible MS. No scribe of any merit
would deliberately omit a final stanza ; one of the most stringent rules of Irish
verse required that the concluding word of a poem should repeat the whole or
part of the first word of the poem.

from § 13 to § 62 inclusive, merely explaining that Suibhne
spent his life in madness through Ireland and Britain 'as
the book written about himself, entitled the *Buile Suibhne*,
affirms.'[1] **L** therefore stands by itself, and I have only made
use of it in the edition here published in a few instances in
which it supplied an interesting reading or assisted in clearing
up difficult passages. As the summary is brief and may
possess interest for students, I have thought it well to print it
in full. It will be found at the close of the Notes. So far as
the present tale is concerned, all three MSS. seem to me to be
immediately independent of each other. On score of date
alone, **L** stands by itself, and, being only a summary, neither
B nor **K** can have been taken from it. **K**, the latest MS. in the
matter of date, might have been copied from **B**, but on internal
evidence this is, I think, out of the question. The verbal
differences, though rarely of importance, are too numerous
to admit of the possibility of its being a copy. Moreover, on
linguistic grounds, **K** seems to me to be nearer the archetype
than **B**. For this same reason, and especially in view of the
omissions from **K** already referred to, I do not think it is
even likely that both texts were taken from the same parent;
it is much more probable that both, perhaps all three, go back
two or three generations to a common ancestor.

III.—DATE OF TALE

The dates of the MSS. afford no criterion as to the probable
date of the tale. From a linguistic point of view the text
belongs to that indefinite period which covers late Middle-Irish
and early Modern-Irish. Until the history of Middle-Irish
has been thoroughly investigated from dated texts it will be
impossible to establish on linguistic grounds with any degree

---

1 See footnote 1, § 12.

of approximation the age of undated Middle-Irish texts. An
odd archaic word or form occurs here and there in our text,
but that proves nothing. Neither does the existence, which
is fairly common, of the infixed pronouns of the first and
second persons singular. These were freely employed down
to the sixteenth and seventeenth centuries. On linguistic
grounds it may be safely said, I think, that the text might
have been composed at any time between the years 1200 and
1500. Further on I endeavour to show that the three tales,
the *Banquet of Dun na nGedh*, the *Battle of Magh Rath*,
and the *Buile Suibhne*, are closely related ; they form in
themselves a small story-cycle, and all the evidence points to
the fact that they have come down, generally speaking, from
the same period. O'Donovan, in the introduction to his
edition of the *Battle of Magh Rath*, discussing the question
of the age of the tale, observes that it was 'unquestionably
intended to flatter the descendants of its hero, king Domhnal,
grandson of Ainmire, while his race were in full power in the
north of Ireland ; and, therefore, that its author must have
lived before the year 1197, when Flaithbhertach O'Muldory,
the last chief of Tirconnell of this monarch's family, died.
How long before that year the date of this composition should
be placed cannot now be well ascertained, but when the whole
case is duly weighed, it will be seen that it could never
have been written after the extinction of the race of the
monarch on whom the exploits described reflect so much
glory.'

Of more importance, however, in this connexion is the
following reference to Suibhne Geilt in the early Irish law
tract entitled the *Book of Aicill*. 'Three were the triumphs
(*buadha*) of that battle (i.e. the battle of Magh Rath) : the
defeat of Congal Claen in his falsehood by Domhnall in
his truth, and Suibhne Geilt having become mad, and
Cennfaeladh's brain of forgetfulness having been taken from
his head. And Suibhne Geilt having become mad is not

a reason why the battle is a triumph, but it is because of the stories and poems he left after him in Ireland."[1]

If, as I think would be generally accepted, the Book of Aicill took shape in the ninth or, at the latest, tenth century, it is evident that the tradition which associated the madness of Suibhne—as well as his poems and the stories respecting him—with the battle of Magh Rath was rife at an earlier date. Of some importance too in this connexion is the curious riddling poem, ascribed to Suibhne Geilt, which exists in an Irish MS. in the monastery of St. Paul in Carinthia.[2]

M'airiuclán hi Túaim Inbir
ni lántechdais bes sestu
cona retglannaib a réir
cona gréin cona escu.

Gobban durigni insin
conecestar duib astoir
mu chridecan dia du nim
is hé tugatoir rodtoig.

Tech inna fera flechod
maigen na áigder rindi
soilsidir bid hi lugburt
ose cen udnucht nimbi.

My little oratory in Tuaim Inbir,
it is not a full house that is   .   .   .
with its stars last night,
with its sun, with its moon.

---

1 *Ancient Laws of Ireland*, Vol. III., p. 89; this is given, though with some differences, in the Banquet of Dun na nGedh, ed. O'Donovan, p. 84.

2 See Thes. Palæohib, Vol. II., pp. xxxII, 294; also Thurneysen, Handbuch des Alt-Irischen, Vol. II., p. 39.

Gobban hath built that—
that its story may be told to you—
my heartlet, God from heaven,
He is the thatcher who hath thatched it.

A house wherein wet rain pours not,
a place wherein thou fearest not spear-points,
bright as though in a garden
and it without a fence around it.

This poem has been variously assigned to the eighth and
ninth centuries. It is worthy of note in passing that, of the
four poems which make up the contents of the St. Paul MS.,
one is ascribed to St. Moling, †697, the friend of Suibhne. Of
this poem the editors of the Thesaurus Palæohibernicus say,
with certain reservations, that it may have actually been
composed by St. Moling himself.

The association of the two names, Suibhne and St.
Moling, in these two poems occurring together in the same
MS. is not without significance when we consider the
friendship between the two as shown in the *Buile Suibhne*.
Both names are found further associated in the interesting
collection of poems ascribed to St. Moling published in
Anecdota from Irish MSS.[1] In a note referring to the first
three poems in that collection it is suggested that it was
Suibhne who composed them, though it was Moling who put
them in the 'old book,' viz.: the Book of Murchadh, son of
Brian.[2] Before passing from these poems it may be remarked
that they bear striking resemblance in many respects to the
poetry in the *Buile Suibhne*, the same phrases occurring in
some cases in both.

---

1 Vol II., p. 20.

2 Murchadh, son of Brian (Boruma), fell in the battle of Clontarf, 1014. Can
it be that Murchadh son of Bran, king of Leinster, ob. 727, is meant? He
must have been a contemporary of Moling.

The evidence so far would seem to point to the fact that the tradition of Suibhne's madness and of his poems and of the stories about him goes back to the time of Suibhne himself, and that Moling may have had a share in the actual moulding of the tradition.

IV.—THE BATTLE OF MAGH RATH

The battle of Magh Rath was fought in the year A.D. 637. That the battle was an historical event and one of considerable significance is without doubt. It is recorded in the Annals of Ulster, the Chronicon Scotorum, and the Annals of Tigernach. It is only in the last-named that mention is made of Suibhne, and there it is recorded that he fell in the battle. Adhamnan, who was thirteen years old when it was fought, mentions it in his Life of Colum Cille,[1] and his words place beyond a doubt any question as to the authenticity of the event. The significance in Irish history of the battle may be inferred from the fact that it gave rise not only to the present tale but also to two long romantic accounts of the battle known as the *Banquet of Dun na nGedh* and the *Battle of Magh Rath*.

Amid the bewildering tangle of events in Ireland in the sixth and seventh centuries it is not easy to determine with any degree of certainty what this significance was. Apart from Adhamnan's Life of Colum Cille,[2] the Irish annals, particularly the Annals of Ulster and the Annals of Tigernach, constitute almost the only available sources of information. Nothing, however, could well be more laconic than the records

---

1 Life of St. Columba, ed. Reeves, p. 200.

2 Nobody can touch this period of Ulidian history without acknowledging his indebtedness to Reeves's splendid edition of Adhamnan's great work. The same scholar's work on the Ecclesiastical Antiquities of Down, Connor, and Dromore is almost equally valuable to the historian and topographer.

in the annals of the period ; events are chronicled, but one looks in vain for a clue to the political forces or motives at work.   Whether a certain battle, for instance, was prompted by deliberate state policy or was merely the outcome of racial, tribal, or even personal rivalry or rancour it is scarcely ever possible to say.[1]

One fact, however, stands out clearly in the records of the century immediately preceding the battle of Magh Rath : it was the remarkable growth in power and dominion which the Scottish portion of the kingdom of Dal Riada attained during the sixth and seventh centuries.   If, as seems probable, the battle was in a large measure[2] the outcome of this growth, the significance in Irish history of the event will be manifest.

The Irish state of Dal Riada comprised roughly the northern half of Antrim.   At an early period in its history —possibly in the fourth century[3]—some of its people passed over to the neighbouring shores of Scotland and established there in the course of the next two or three centuries the Scottish kingdom of Dal Riada, an event of great importance in the history of Scotland.   Both the Irish and Scottish Dal Riada were under one ruler, who appears to have been subject to the High King of Ireland,[4]

---

1 The systematic study of the genealogies, carried out on the lines of Mac Neill's *Early Irish Population-Groups*, will help to clear up much of this.

2 No doubt, other circumstances contributed, such as the rivalry between the Ulaidh and the Picts of Dal Araidhe.

3 There are many evidences against Tigernach who gives 502 as the date of the migration.   For one thing, it is scarcely possible that the Scottish Dal Riada could have achieved in seventy years the position of importance it had attained under Aedhan son of Gabhran.   Furthermore, the migration must have taken place at a time when the Irish Dal Riada was a much larger territory than it was in 502.   A line drawn from the village of Glynn, a little to the south of Larne, to the northern slopes of Slemish, thence—keeping to the west of the mountains —to the source of the Bush, and following that river to the sea, would probably give the boundary between Dal Araidhe and Dal Riada.

4 The accounts of the Convention of Druim Ceata seem to point to the fact that the questions at issue lay between the High King of Ireland and the king of Dal Riada.   The king of Ulaidh does not figure in the accounts of the Convention.

at least as far as the Irish Dal Riada was concerned. The
Dalriadic dynasty may be said to have been firmly established
in Scotland by Aedhan, son of Gabhran, who is reckoned
as its seventh king. Aedhan was solemnly inaugurated by
Colum Cille, Abbot of Iona, in 575. Immediately after
his accession to the throne he appears to have set himself
to the task of making the Scottish portion of his kingdom,
if not indeed the whole of it, independent. There can be
no doubt that it was largely to settle the dispute between
Aedhan and the Irish monarch respecting the tributes of
Dal Riada that the Convention of Druim Ceata was held
in 575. Colum Cille, who was present[1] at the Convention,
pleaded the cause of Dal Riada. The result of the
Convention is not very clear, but it would seem that
Aedhan succeeded in obtaining some measure of indepen-
dence. 'Their expeditions and their hosting with the men
of Ireland—for hosting is always with the founders—and
their tribute with the men of Scotland'; such is one version
of the judgment given.[2] His action in this respect was in
keeping with the activity displayed by him in other
directions. The annals record that he made an expedition

---

1 It is unlikely that Aedhan was present, although Keating in his account of
the Convention states that it is recorded in the Book of Glendalough that he was
present.

2 *Lismore Lives*, ed. Stokes, page 314. I am indebted to Professor
John Mac Neill for the following note on the import of this judgment :—'This
law cannot refer to Fir Alban (which name was appropriated to the Dal Riada
of Scotland). Their hostings were not with Ireland, and such a judgment in
their case would have been, not a compromise, but an open mockery of the Irish
king. But the import of the law becomes clear and reasonable if we understand
it to apply to the Irish Dal Riada. In their case, to have to attend the Scottish
king in war would have been a grievous burden to themselves, and a breach of
the Irish monarchical theory. Therefore, so far as they were obliged to aid a
suzerain in war, their aid was due to the Irish king only. But since the Scottish
dynasty was their dynasty too, their tributes, i.e. the rents paid to their kings
and nobility by the vassal population of Irish Dal Riada continued to be paid,
or at all events payable, to the king and his nobles, though these were resident in
Scotland. When Irish writers lost touch with the early conditions of eastern
Ulster, they must have failed to understand the treaty of Druim Ceata.'

to the Orkneys in 581, that he was victor in the battle of Mano in the following year, and in the battle of Lethreid in 590, and that he was defeated a year or two later in a battle against the Saxons.[1] At his death in 606 he was succeeded by his son Eochaidh Buidhe, whom the annals, in recording his death in 629, style king of the Picts. His son Conadh Cerr followed in the kingship of Dal Riada. Conadh was slain at the battle of Fidheoin in 629, and was succeeded by his brother Domhnall Brecc, who reigned until 642, and was thus king of Dal Riada at the date of the battle of Magh Rath, in which, as we shall see later, he took a prominent part.

So far as Dal Riada is concerned, the records of the sixth century go to show that, side by side with the growth of the Scottish state, the parent kingdom was steadily waning in power and importance, until it eventually ceased to be more than a name. It is certain that at an early date—possibly by the close of the sixth century—the native dynasty became merged in that of Argyle; and, with the transfer of the dynasty, the nobles of the Irish Dal Riada passed over to Scotland.[2] No doubt, the new country across the narrow

---

[1] In the story of the birth of Brandubh (Zeit. C.P. II, 134) it is stated that Aedhan went on a hosting to Ireland to contest the kingship of Ireland, taking with him men of Scotland, Britons, and Saxons. The Irish annals have no record of such expedition. It is recorded also (see Reeves, *Adhamnan*, p. 373) that Aedhan submitted to Baedan, king of Ulaidh, at Rossnaree in Seimhne.

> Giallastar do Baetan ban
> arddri na hAlban Aedan
> ic Ross na rig, rad ṅglan ṅgle,
> in airthiur tuaisciurt Semne.
> Rawl. B 502, Fo. 156b.

[2] The genealogies under the heading of Dal Riada ('race of Conaire Mor contain no pedigrees, no kindreds or septs, but those of Fir Alban (i.e. the Dal Riada of Scotland). This indicates that by the time when the corpus genealogical began to be assembled, the nobles of the Irish Dal Riada were no longer known to exist, or at all events had fallen into obscurity. This must have been the case when the Laud 610 tract was compiled, i.e. about 1050, for

strip of sea offered a wider field for enterprise and adventure
than they could find at home. Moreover, the Irish Dal Riada
must have constantly suffered from the pressure of its
neighbours, the warlike Picts of Dal Araidhe on the west
and the equally warlike Ulaidh to the south.   Ever since the
fall of Emain in the fourth century—when the power of
Ulaidh was well-nigh crippled—the Picts of Dal Araidhe had
been rising into prominence. They who had once been
subjects of the Ulaidh were now their rivals, and the history
of the two states from the fifth to the eighth century is one
long struggle for supremacy. Within so circumscribed an
area it was inevitable that Dal Riada should be brought into
the conflict. During the decade immediately preceding the
battle of Magh Rath there is evidence of the struggle between
them. The battle of Lethet Midind was fought in 626
between Ulaidh and Dal Araidhe. A year later Ulaidh
was defeated by Dal Riada in the battle of Ard Corainn.
Dal Riada, on the other hand, suffered severely at the hands
of Cruithni in the battle of Fidheoin,[1] fought in 629.

---

that tract gives special prominence to the genealogies of East Ulster; it was
compiled in or near Armagh, and is the source of the material for that region in
LL., BB., and Rawl. B. 502.   But it ignores the Irish Dal Riada.   Again, the
Laud tract draws on eighth-century sources, and would have copied any Dal
Riada pedigrees found in them. Hence we may infer that even in the eighth
century, the nobles of Dal Riada had probably ceased to be of account in
Ireland.   Their disappearance is easily explained once we grasp the fact that the
Irish Dal Riada maintained to the full their political and social unity with the
' Fir Alban,' living even under the same government.   In Ireland their territory
was narrow and unfertile, and they were hemmed in by the warlike Picts and
Ulaidh.   In Scotland their kings kept gaining ground steadily until the final
conquest of the Picts, Britons, and Angles by Cinaeth Mac Ailpin in the ninth
century. The topography of the Scottish Lowlands proves that that region,
including even the Anglian territory of Bernicia (the Lothians), was extensively colonized by the Irish (Scots) after they conquered it. We can imagine
that the people of the Antrim Glens were glad to leave those cramped and
wooded fastnesses to become possessors of wide domains in various parts of
Scotland, and that they carried off with them the genealogical traditions which
find no place in the very copious Irish record. [Note by Prof. John MacNeill.]

1 The battle of Fidheoin seems to have been a most important event.
Unfortunately the place has not been identified; it cannot even be said that it is

Let us now turn to Congal Claen and the events leading up to the battle of Magh Rath. Congal was a prince of the great Ulidian race of Rudraige Mor. From an early age he had been fostered by Domhnall, who succeeded his father Aedh, son of Ainmire, as High King of Ireland in 598. The romantic accounts of the battle of Magh Rath dwell at considerable length on the causes which led to a quarrel between Congal and his foster-father, but these may for the most part be dismissed as bardic fictions. There is one passage, however, in the *Banquet of Dun na nGedh*[1] which is worth quoting here, as it may well represent the traditional view of the relations of Congal and Domhnall. Congal in a moment of anger, through being, as he thinks, slighted at the famous banquet, says to the king :

' I will now state, before all, the injuries thou hast done to me. The king who preceded thee over Erin was Suibhne Menn . . . thou wert not obedient to that king, and thou didst go to make a treaty with the Ultonians, and I was given in fosterage to thee by my father and my own tribe ; a woman of my own tribe was sent with me to nurse me with thee, but when she reached thy house thou didst send the Ultonian woman back to her own country, and thou didst place a woman of thine own tribe to nurse me in the garden of the fort in which thou dwellest. It happened on a certain day that I was left in the garden without anyone to take care of me, and the little bees of the garden rose up with the heat of the sun, and one of them put its venom in one of my eyes, so that my eye became awry, from which I have been named Congal Claen. I was nursed by thee until thou wast expelled

---

in Ireland Moreover, it is doubtful that Maelcaich (or Maelcaith) was king of the Cruithni, as he is described, at the time. Tigernach gives the fullest record of the battle. There fell in the battle Conadh Cerr, king of Dal Riada, Dicull mac Eachach, who is described as king of the kindred of the Picts, two grandsons of Aedhan as well as Oisiric mac Albruit, crown prince of England (rigdomna Saxan).

1 ed. O'Donovan, p. 33.

by the king of Erin, Suibhne Menn . . . and then thou
didst repair to the king of Alba, taking me along with thee in
that exile ; and thou didst receive great honour from him,
and you formed a treaty, thou and the king of Alba, and he
protested to thee that he would not oppose thee as long as
the sea should surround Erin.   Thou didst afterwards return
to Erin, and I returned along with thee, for I was in exile
along with thee.   We put into port at Traigh Rudhraighe,
and here we held a short consultation.   And what thou didst
say was, that whoever thou shouldst get to betray the king of
Erin, thou wouldst be bound to restore his territory to him
whenever thou shouldst become king of Erin.   I went on the
enterprise, O king, for a promise that my patrimony should be
wholly restored to me, whenever thou shouldst become
monarch of Erin ; and I delayed not until I reached Aileach
Neid, where the king held his residence at the time.   The
king came out upon the green surrounded by a great
concourse of the men of Erin, and he was playing chess
amidst the hosts, and I came into the assembly, passing
without the permission of anyone through the crowds and
made a thrust of my spear, Gearr Congail, which I held in my
hand, at the breast of the king, and the stone which was at
his back responded to the thrust, his heart's blood was on the
head of the javelin, so that he fell dead.   But as the king was
tasting of death he flung a chess-man which was in his hand
at me, so that he broke the crooked eye in my head.   I was
squint-eyed before, I have been blind-eyed since.   The host
and people of the king fled, thinking that thou and the men
of Alba were with me, as I had killed Suibhne Menn, the
king.   I then returned to thee, and thou didst, after this,
assume the sovereignty of Erin.   My father, Scannall of the
Broad Shield, died soon after, and I came to thee to be made
king as thou hadst promised me.   Thou didst not perform
thy promise except to a small extent, for thou didst deprive
me of Cenel Conaill and Cenel Eoghain and also of the nine

cantreds of Oirghiall, the land of Maelodhar Macha, who now sits at my shoulder, and whom thou hast seated in the place of a king, in preference to me, this night, in thine own house, O king, said he. And a goose egg was placed before him on a silver dish, while a hen egg was placed on a wooden dish before me. And I will give battle to thee and the men of Erin in consequence, as thou hast them assembled around thee to-night, said Congal. And he went out of the house and the Ultonians followed him.'

What are the facts as recorded in the annals? Suibhne Menn, son of Fiachna, became High King in 615 in succession to Maelchoba, son of Aedh, whom he dethroned. He defeated Domhnall, son of Aedh, at Both in 628, but was slain the same year by Congal Claen on the shores of Lough Swilly near Aileach. He was succeeded by Domhnall, brother of Maelchoba and son of Aedh. As to the kingship of Ulaidh, the annals record that Fiachna, son of Demman, was killed in the battle of Ard Corainn in 627. Congal appears as next king of Ulaidh[1]; he also figures as king of Dal Araidhe.

The battle of Dun Cethirn, which was fought in 629 between Congal Claen and the High King, Domhnall, son of Aedh, marks the next stage. The annals merely record that Domhnall was victor and that Congal fled, but Adhamnan in his Life of Colum Cille[2] records the fulfilment of one of the saint's prophecies to the effect that Ui Neill and Cruithni would wage war fighting in the vicinity of the fortress of Cethern.

Dun Cethirn lies some five miles to the west of the Bann in territory which had long been a source of strife,[3] but which

---

1 See LL. fo. 41; also the 'Comaimserad righ nErenn,' Book of Lecan, fo. 23a1.

2 ed. Reeves, p. 93.

3 One of the *geasa* or 'prohibitions' of the king of Eogain was ' to make peace with Dal Araidhe ever '; *Book of Rights*, p. 267.

had been ceded by the Cruithni to the Cenel Eogain as a
result of the battle of Moin Daire Lothair in 563. This
was Congal's first move against the High King. After his
defeat he fled to Scotland. The annals are silent about
him until the battle of Magh Rath; but if the account
given in the *Banquet of Dun na nGedh* can be accepted,
he spent the interval in collecting an army among the
Scots of Dal Riada, the Picts and Strathclyde Britons,
with a view to avenging his defeat at Dun Cethirn and
establishing himself again in Ireland. Domhnall Brecc
was king of Dal Riada at the time ; he was Congal's
uncle, and, judging by subsequent events, appears to have
lent a willing ear to the designs of Congal. There is
some slight evidence that both Domhnall and his father
Eochaidh Buidhe had acquired influence, if not actual
dominion, over a section of their Pictish neighbours. In the
annals of Ulster at the year 629, Eochaidh is called king of
the Picts, and an earlier entry in the same year records the
death of Conadh Cerr, king of Dal Riada, in the battle of
Fidheoin. Tigernach records that Conadh Cerr, king of Dal
Riada, defeated Fiachna, son of Demman, king of Ulaidh, in the
battle of Ard Corainn (A.U. 627). These entries go to show
that Conadh was regarded as king of Dal Riada during the
lifetime of Eochaidh Buidhe. The explanation may be, as
Skene points out,[1] that Eochaidh had acquired some measure
of authority over the Picts of Galloway, and had placed his
son Conadh Cerr on the throne of Dal Riada. Domhnall
Brecc succeeded his brother on the throne of Dal Riada in
629. He is nowhere styled king of the Picts ; it is probable

---

1 *Celtic Scotland*, Vol. I., p. 241. Skene's transcription of Tigernach's
record of the battle of Fidheoin is erroneous in one important point. He has
" Eochaidh Buidhe mac Aidan victor erat," whereas it should be : " mors E.B.
maic Aidan," an event which appears to have no connection with the battle of
Fidheoin. This disposes of Skene's ingenious theory about Eochaidh fighting
on the side of the Picts of Dal Araidhe while his son Conadh was fighting
on the side of Dal Riada.

that the Pictish law of succession in the female line was followed. Nevertheless Domhnall's activities were by no means confined to his own dominions of Argyle. The period was one of considerable ferment in north Britain amongst the Picts, Scots, and Britons; and Domhnall, no doubt, took advantage of this ferment to extend his oversea dominions, to the neglect of his Irish territory. We find him fighting at Calathros in 634—in the land of the Picts or Britons it is surmised—where he suffered defeat. His incursions into Pictish or British territory subsequent to Magh Rath were not more successful.

We come now to the battle of Magh Rath. The Irish annals have very little to say about it. The Annals of Ulster barely mentions it. Tigernach says that it was fought by Domhnall, son of Aedh, and by the sons of Aedh Slane; that Congal Caech (Cael), king of Ulaidh and Faelan, as well as many other nobles, and Suibhne, son of Colman Cuar, fell in it. No mention is made of Domhnall Brecc, king of Dal Riada. Let us see, however, what Adhamnan has to say about it. Adhamnan was thirteen years old when the battle was fought, and must have had memories of it when he wrote some fifty years later. Speaking of the prophecy of Colum Cille uttered on the occasion of the inauguration of Aedhan as king of Dal Riada, he says:—"Now this prophecy has been fulfilled in our times in the battle of Roth, when Domhnall Brecc, grandson of Aedhan, devastated without cause the province of Domhnall, grandson of Ainmire. And from that day to this they (i.e. the descendants of Aedhan) are in decadence[1] through pressure from without, a thing which convulses one's breast, and moves one to painful sighs."[2] In face of so positive a statement, coming from such a source, the silence of the Irish annals is strange. Adhamnan must here

---

1 This, no doubt, refers to their power *in Ireland*, as there is no evidence that they were in decay in Scotland in the time of Adhamnan.

2 The Life of St. Columba, ed. Reeves, p. 200.

be taken as the soundest authority, and he makes it sufficiently clear that Domhnall Brecc took a prominent part in the battle.

According to the traditional accounts of the battle, the invading army was composed of the Scots of Dal Riada assisted by the Picts and Britons. It is not necessary here to inquire what forces the High King had behind him. The romantic accounts tell us that the whole of Ireland rallied to him.[1] Whatever the facts, it is evident that the battle was a desperate one. It is said to have lasted several days, victory ultimately falling to the High King, Domhnall, son of Aedh. Congal fell fighting, and Domhnall Brecc escaped to Scotland with a remnant of his army.

Magh Rath (Moira) is situated on the Lagan, some five miles to the east of the south-eastern angle of Lough Neagh. It was within the territory of Dal Araidhe, the Bann which separated it from Airghialla (Oriel) being only some ten miles to the west. In one of the romantic accounts of the battle it is stated that the Scots arrived a fortnight before the battle, and that they were quartered out every night for a week. The Ulaidh, however, thought this nightly quartering oppressive, so the army set out to Magh Glass, to Domhnall's mother, and they left "not a cow or an ox, or a woman or a boy in the place."[2] The precise situation of Magh Glass has not been ascertained, but it seems clear from the reference to to it in the *Circuit of Ireland*[3] that it was somewhere in the vicinity of Raphoe, that is, in Tir Conaill. Adhamnan says that Domhnall Brecc devastated the province of the High King, Domhnall, son of Aedh; and as Tir Conaill was the High King's domestic state, the remarks of Adhamnan are probably literally correct. It may be that Domhnall Brecc invaded Airghialla and penetrated as far as Tir Conaill, and that when Domhnall, son of Aedh, took the field, the Scots

---

1 But see note below on the battle of Saltire.

2 Ériu v, p. 237.

3 ed. Hogan, p. 32.

retreated across the Bann and were overtaken and defeated at Magh Rath.[1]

The victory of th~ High King saved perhaps Ireland or at least the great dynasty of the Ui Neill, which had controlled the destinies of a large portion of Ireland for many centuries. Whatever may have been the immediate intentions of the invaders, it is sufficiently clear that a most determined effort was made by them to obtain a footing in the government of Ireland. Herein I venture to think lies the significance which native writers attached to the battle of Magh Rath.

As a consequence of the battle, the Argyle dynasty appear to have relaxed their interest in the Irish Dal Riada. A century and a half later (792) kings of the territory cease to be mentioned in the Annals of Ulster. Certainly after the eighth century Dal Riada in Ireland was hardly more than a geographical term in the annals.[2]

V.—SUIBHNE GEILT.

When we consider the prominent part assigned to Suibhne in the present tale, it is singular that so little is known of him. It is true that his connection with the battle of Magh Rath is mentioned in that early Irish law tract the *Book of Aicill*. He is also named in the Annals of Tigernach,[3] where it is stated

---

1 It is worthy of note that the battle of Saltire was won by Conall Coel, "socius Domnaill," over the Cenel Eoghain on *the same day* as the battle of Magh Rath. It i~ significant that at the moment when Domhnall mac Aedha was engaged in crushing the Scots and their allies in the east, his "socius" and nephew was also overcoming the resistance of the Cenel Eoghain. It is possible that the latter were acting in consort with the eastern confederates.

2 See Mac Neill's *Early Irish Population-Groups*, § 114 ; the general description therein given of the ruling races of northern Ireland makes no mention of Dal Riada.

3 The reference to him in the Martyrology of Donegal is evidently taken from the *Buile Suibhne*.

that he fell in the battle.   He is mentioned in the Acallamh na Senórach[1] in connection with St. Moling and Ros Brocc. He peers now and again, a dim, mysterious figure, out of the pages of one[2] of the romantic accounts of the battle, and at least two Irish poems, both of considerable antiquity, are attributed to him.[3]   He is described in the present tale and in the *Battle of Magh Rath* (ed. O'Donovan) as king of Dal Araidhe, but his name does not appear, so far as I am aware, in any of the lists[4] of kings of that territory.   In fact, if we are to trust the list given in the Book of Leinster, Congal Claen was king both of Dal Araidhe and Ulaidh at the time of the battle.   Congal fled from Ireland after the battle of Dun Cethirn in 629, and appears to have remained in exile until he returned to Ireland to fight at Magh Rath in 637.   After the defeat of Congal at Dun Cethirn, Domhnall, the High King, may have taken under his immediate control the affairs of Ulaidh.   The kingdom of Dal Araidhe, however, was peopled by Cruithni or Irish Picts, and it is not improbable that these people may have chosen Suibhne to act as regent during the absence of Congal.   Suibhne is called king, but the word is used loosely in the annals ; the designation of lord may have more closely represented the position.

In one of the Moling poems, to which reference has already been made, there occurs a stanza[5] in which Suibhne is called 'the Albanach':

---

1 ed. Stokes, Irische Texte IV (I), p. 75.   Stokes shows (Notes, p. 273) that the Acallamh cannot have been compiled earlier than the latter half of the twelfth century.

2 He is not mentioned in the shorter account edited by Prof. Carl Marstrander and published in *Ériu* v, p. 226.

3 One is the Old-Irish poem beginning M' airiuclán hi Túaim Inbir, see above, p. xvii; the other is given in *Ériu* II, p. 95.

4 e.g., B. of Leinster, B. of Ballymote, B. of Lecan, Rawlinson B 502, IacFirbis, &c.   Any close investigation shows that these lists require to be indled with caution.

5 *Anecdota* ii, p. 22, § 17.

' Suibhne, is é an fer fartalach,
aife tri immain cen luge,
is inmain an t-Albanach,
na tabair taobh re duine.'

In the present tale he is described as son of Colman
Cuar, and in the *Battle of Magh Rath* as son of Colman
Cuar, son of Cobhthach. But the names of father and
grandfather—if they may be accepted at all—carry us no
further. The Annals of Ulster states that Colman, son of
Cobhthach, was slain in the battle of Cenbuigh in 622. The
Annals of the Four Masters, recording the same event under
the year 617, mentions in addition that Cobhthach was father
of Guaire Aidhne. It is possible that there is some confusion
due to the fact that the names Suibhne and Colman are very
common in the sixth and seventh centuries. It is a well-known
fact that this confusion arising from a general use of certain
names is one of the most persistent sources of error in early
Irish history.[1] In the case of Suibhne and his father Colman
Cuar, for example, the two names are associated in the case
of Suibhne who was slain in 600, and whose father was Colman
Mor. It is probably due to the same cause that he is referred
to in our tale as son of Colman Cas and descendant of
Eochaidh Salbuidhe.

VI.—ORIGIN.

On the interesting question of the origin of the
Buile Suibhne I do not feel entitled to speak with any
authority. I shall therefore confine myself to setting down
a number of points which have occurred to me in this
connection in the course of my work. At the outset it seems

---

1 See Plummer's *Vitae Sanctorum Hiberniae* I, p. xc, and Kuno Meyer's
Betha Colmáin Maic Lúacháin, p. xiii.

clear that the origin of the *Buile Suibhne* cannot be settled
without taking into account the other extant tales which
treat of the battle of Magh Rath, more especially as Suibhne's
madness occupies a prominent place in one of the tales.
Two more or less distinct versions of the tale known as
the *Battle of Magh Rath* are extant; one a long and highly
coloured version,[1] the other a brief and comparatively sober
account.   Professor Carl Marstrander, in his edition of the
latter,[2] shows that the sources of both versions were partly
or wholly different, that the shorter version appears to be an
abridgment of several older and varying sources, and that the
longer version has obviously been drawn from different
sources.   The shorter version stands alone ; it bears no
special relation either to the longer version or to the
Buile Suibhne.   On the other hand, the longer version has
some points in common with the *Buile Suibhne* to which it
is necessary to draw attention.   The two single stanzas, one
at p. 234, beginning :

Ba he guth cach aenduine,

and the other at 236 beginning :

Rop e sin mo ced-rithsa,

are introduced by the words 'as Suibhne said in another
place.'   The other place is evidently the *Buile Suibhne* as
both stanzas occur in it.[3]   From this it would appear that the
Buile Suibhne, in one shape or another, was in existence
before the long version of the *Battle of Magh Rath* was
composed.   On the other hand, five stanzas out of the whole
poem at § 16 of the *Buile Suibhne*[4] occur in the long poem,

---

1 *Banquet of Dun na nGedh and Battle of Magh Rath,* ed. O'Donovan.

2 *Ériu,* Vol. v., p. 226.

3 See Notes, pp. 168 and 169.

4 The poem in the *Buile Suibhne* in which the stanzas occur seems somewhat
out of place ; it is possibly a later interpolation.

which extends from p. 126 to p. 141 of O'Donovan's edition.
Again, the description of Suibhne's madness, with all its
wealth of detail, corresponds so closely in both texts[1] that it
is scarcely possible for one to have been written independently
of the other.

Apart from the foregoing, there are other evidences that
the tale in its present form is a composite one. It is possible
to trace the interweaving of two versions differing in many
details. At the outset of the tale we are presented with two
different accounts of the manner in which Suibhne offended
St. Ronan, one by drowning his psaltair, the other by slaying
one of his followers. We find also two 'lucid intervals' in the
tale of Suibhne's madness of which the second seems to know
nothing of the first. In a general way, too, it may be said
that the distinctly Christian passages could be omitted
without any serious distortion of the tale. In this connection
and in view of the reference in the *Book of Aicill* to Suibhne's
madness, I venture to suggest that the original story attributed
the madness to the horrors which he witnessed in the battle of
Magh Rath, and that the introduction of St. Ronan and
St. Moling may be a later interpolation. At the same time,
it must be borne in mind that 'levitation' plays a considerable
part in the development of the tale, and levitation—or, at
least, extraordinary bodily agility—was not an uncommon
phenomenon of religious mysticism in the Middle Ages. It is
only necessary to cite the case of St. Joseph of Cupertino,
whose feats of flying are recorded in the *Procès* of the saint.
I know of no instance of similar levitation in Irish literature,[2]

---

1 Cf. pp. 231–237 of *Battle of Magh Rath* (ed. O'Donovan) with § 11 of the
Buile Suibhne.

2 Prof. Kuno Meyer has drawn my attention to the following passage from
the Irish mirabilia in the 'Speculum Regale,' an old Norse book written about
1250 A.D., *Ériu*, iv, p. 11, § 18 :—'There is also one thing which will seem very
wonderful about men who are called *gelt*. It happens that when two hosts meet
and are arrayed in battle-array, and when the battle-cry is raised loudly on
both sides, that cowardly men run wild and lose their wits from the dread and

and of course the bodily agility of Suibhne is to be
distinguished from such phenomena as the flight of the soul
described in a number of Irish ' Visions,' as, for example, the
Vision of Fursa. In the *Buile Suibhne* the levitation element
is curious. It takes the form of Suibhne imagining himself as
flying about from place to place, imagining, too, that feathers
have grown on him. It may be observed that until quite
recent times it was the general belief in Ireland that madmen
were as light as feathers and could climb steeps and
precipices.[1]

The account of Suibhne's madness seems to bear some
resemblance to the widely dispersed story of the Wild Man
of the Woods,[2] of which the Merlin legend is perhaps the
most conspicuous offshoot. The story on the whole seems
to be made up of a small folk element, probably deriving
from the same source as the Merlin legends, and a historical
element, with the battle of Magh Rath for a background.
Beyond the curious notion of levitation, the tale may be said
to be devoid of conventional folk elements or episodes.
The theme is treated throughout in so unconventional and
natural a way, that it may well owe nothing more to legend
than the central idea.

---

fear which seize them. And then they run into a wood away from other men,
and live there like wild beasts, and shun the meeting of men like wild beasts.
And it is said of these men that when they have lived in the woods in that
condition for twenty years, then feathers grow on their bodies as on birds,
whereby their bodies are protected against frost and cold, but the feathers are
not so large that they may fly like birds. Yet their swiftness is said to be so
great that other men cannot approach them, and greyhounds just as little as men.
For these people run along the trees almost as swiftly as monkeys or squirrels.'
(From this it would seem probable that the Norsemen had heard of the story of
Suibhne.)

    1 See note on page 234, *Battle of Magh Rath*, ed. O'Donovan; cf. in this
connection the gloss—*gealta*—to the word *volatiles* in the Chronicon Scotorum,
p. 122.

    2 See e.g., *The Story of Grisandole, a Study in the Legend of Merlin*, by
Lucy Allen Paton, in the publications of the Modern Language Association of
America, xxii. 2 (1907).

VII.—THE COMPOSITION.

The present tale, like many early Irish compositions, consists of alternate prose and verse, the latter constituting by far the greater part of the work. The events making up the somewhat slender framework of the tale are, as a rule, recorded in both the prose and verse, but the latter is devoted in the main to recounting the changing moods and manifold sorrows of the madman.

As a work of art it must be admitted that the *Buile Suibhne* is marred by a certain lack of unity. In the matter of the general framework, the story as a whole is intelligible enough, and proceeds smoothly and naturally from stage to stage, but occasionally in the verse one is brought face to face with sudden and violent changes of subject. The long poem (§ 40) which opens with a description of the trees of Ireland furnishes a good instance of this lack of artistic coherence. It is possible that this may be due to an incomplete text, or it may be the author's way of representing the incoherent mind of the madman.[2] In the verse portions, too, one feels that matter has to some extent been subordinated to form. It is some compensation that the verse forms throughout are excellent. In many of the poems difficult metres are handled with remarkable skill.[3] On the other hand, the whole is not lacking in imaginative

---

[1] The *Book of Rights* is a good example. For references to other examples, see Rev Celt., vol. xii., p. 519.

[2] On the other hand, this lack of coherence and restraint is a characteristic of many medieval compositions; see, for example, the remarks at p. xv of the Introduction to the *Vision of MacConglinne*.

[3] I have indicated in the Notes the metres of the poems. For descriptions of the various metres, readers are referred to Professor Kuno Meyer's *Primer of Irish Metrics*.

power, and there is genuine pathos displayed in recounting the madman's sufferings.

Perhaps the outstanding feature of the composition is the extraordinary love of place which it reveals. I venture to say that this is one of the most distinctive features of early Irish literature. It is only necessary to recall in this connection the vast number of compositions which have for subject the origin of place-names.[1] Nor was this love of place a mere convention ; I believe it sprang from a very intimate knowledge of the actual place or of the spirit of the place ; and I suggest that it will be found on investigation that the descriptions of places given in early Irish literature are in the main accurate.

In one respect the *Buile Suibhne* possesses special interest. Unlike the large mass of early Irish literary remains, it seems to owe but little to traditional lore. Whatever folk-beliefs and superstitions it may enshrine, the tale in its broad outline seems to be largely independent of floating myth, and the theme is treated in a way that is free from the literary conventions of the time. In a word, the *Buile Suibhne*, like the Vision of MacConglinne—to cite a well-known example —is a sustained literary *tour de force*, and, as such, furnishes an interesting example of the medieval attitude of mind towards literary creation.

In conclusion, I desire to express my gratitude to those who have assisted me in various ways in the preparation of this book. I am in a very special way indebted to Professor Kuno Meyer for constant encouragement and assistance, and I offer him my most sincere thanks. To Professor Osborn Bergin and the Rev Charles Plummer, I am also deeply

---

[1] The numerous ' Dinnsenchus ' poems and prose tales form the most important portion of these compositions, but, in addition, the ' Dinnsenchus ' motive plays an important part in early Irish literature in general.

indebted for considerable help. I have to thank Professor John MacNeill for his kindness in placing at my disposal a mass of valuable historical notes, bearing specially on the battle of Magh Rath. Lastly, I desire to thank Miss Eleanor Knott for her assistance in collating a portion of the text with the manuscripts.

J. G. O'KEEFFE

DUBLIN, *December* 1912.

BUILE SUIBHNE

BUILE ŚUIBHNE ANNSO SÍOS

1 DÁLA SHUIBHNE mhic Colmáin Chúair, rígh Dál Araidhe, roaisneidhsem remhainn do dhul ar fainneal 7 ar folúam*ain* a cath. Ba h*edh* ann fochann 7 tucaitt t*re*sa ttangattar na hairrdhena 7 na habarta fúalaing 7 foluaimhn*igh*e sin faói-siumh tar chách a ccoitchinne 7 febh tecómhnaccair dhó iaromh.

2 Baói aroile naoimh-erlumh uasal oirdn*idh*e hi tir nErenn .i. Ronán Fionn, mac Beraigh, mic Criodáin,[1] mic Earciogha, mic Érnainne, mic Urene, mic Seachnusaigh, mic Coluim Chúile, mic Muiredhaigh, mic Laogaire, mic Néill, .i. fer comhailte tiomna Dé 7 congm*al*a cuinge crab*uidh* 7 fuilngthe ingreama ar sgáth an Choimd*edh* an fer sin. Ba mogh-sén diles[2] diongm*al*a do Dhia, ar no bhiodh ag crochadh a chuirp ar grádh Dé 7 do tuill*edh* fochraicciu dia anmain. Ba sgíath dhidin fri drochaimsibh diabhail 7 doailc[h]ibh an fer mín muinterrdha mormhonarach sin.

3 Robaoi-sidhe fecht ann ag torainn chille i nDál Araidhe .i. Ceall Luinni[1] a comhainm. As é robadh righ ar Dhál Araidhe an ionbaidh sin .i. an Suibhne, mac Colmáin, adru[b]rumar. Rocuala 'diu[2] Suibhne airm a raibhi gut[h] chluig Rónáin ag tórainn na cille, go rofhíarfa*cht* dia muint*ir* cidh adchualadar.[3] 'Rónán Fionn mac Bearaigh,' ar síad, 'ata ag tórainn chille it chrich-si 7 it fheronn 7 as é guth a chluig itchluini-si anosa.' Rolonnaig*edh* 7 rofergaig*edh*

2—1 Criothainn, altered later to Criomthainn K   Criomthainn L   2 sén diles BK ; naoimhdiles L

3—1 Lainni L   2 dia K   3 *sic* L : adchuala B ; atchual K

THE FRENZY OF SUIBHNE HERE

1 As to Suibhne, son of Colman Cuar, king of Dal Araidhe, we have already told[1] how he went wandering and flying out of battle. Here are set forth the cause and occasion whereby these symptoms and fits of frenzy and flightiness came upon him beyond all others, likewise what befell him thereafter.

2 There was a certain noble, distinguished holy patron in Ireland, even Ronan Finn, son of Bearach, son of Criodhan, son of Earclugh, son of Ernainne, son of Urene, son of Seachnusach, son of Colum Cúile, son of Mureadhach, son of Laoghaire, son of Niall ; a man who fulfilled God's command and bore the yoke of piety, and endured persecutions for the Lord's sake. He was God's own worthy servant, for it was his wont to crucify his body for love of God and to win a reward for his soul. A sheltering shield against evil attacks of the devil and against vices was that gentle, friendly, active man.

3 On one occasion he was marking out a church named Cell Luinne in Dal Araidhe. (At that time Suibhne, son of Colman, of whom we have spoken, was king of Dal Araidhe.) Now, in the place where he was, Suibhne heard the sound of Ronan's bell as he was marking out the church, and he asked his people what it was they heard. ' It is Ronan Finn, son of Bearach,' said they, ' who is marking out a church in your territory and land, and it is the sound of his bell you

---

[1]—1 In MSS. B and K this tale follows that entitled the Battle of Magh Rath, in which reference is made to the frenzy of Suibhne. See the *Battle of Magh Rath*, ed. O'Donovan, p. 231.

go mor antí Suibhne 7 roeirigh go dian deinmneadhach do dhiochar an chleirigh oṅ chill. Tarr*aidh* a bhainc[h]eile .i. Eorann ingen Chuinn Chiannachta eiti³ an bhrait chortharaigh chorcra robhúi ime dia fhosd*udh*, go rosging fón teach an sioball⁴ airgid aeinghil co míneagur⁵ óir robhaói san brat os a bruinne. Lasodhain fágb*aidh* a bhrat ag an riogain 7 dothaod roimhi lomnocht ina reim roiretha do dhíochar an chleirigh on chill co riacht áit ina raibhe Ronán.

4 As amhlaidh robhúi an cléirech ar cionn Suibhne an ionbaidh sin, ag moladh righ nimhe [7] talman .i. ag sol*us*ghabáil a ṗsalm 7 a¹ ṗsaltair líneach lánáluinn ina fhiadhnuisi. Dosfuairgaibh² Suibhne an ṗsaltair go rotheilg a bfudhomhuin an locha lionnfuair robhaoi 'na fharradh go robáid*edh* ann í. Rogabh Suibhne lamh Ronáin iarsin co rotharraing ina dhiaigh é tar an ccill amach 7 nior leicc láimh an chlerigh úaidh fós no go ccúala³ an eighemh. As e dorinne an eighemh sin .i. giolla Congáil Chlaoin mic Sgannláin, arna thecht ar cenn Suibhne o Chong*al* fe[i]n do chur chatha Mhuighe Rat[h]. O rainic an giolla co hait n-iomagallmha fri Suibhne adf*éd* sgéla dhó o thús go deredh. Téit tra Suibhne lasan ngiolla 7 fágbaidh⁴ an clérech go dubhach dobronach ar mbád*udh* a ṗsaltrach 7 iar ndénamh a dhimigni 7 a esonora.

5 Diuidh laoi co n-oidhche iarsin doriacht dobarchú robui isin loch dochum Ronáin 7 a ṗsaltair leis gan mill*edh* líne na litri inte. Dob*er*t Ronán altugudh buidi do Dia tresan mirbuile sin 7 mallachais Suibhne iaromh, conadh *edh* roraidh: 'Mo ched-sa fri ced an Choimd*edh* chumachd*aigh*,' ar sǽ, 'amail tainic-siomh dom dhiochur-sa 7 é lomnocht, gurab amhlaidh sin bhías [82 b] doghrés lomnocht ar faoinnel 7 ar fuluamhain sechnóin an domhain,

---

3—3 err L   4 .i. dealg *add.* L   5 *sic* B mioneccur K

4—1 pṡaltrach 7 a *add.* B   2 tuargaib .i. do thogaibh L   3 From this point to the word *da* in line 4   § 9 is omitted from K   4 fagbais L

now hear.' Suibhne was greatly angered and enraged, and he set out with the utmost haste to drive the cleric from the church. His wife Eorann, daughter of Conn of Ciannacht, in order to hold him, seized the wing of the fringed, crimson cloak which was around him, so that the fibula of pure white silver, neatly inlaid with gold, which was on his cloak over his breast, sprang through the house. Therewith, leaving his cloak with the queen, he set out stark-naked in his swift career to expel the cleric from the church, until he reached the place where Ronan was.

4 He found the cleric at the time glorifying the King of heaven and earth by blithely chanting his psalms with his lined, right-beautiful psalter in front of him. Suibhne took up the psalter and cast it into the depths of the cold-water lake which was near him, so that it was drowned therein. Then he seized Ronan's hand and dragged him out through the church after him, nor did he let go the cleric's hand until he heard a cry of alarm. It was a serving-man of Congal Claon, son of Scannlan, who uttered that cry; he had come from Congal himself to Suibhne in order that he (Suibhne) might engage in battle at Magh Rath. When the serving-man reached the place of parley with Suibhne, he related the news to him from beginning to end. Suibhne then went with the serving-man and left the cleric sad and sorrowful over the loss of his psalter and the contempt and dishonour which had been inflicted on him.

5 Thereafter, at the end of a day and a night, an otter that was in the lake came to Ronan with the psalter, and neither line nor letter of it was injured. Ronan gave thanks to God for that miracle, and then cursed Suibhne, saying: ' Be it my will, together with the will of the mighty Lord, that even as he came stark-naked to expel me, may it be thus that he will ever be, naked, wandering and flying throughout the world ; may it be death from a spear-point

gurab bás do rinn nosbéra.[1] Mo mallacht-sa for Suibhne
bheós 7 mo bhennacht for Eorainn rothriall a fhost*udh*
7 [2]fós fágbhaim-si do chloinn Cholmáin an lá atchífit an
psaltair si [robaidedh] la Suibhne gurab díth 7 dilghenn
doibh ' ;[2] 7 a[t]bert in laid :

> 6 ' Suibniu mac Colmáin romc*hrá*idh,
>   romt[h]arraing leis ar leathláimh,
>   d' fhágbháil Chille Luinne lais
>   dom beith ath*aigh* 'na hégmais.
>
> Tainig chugum 'na rith rod
>   amail rochóala mo chlog,
>   tug leis feirg n-adhbhal n-anba
>   dom athchar, dom ionnarba.
>
> Leasg lem-sa mh'athchar abhus
>   ón bhaile céda rabhus,
>   gerbo lium-sa rob*adh* lesg
>   do Dhía táinic a thoirmesg.
>
> Nior leig mo lámh as a láimh
>   co ccóalaidh an eighemh n-áin,
>   go n-ébreadh ris : 'tair don chath,
>   doriacht Domhnall Magh r*án*-Rath.'
>
> Dodheachaidh maith dhamh-sa dhe,
>   ni ris rugus a bhuidhe,
>   o doriacht fios an chatha
>   do ṡoigh*idh* an ardflat[h]a.
>
> Ro-ionnsaigh an cath go cían
>   dar chláon a chonn [i]s a chíall,
>   sirf*idh* Éirinn 'na[1] gheilt ghlas
>   agus bidh do rinn raghas.

5—1 notbéra B ; bhéras K   2–2 an la adcífet clanna Colmain an tsaltair
robaidedh gurab díth 7 dílgenn doibh L
6—1 Eire an B

that will carry him off. My curse once more on Suibhne,
and my blessing on Eorann who strove to hold him ;
and furthermore, I bequeath to the race of Colman that
destruction and extinction may be their lot the day they
shall behold this psalter which was cast into the water by
Suibhne'; and he uttered this lay :

6 ' Suibhne, son of Colman, has outraged me,
    he has dragged me with him by the hand,
    to leave Cell Luinne with him,
    that I should be for a time absent from it.

    He came to me in his swift course
    on hearing my bell ;
    he brought with him vast, awful wrath
    to drive me out, to banish me.

    Loth was I to be banished here
    from the place where I first settled ;
    though loth was I,
    God has been able to prevent it.

    He let not my hand out of his
    until he heard the loud cry
    which said[1] to him : ' Come to the battle,
    Domnall has reached famous Magh Rath.'

    Good has come to me therefrom,
    not to him did I give thanks for it
    when tidings of the battle came
    for him to join the high prince.

    From afar he approached the battle
    whereby were deranged his sense and reason,
    he will roam through Erin as a stark madman,
    and it shall be by a spear-point he will die.

6—1 lit. ' so that it was said.'

Mo psaltair doghabh 'na láimh
dusfarlaic[2] fon linn láin,
dorad Críst chugum gan chair
conar bhó misdi an psaltair.

Lá co n-oidhche fán loch lán
is nir mhisdi an breac-bán,
dobhrán do dheóin Mic Dé dhe
doroidhnacht damh dorisse.

An psaltair doghabh 'na láimh
fágbuim-[se] do chloinn Cholmháin,
b*idh* [olc] do chloinn Cholmáin chain
an lá dochífed[2a] an psaltair.

Lomnocht dodheachaidh sé sonn
dom thochradh is dom thafonn,
as *edh* doghéna[3] Día dhe,
bidh lomnocht dogres Suibhne.

Rogabh ga astadh a brat
Eorann, ingen Chuinn Chiannacht,
mo bhennacht ar Eorainn de
is mo mallacht ar Suibhne.' S.

7 Dodheachaidh[1] Rónán iarsin go Magh Rath do denamh
síodha eitir Dhomhnall mac Aodha 7 Congal Claon mac
Sgannláin 7 nior fhéd a siodhug*udh*. Doberthaoi im*morro*
an cléreach i ccomairci eaturra gach laói go nach marbhtha
neach and[2] on[3] uair rotoirmisgthi an cathug*udh* 'go ccead-
aighthi doibh doridhisi. Nomhill*edh* tra Suibhne cumairce
an chleirigh,[4] uair gach sidh 7 gach os*adh* fogníodh Rónán
robris*edh* Suibhne, ar nomharb*adh* fer re trath an chomh*lainn*
gach laoi 7 fer eile re sgur an chomh*lainn* gacha nóna. An

6—2 leg. dodasfarlaic ?   2[a] leg. dochífe   3 dodhéna B
7—1 dochuaidh L   2 marbhthaoi neach ettorra L   3 *sic* L *om.* B   4–4 no

He seized my psalter in his hand,
he cast it into the full lake,
Christ brought it to me without a blemish,
so that no worse was the psalter.

A day and a night in the full lake,
nor was the speckled-white [book] the worse ;
through the will of God's Son
an otter gave it to me again.

As for the psalter that he seized in his hand,
I bequeath to the race of Colman
that it will be bad for the race of fair Colman
the day they shall behold the psalter.

Stark-naked he has come here
to wring my heart, to chase me ;
on that account God will cause
that Suibhne shall ever naked be.

Eorann, daughter of Conn of Ciannacht,
strove to hold him by his cloak ;
my blessing on Eorann therefor,
and my curse on Suibhne.'

7 Thereupon Ronan came to Magh Rath to make peace
between Domnall son of Aodh, and Congal Claon son of
Scannlan, but he did not succeed. Howbeit, the cleric used
to be taken each day as a guarantee between them that
nobody would be slain from the time the fighting was stopped
until it would be again permitted. Suibhne, however, used
to violate the cleric's guarantee of protection inasmuch as
every peace and truce which Ronan would make Suibhne
would break, for he used to slay a man before the hour
fixed for combat each day, and another each evening when

go ngabtha doridhisi.   Ticcedh thrá Suibhne tar lamha an chleirigh gacha
trátha L

lá do*no* rocinn*edh* an cath mor do thabairt tainic Suibhne ria
gcách dochum an chatha.

8 As amhlaidh robaoi 7 leine sreabhn*aidh*e śíodae i cusd*ul*
fri gheilchnes dó 7 fúathróig do śrol righ uime 7 an t-ionar
tuc Congal dó an lá romarbh Oilill Céd*ach* rí Úa bFaoláin for
Magh Rath, ionar corcra comhdatha esein co cciumhi*us* dluith
deghfhighthi d'ór aluinn órloisghthi ris, co sreithegar gem
ccaomh ccarrmhogail on chionn gór araill don chiumhais
sin, go stúaghlúbaibh sioda dar cnaip*idh*ibh caoimettrochta
re hiadh*adh* 7 re hosgl*adh* and, [83 a] go bfoirbreachtadh
airgid aóingil gacha caói 7 gacha con*air*e imtheigh*edh*;
cr*í*aidhrinn chaoilśnáithaide don ion*ar* sin. Dhá śleigh
śithfhoda slinnleathna ina lámhaibh, sgíath breacbhuidhe
bhúabhallda for a mhuin, claideamh órdhoirn for a chlíu.

9 Tainic roimhe fón toichim sin co ttarla Rónán dó 7
ochtar psa[l]mchetl*aidh* da muintir ina fharradh 7 íad ag
crothadh uisge coisreagtha dar na slúaghuibh 7 roscroithset
ar Śuibhne hi ccuma cháich. Agus andar leis-siomh bá da
ḟochuidm*edh* rocroith*edh* an t-uisge fair, 7 dorad a mhér a
suainemh[1] na sleighe seimn*idh*e[1a] robhúi ina laimh 7 rosdiubhraic do pśalmc[h]eadl*aidh* do muintir Rónáin go romarbh
don oenorch*ar* sin é. Dorad andara hurchar don fhogha
faobrach uillenngér dochum an chlérigh budhdhén go rosben
isin chlog robhaói for a ucht, go rosging a cr*ann* as a n-airde
isin aer, co n-ébairt an cléireach: 'Guidhim-si an Coimde[2]
cumachtach,' ar sé, 'an ccomhairde dochúaidh crann an
fhogha isin aer 7 a nellaibh nimhe co ndeachair-si[3] amail
gach n-ethaid 7 an bás roimris-[s]i[4] for mo dhalta-sa, gurab
eadh notbéra[5] .i. bas do rinn[6], 7 mo mhallacht-sa fort 7 mo
bhennacht for Eorainn, Uradhrán[7] 7 Telli[8] uaim i n-aghaidh
do śil[9] 7 chloinne Colmain Chuair,' 7 itbert:

9—1 sioda *add.* K   1a *sic* K seim*h*nidhe B   2 *sic* K *om.* B   3 sī B ar
gealtacht *add.* L   4 roimbreisi K   5 nosberai-si L   6 fodhein *add.* B
7 Furadhrán L   8 Teilli K   9 śiola L

the combat ceased. Then on the day fixed for the great battle Suibhne came to battle before the rest.

8 In this wise did he appear. A filmy shirt of silk was next his white skin, around him was a girdle of royal satin, likewise the tunic which Congal had given him the day he slew Oilill Cedach, king of the Ui Faolain, at Magh Rath; a crimson tunic of one colour was it with a close, well-woven border of beautiful, refined gold set with rows of fair gems of carbuncle from one end to the other of the border, having in it silken loops over beautiful, shining buttons for fastening and opening it, with variegation of pure white silver each way and each path he would go;[1] there was a slender-threaded hard fringe[2] to that tunic. In his hands were two spears very long and (shod) with broad iron, a yellow-speckled, horny shield was on his back, a gold-hilted sword at his left side.

9 He marched on thus until he encountered Ronan with eight psalmists of his community sprinkling holy water on the hosts, and they sprinkled it on Suibhne as they did on the others. Thinking it was to mock him that the water was sprinkled on him, he placed his finger on the string of the riveted spear that was in his hand, and hurling it at one of Ronan's psalmists slew him with that single cast. He made another cast with the edged, sharp-angled dart at the cleric himself, so that it pierced the bell which was on his breast and the shaft sprang off it up in the air, whereupon the cleric said : 'I pray the mighty Lord that high as went the spear-shaft into the air and among the clouds of Heaven may you go likewise even as any bird, and may the death which you have inflicted on my foster-child be that which will carry you off, to wit, death from a spear-point; and my curse on you, and my blessing on Eorann; (I invoke) Uradhran[1] and Telle on my behalf against your seed and the descendants of Colman Cuar'; and he said :

8—1 i.e. it flashed as he went.   2 lit. hard-point.
9—1 Furadhrán L

10 ‘ Mo mallacht for Ṡuibhne,
rium is mor a chionaidh,
a fhogha blaith builidh
doṡaith trem c[h]log creadhail.

An clog sin roghonais
notchurfi-si ar cráobhaibh
gurbat¹ aon re henaibh,
an clog náomh re náomhaibh.

Mar dochuaidh i cédóir
crann an fhogha a n-airde
co ndeachair-si, a Ṡuibhne,
re² gealtacht gan chairde.

Roghonais mo dhalta,
rodergais as t’fhogha,
bíaidh dhuit ann do chomha
gurab do rinn ragha.

Madh dá ttísat riom-sa
siol nEoghain go tteinne,
noscuirfet a ccran[n]acht
Uradhran is Teille.

Uradhran is Teille
roscursiod³ i ccran[n]acht,
an ced-sa, tre chorracht,
as let-sa mo mhallacht.

Bennacht uaim for Eorainn,
Eorann chaemh gan crannacht,
tre dhuilghe gan domacht
for Ṡuibhne mo mhallacht.’   Mallacht.

10 ' My curse on Suibhne!
    great is his guilt against me,
    his smooth, vigorous dart
    he thrust through my holy bell.

    That bell which thou hast wounded
    will send thee among branches,
    so that thou shalt be one with the birds—
    the bell of saints before saints.

    Even as in an instant went
    the spear-shaft on high,
    mayst thou go, O Suibhne,
    in madness, without respite!

    Thou hast slain my foster-child,
    thou hast reddened thy spear in him,
    thou shalt have in return for it
    that with a spear-point thou shalt die.

    If there should oppose me
    the progeny of Eoghan with stoutness
    Uradhran and Telle
    will send them into decay.

    Uradhran and Telle
    have sent them into decay,
    this is my wish for all time:[1]
    my curse with thee!

    My blessing on Eorann!
    Eorann fair without decay:
    through suffering without stint
    my curse on Suibhne!'

10—1 lit. ' through restlessness '.

11 O rochomhracsiot iarom na catha cechtarrdha ro-
bhúirs*et* an damhr*adh* dermhair adíu 7 anall amail dámha
damhghoire co ttuarg*aibh*set tri tromghaire os aird.
O'dchúala thrá Suibhne na gaire mora sin 7 a fhuamanna
7 a freagartha i nellaibh nimhe 7 i fraight*ibh* na firmaminnte
rofhéch Suibhne suas iarum co rolíon nemhain 7 dobhar 7
dásacht 7 fáoinnel 7 fúalang 7 foluamain 7 udmhaille,
anbsaidhe 7 anfhoistine, miosgais[1] gach ionaidh ina mbiodh
7 serc gach ionaidh noco roichedh ; romheirbhlighset a meoir,
rocriothnaighsiot a chosa, roluath*adh* a chroidhe, roclódhadh
a c*hedfadh*a, rosaob*adh* a radharc, rot*uit*set a airm urnocht
asa lámhuibh co ndeachaidh la breithir Rónáin ar gealtacht 7
ar geinidecht amail gach n-ethaid n-æerdha.

12 A'n tan im*morro* doriacht asin ccath amach ba hainminic nothaidhl*edh* a c[h]ossa lár ar lúas a réime 7 an tan
nothaidhl*edh* ni bhenf*adh* a drucht do bharrúachtar an fheóir
ar ettroma 7 ar aerrdhacht an chéme nochinge*dh*. Ni roan
don reim roiretha sin co nár fág magh na machairi na maol-
sliabh, móin na muine na mothar, cnoc na cabhán, na coill
chlithardhlúith a nEirinn gan taisdeal an lá sin[1], go rainig co
Ros Beraigh[2] i nGlenn Earcáin co ndeachaidh isin iobhar
robhaoi isin glinn.

13 Romheabh*aidh* an cath re nDomhnall mac Aodha an
lá sin amail adru[bru]mar 7 rohaisnéidh*sem* remhainn. Robhaoi éimh clíam*uin* do Suibhne isin chath .i. Aonghus
Remhar mac Ardghail mic Macníadh [83 b] mic Ninnedha
do thoathaibh Úa Ninnedha do Dhál Aruidhe. Tainic sidhe

11—1 Ciodh t*r*á acht ó rochomraicsiot na catha fochedóir robhúirsett 7
rogairset na sluaigh da gach leith. O'dchuala Suibhne na gáire mora sin 7 a
bfreccartha 7 a bfuaim 7 a macalla a nellaibh nimhe 7 a bfroighthibh na firminnte
rofech suas 7 rolion nemhain 7 dásacht 7 faindeal 7 fualang 7 foluamhain é 7
miosgais L

12—1 For the portion of the tale from this point to the commencement of
§ 63 the following is all that occurs in L :—Agus rochaith a aois 7 a aimser ar
gealtacht in Eirinn 7 a mBretain an ccein romair gan furtacht gan fóiridhin gan
taobh do tabairt le daoinibh amhail dherbhas an leabhar sgriobhthar air fein
darab ainm *Buile Suibhn*   Ró Meraigh B Ros mBeraigh K

11 Thereafter, when both battle-hosts had met, the vast army on both sides roared in the manner of a herd of stags so that they raised on high three mighty shouts. Now, when Suibhne heard these great cries together with their sounds and reverberations in the clouds of Heaven and in the vault of the firmament, he looked up, whereupon turbulence (?), and darkness, and fury, and giddiness, and frenzy, and flight, unsteadiness, restlessness, and unquiet filled him, likewise disgust with every place in which he used to be and desire for every place which he had not reached. His fingers were palsied, his feet trembled, his heart beat quick, his senses were overcome, his sight was distorted, his weapons fell naked from his hands, so that through Ronan's curse he went, like any bird of the air, in madness and imbecility.[1]

12 Now, however, when he arrived out of the battle, it was seldom that his feet would touch the ground because of the swiftness of his course, and when he did touch it he would not shake the dew from the top of the grass for the lightness and the nimbleness of his step. He halted not from that headlong course until he left neither plain, nor field, nor bare mountain, nor bog, nor thicket, nor marsh, nor hill, nor hollow, nor dense-sheltering wood in Ireland that he did not travel that day,[1] until he reached Ros Bearaigh, in Glenn Earcain, where he went into the yew-tree that was in the glen.

13 Domnall, son of Aedh, won the battle that day, as we have already narrated.[1] Suibhne had a kinsman in the battle, to wit, Aongus the Stout, son of Ardgal, son of Macnia, son of Ninnidh, of the tribes of Ui Ninnedha of Dal Araidhe; he

---

11—1 perhaps ' goblin-like'.

12—1 see note 1, § 12, on opposite page ; ' and he spent his life and his time in madness in Ireland and Britain while he lived, without aid, without succour, without trusting people, as the book which is written on himself, called *Buile Suibhne*, proves.'

13—1 i.e. in the *Battle of Magh Rath*, ed. O'Donovan ; see note 1 p. 3, supra.

a ráon madhma asin ccath go mbuidhin[1] dia muintir imalle fris 7 as í conair tainic a nGlionn [E]arcáin. Baoi siumh tra cona muintir ag iomradh ar Suibhne ara iongantaoi leo gan a bheo no a mharbh d'fhaicsin o rochomraicset na catha, acht chena ba derbh leó gurab tre esgcáoine Rónáin fodrúair gan fios a oidhedha. Rochualaidh éimh Suibhne ar chansat 7 e isin iobar osa ccionn, 7 itbert[2]:

14 'A óga, tigidh a lle,
   a fhiora Dhál Araidhe,
   foghebhthaoi isin bhile a bfuil
   an fer forsatáoi iarraidh.

   Dodheónaidh Dia dhamh-sa sunn
   betha iomnocht iomchumhang,
   gan ceól is gan codladh sáim,
   gan banchuire, cen bandáil.

   Misi sunn ag Ros mBearaigh,
   domrad Ronán fo mheabhail,
   romsgar Dia rem dheilbh nad ró,
   sgaraidh re mh'eol, a ogó.'   A óga.

15 O'dchualadar na fir Suibhne ag gabáil na rann tugsat aithne[1] fair 7 roráidhset fris taobh do thabairt friu. Adbertsom nach ttiubradh tre bhith sior. O robhádar-somh iarumh ag iadhad im an mbile rotogaibh Suibhne uime co háithétrom áerda othá sin co Cill Ríagain i tTir Chonuill 7 rothoirinn iarumh a mbile na cille. As ag an mbile sin dorala do Dhomhnall mac Aodha cona sluagaibh do ueith a haithle an chatha 7 o'dchonncadar an gheilt ag dol isin mbile tangadar drong dona slóghaibh go roiadhsat ina iomthacmhang ina ccuairt; gabhaid iarumh ag tabairt túarusgbála na geilti os aird, adberedh fer ann ba ben, adberedh fer eile ba fer robhúi ann, go ttarad[2] Domhnall féi]n aithne[1] fair,

13—1 sic K mbuighin B   2 go nebhairt an laoidh go truagh K
15—1 aithghni K   2 tard K

came in flight with a number of his people out of the battle, and
the route he took was through Glenn Earcain. Now he and his
people were conversing about Suibhne (saying) how strange it
was that they had not seen him alive or dead after the battle-
hosts had met. Howbeit, they felt certain it was because of
Ronan's curse that there were no tidings of his fate. Suibhne in
the yew-tree above them heard what they spoke, and he said:

14 'O warriors, come hither,
      O men of Dal Araidhe,
      you will find in the tree in which he is
      the man whom you seek.

      God has vouchsafed me here
      life very bare, very narrow,
      without music and without restful sleep,
      without womenfolk, without a woman-tryst.

      Here at Ros Bearaigh am I,
      Ronan has put me under disgrace,
      God has severed me from my form,[1]
      know me no more, O warriors.'

15 When the men heard Suibhne reciting the verses, they
recognized him, and urged him to trust them. He said that
he would never do so. Then, as they were closing round the
tree, Suibhne rose out of it very lightly and nimbly (and
went) to Cell Riagain in Tir Conaill where he perched on the
old tree of the church. It chanced that it was at that tree
Domnall, son of Aedh, and his army were after the battle,
and when they saw the madman going into the tree, a portion
of the army came and closed in all round it. Thereupon
they began describing aloud the madman; one man would
say that it was a woman, another that it was a man, until
Domnall himself recognized him, whereupon he said : ' It is

14—1 lit. 'from my form which is not too much '.

C

conadh ann adbert: 'As é Suibhne fil ann,' ar sé, '.i. righ
Dal Araidhe roesgcáoin Rón[án] an lá tug*adh* an cath.
Maith éimh an fer fil ann,' ar sé, '7 da madh áil leis seóide³
7 máoini d'fhag*bail* fogeb*adh* úainne da ttug*adh* taobh frinn.
Truag lem,' ar sé, 'iarsma muintire Congail amlaidh sin, ar
robtar maith 7 robtar mora mo chomh*ad*a-sa⁴ do Chongal,'
ar se, 're cc*ur* an chatha, et robadh maith do*no* comairle
Choluim Chille don ghille úd fe[i]n da ndeachaidh le Congal
do chuingidh sochraidhe co righ Alban im agh*aidh*-si';
conadh ann adbert Domhnall an laid:

> 16 'Cionnus sin, a Ṡuibhne ṡeing?
> robadh¹ tóiseuch mór ndíreim²
> an la tugadh an cath clóen,
> ar Macc Rath robadh¹ rochoemh.
>
> Cosmhuil do ghnúis ergna iar n-ól
> re corcair no re coemhor,
> cosmhuil do chúl gan chaire
> re cluimh no re casn*aidh*e.
>
> Cosmhuil gne³ do ch*uir*p choidche
> re sneachta n-úar n-áenoidhche,
> do rosg rogormadh mar ghloin,
> mar oighreadh seimh snúadhamail.
>
> Aluinn cuma do da chos,
> dar liom ni trén th'urradhus,
> t'airm rathmara, ruicthis⁴ fuil,
> robsat athlumha i n-iomghuin. [84a]
>
> Targaidh Colaim Cille dheit
> nemh agus righe, a romheic,
> diogháir tangais isin magh
> o priomh[f]áidh nimhe is talmhan.

15—3 seoid K   4 *sic* K comhadhsa B

16—1 robat K   2 ineirinn K   3 *sic* K; *om.* B   4 ruictis K

Suibhne, king of Dal Araidhe, whom Ronan cursed the day the battle was fought. Good in sooth is the man who is there,' said he, ' and if he wished for treasures and wealth he would obtain them from us if only he would trust us. Sad is it to me,' said he, ' that the remnant of Congal's people are thus, for both good and great were the ties that bound me to Congal before undertaking the battle, and good moreover was the counsel of Colum Cille to that youth himself when he went with Congal to ask an army from the king of Alba against me '; whereupon Domnall uttered the lay :

16 ' How is that, O slender Suibhne?
   thou wert leader of many hosts ;
   the day the iniquitous battle was fought
   at Magh Rath thou wert most comely.

   Like crimson or like beautiful gold
   was thy noble countenance after feasting,
   like down or like shavings
   was the faultless hair of thy head.

   Like cold snow of a single night
   was the aspect of thy body ever ;
   blue-hued was thine eye, like crystal,
   like smooth, beautiful ice.

   Delightful the shape of thy feet,
   not powerful methinks was thy chieftainship ;
   thy fortunate weapons—they could draw blood—
   were swift in wounding.

   Colum Cille offered thee
   Heaven and kingship, O splendid youth,
   eagerly (?) thou hast come into the plain
   from the chief prophet of Heaven and earth.

C 2

Adubairt Colum Cille,
fáidh fosaidh na firinne,
lion ticcthi tar tuile theinn
ni riccthi uile a hEirinn.

Targus-sa do Chongal Chlaon
tan robamar imaráon
bennacht fer nErenn uile,
ba mor an t-ioc enuige.⁴

Muna gabha uaim-si sin,
a Chonghail chaoimh mic Sgannail,
ga breith bheire, mor an modh,
orm-sa, más eadh, it aonor?

[Congal :] Gébhad-sa úait madh maith lat,
tabhair dhamh-sa do dhá mac,
do lámh dhiot⁵ is do bhen mhas,
t'ingen is do rosg rinnglas.

[Domnall:] Nocha béra acht rinn fri rind,
béd-sa choidche in bhar n-oirchill,
as e ar ccomhradh iman ccacht,
beir-si lomnán mo mallacht.

Bidh cuid do chuifir⁶ do chorp,
beittid fiaich ar do t[h]romthocht,
nodgonfa ga dremhan dubh
agus beir-si faon folumh.

Atáoi it áonar seach gach righ
gum aimhles o thír do⁷ thír,
rodlesaighes thairis sin
on lo rondug do mháthair.

16—4 enuig*he* K   5 *sic* K ; duit B   6 *sic* B ; chiufir K   7 co K

Said Colum Cille,
steadfast prophet of truth,
' as many of you as come over the strong flood
will not all return from Erin.' [1]

I offered Congal Claon
when we were together
the blessing of all the men of Erin ;
great was the mulct for one egg.[2]

If thou wilt not accept that from me,
O fair Congal, son of Scannal,
what judgment then—deed of great moment—
wilt thou pass upon me ?

Congal :   (These) will I accept from thee if thou deemest it
                 well :
             give me thy two sons,
             thy hand from thee, likewise thy stately wife,
             thy daughter and thy eye blue-starred.

Domnall : Thou shalt not have but spear to spear,
             I shall be evermore lying in wait for you,
             this is our speech about the bondage ;
             take thou the full of my curse !

             Thy body will be a feast for birds of prey,
             ravens will be on thy heavy silence,
             a fierce, black spear shall wound thee,
             and thou shalt be laid on thy back, destitute.

             My bane from land to land
             art thou alone beyond each king,
             yet I have befriended thee
             since the day thy mother brought thee forth.

16—1 lit. 'the number ye come over the strong flood ye do not all return from
Erin '.
    2 see Notes.

As ann fós tugadh an cath
ar an maighin a Muigh Rath,
robhúi bráon dar claideamh nglas,
torc[h]air Congal Cláon cionnus.' Cionnus.

17 Ó'dchuala tra Suibhne sésdan na sochaidhe 7 muirn an morślúaigh nostogb*aidh* uime asin mbile re fraisnell*aibh* na fírmaiminti ós mullaighibh gacha maighni 7 os fheigi gacha ferainn. Baoi fri re chein iarsin seachnoin Erenn ag tadhall 7 ag t*ur*rag a sgalpaibh cruadhcharrag 7 a ndosaibh crann urard eidhn*each* 7 i ccuasaibh caolchumhguibh cloch o inber do inber 7 o binn do binnd 7 o glinn do glionn go rainic Glenn mbit[h]aluinn mBolcáin. Ann nothaigtais[1] gealta Eirenn o robadh slán a mbliadhain ar gealtacht, ar as ionadh aoibhnesa móir an glenn sin do gheltaibh dogrés. Uair as amlaidh ata Glenn mBolcáin 7 ceithre doirsi ag an ngaoith ann 7 roschoill roaluinn rocháoin ann bheós 7 tiobrada táobhghlana 7 uarána ionnfhuara 7 glaisi gainm*idh*e glanuisg*idh*e 7 biorar barrghlas 7 fothlocht fann foda for a lár. Iomda fhos a śamha[2] 7 a śiomsáin 7 a lus-bían[3] 7 a biorragáin,[4] a chaora 7 a chreamh, a mhelle 7 a miodhbhun 7 airn*idh*e[5] dubha 7 a dercain donna. Nobidh do*no* gach æ dona gealtaibh ag tuarg*ain* a chéile im thogha biorair an ghlenna sin 7 im roignibh a leptach.

18 Robúi do*no* Suibne athaigh fhoda isin ghlenn sin conustarla aen na n-oidhche ann a mullach sgíach urairde eidhn*idh*e robhaoi isin glinn.[1] Roba deacair do-sumh iumfhulang na leaptha sin, uair gach cor 7 gach iompodh nochuir*edh* dhe nothegmadh frais do dhealgaibh sgiach ann, co mbittis ag tolladh 7 ag treaghd*adh* a thaoibh 7 ag comhghuin a c[h]nis. Roaitherr*aigh* Suibne iarum asin leabaidh sin dochum ionaidh ele. As amhlaidh eimh robhúi an

---

17—1 *sic* K ; nothiadhtais B   2 śamadh K   3 luis-bian K   4 biorragaind K   5 *sic* K ; airne B
18—1 *add*. é B

'Tis there the battle was fought—
at the stead in Magh Rath—
there was a drop on a gleaming sword ;
so fell Congal Claon.'

17 Now when Suibhne heard the shout of the multitude
and the tumult of the great army, he ascended from the tree
towards the rain-clouds of the firmament, over the summits
of every place and over the ridge-pole of every land. For a
long time thereafter he was (faring) throughout Ireland,
visiting and searching in hard, rocky clefts and in bushy
branches of tall ivy-trees, in narrow cavities of stones, from
estuary to estuary, from peak to peak, and from glen to glen,
till he reached ever-delightful Glen Bolcain. It is there the
madmen of Ireland used to go when their year in madness
was complete, that glen being ever a place of great delight for
madmen. For it is thus Glen Bolcain is : it has four gaps to
the wind, likewise a wood very beautiful, very pleasant, and
clean-banked wells and cool springs, and sandy, clear-water
streams, and green-topped watercress and brooklime bent and
long on their surface. Many likewise are its sorrels, its
wood-sorrels, its *lus-bian* and its *biorragan*, its berries, and its
wild garlic, its *melle* and its *miodhbhun*,[1] its black sloes and
its brown acorns. The madmen moreover used to smite
each other for the pick of watercress of that glen and for the
choice of its couches.

18 Suibhne also remained for a long time in that glen
until he happened one night to be on the top of a tall ivy-
clad hawthorn tree which was in the glen. It was hard for him
to endure that bed, for at every twist and turn he would give,
a shower of thorns off the hawthorn would stick in him, so
that they were piercing and rending his side and wounding
his skin. Suibhne thereupon changed from that bed to another

17—1 *Melle* (*melne*) is atriplex or golden herb ; what the other plants are I
cannot ascertain.

t-ionadh sin 7 motharmhuine móirdreasa mindeilgneach
ann 7 áonc[h]raobh dhioghainn droighin ar na hionfhás
[84 b] na hénur tresan muine suas. Tairis*edh* Suibhne for
barr na c*r*aoibhe sin, sdúaghais 7 lúbais an c*r*aobh chomh-
cháol robháoi faoi go ttarla beim n-asglainn de tresan muine
go ttorc*hair* go lár talman, co nach raibhe méd n-orl*aigh* ann
o a bhonn go a bhathais gan fhuiliúgudh, gan forrdergudh fair.
Adráigh iaromh go heneirt anfann 7 dothoed tresan muine
amach, co n-ébairt : ' Mo chubhais eimh,' ar sé, ' as deacair an
bheatha so d'fhulang tar éis deghbhethad 7 bliadhain gus aréir
damh-sa forsan mbethaidh-si'; conadh ann adbert an laoi[dh]:

19 ' Bliadhain gus aréir
   dhamh fo chiamhair chraobh[1]
   eitir tuile is traigh
   gan tuighe fom tháobh.

Gan cerchaill fom chionn
eitir ferchloinn fhinn,
baeghal, a Dhé, dhuinn,
gan fhaobar, gan rinn.

Gan comhthocht fri mnáibh,
acht madh fothlacht fían,
as cuid iodhan óg,
biolar, as é ar mían.

Gan rúat*har* co righ
am úathadh im eól,
gan airgni go hán,
gan chairde, gan cheol.

Gan chodladh, monúar,
go n-abrar a fhíor,
gan chobhair co cían,
as doraidh mo dhíol.

19—1 ceimair craebh K

place, where there was a dense thicket of great briars with fine thorns and a single protruding branch of blackthorn growing alone up through the thicket. Suibhne settled on the top of that tree, but so slender was it that it bowed and bent under him, so that he fell heavily through the thicket to the ground, and there was not as much as an inch from his sole to the crown of his head that was not wounded and reddened. He then rose up, strengthless and feeble, and came out through the thicket, whereupon he said: 'My conscience!' said he, 'it is hard to endure this life after a pleasant one, and a year to last night I have been leading this life,' whereupon he uttered the lay:

19 ' A year to last night
     have I been among the gloom of branches,
     between flood and ebb,
     without covering around me.

Without a pillow beneath my head,
among the fair children of men ;
there is peril to us, O God,
without sword, without spear.

Without the company of women ;
save brooklime of warrior-bands—
a pure fresh meal—
watercress is our desire.

Without a foray with a king,
I am alone in my home,
without glorious reavings,[1]
without friends, without music.

Without sleep, alas !
let the truth be told,
without aid for a long time,
hard is my lot.

19—1 perhaps ' spoils.'

Gan tegh lomnán lán,
gan comhrádh bfher bfhíal,
gan righ riom da rádh,
gan lionn is gan bíadh.

Trúagh romt[h]earb*adh* sunn
rem ślúagh trealmach trom,
im geilt gé[i]r tar gleann
gan chéill is gan chonn.

Gan bheth ar cuairt righ
acht rúaig ar gach ráon
as í an mhire mhór,
a rí nimhe naomh.

Gan áos comhlán ciúil,
gan comhrádh fri mnáibh,
gan tiodhnacal séd,
tuc mh'ég, a Chríst cháidh.

Robadhus-sa feacht,
ge béo mar 'tú anocht,
ba neamhfhann mo nert
ar ferann nárbh olc.

Ar eachaibh co hán
i mbeathaid can bhrón,
ar mo righe raith²
robsam³ righ maith mór.

Beith mar 'tu 'na dhíaid
dot chreic, a Chríst cáidh,
im⁴ bhochtán gan brígh
a nGlionn Bolcáin báin.

---

2 *sic* K, righi (?) raith B   3 robam K   4 am K

Without a house right full,
without the converse of generous men,
without the title of king,
without drink, without food.

Alas that I have been parted here
from my mighty, armed host,
a bitter madman in the glen,
bereft of sense and reason.

Without being on a kingly circuit,
but rushing along every path ;
that is the great madness,
O King of Heaven of saints.

Without accomplished musicians,
without the converse of women,
without bestowing treasures ;
it has caused my death, O revered Christ.

Though I be as I am to-night,
there was a time
when my strength was not feeble
over a land that was not bad.

On splendid steeds,
in life without sorrow,
in my auspicious kingship
I was a good, great king.

After that, to be as I am
through selling Thee, O revered Christ !
a poor wretch am I, without power,
in the Glen of bright Bolcan.

An scé nach máoth bárr⁵
romthraoth is romt[h]oll,
súaill nach ttuc mh' oid*idh*,
an craobh droighin dhonn.

Cath Congail co cclú,
ba liach dhún fo dhí,
ba día mairt an maidhm,
lía ar mairbh 'naid⁶ ar mbí.

Ar fǽinnel go fíor
gerbham sǽir*fher* séimh,
isam triamhain trógh
bliadhain gus aréir.'   Bliadhain.

20 Robháoi-siumh amlaidh sin a nGlinn Bolcáin go
rostógaibh uime feacht ann co ráinic Cl*úain* Cilli a ccoiccrich
Thíre Chonaill 7 Thire Bóghain[e].¹ Dochuaidh iarumh for
s*rai*th na tiopraidi² gur chaith biorar 7 uisge ann an oidhche
sin. Téit iarumh a mbile na cilli. As é ba hoirchinneach isin
chill sin Fáibhlen do muintir B*rughaigh* mic Deagh*aidh* 7
tainic doinenn mór dermhair ann an oidhche sin gur ro*chuir*
ar Suibhne go mor méd an*ṡ*óidh na hoidhchi sin 7 adbert-
somh : ' Trúagh ámh,' ar sé, 'nach air Muigh Rath rommhar-
badh-sa resíu nobheinn isin deacair-si'; go n-ébairt an
laoi[dh] annso siosana go leig³ :

21 ' Anocht is fúar an snechta,
      fodeachta is búan mo bhochta,
      nidom n*ei*rt isin deab*uidh*
      im¹ geilt romgeoghuin gorta.

19—5 *sic* B barr K.   6 nait K
20—1 heoguine K   2 tiopratt K   3 an laoidh go truagh annso sios K
21—1 am K

The hawthorn that is not soft-topped
has subdued me, has pierced me ;
the brown thorn-bush
has nigh caused my death.

The battle of Congal with fame,
to us it was doubly piteous ;
on Tuesday was the rout ;
more numerous were our dead than our living.

A-wandering in truth,
though I was noble and gentle,
I have been sad and wretched
a year to last night.'

20 In that wise he remained in Glen Bolcain until at a
certain time he raised himself up (into the air) and went to
Cluain Cille on the border of Tir Conaill and Tir Boghaine.
He went then to the brink of the well where he had for food
that night watercress and water. Thereafter he went into
the old tree of the church. The erenach of the church was
Faibhlen of the family of Brughach, son of Deaghadh. That
night there came an exceeding great storm so that the
extent of the night's misery affected Suibhne greatly, and he
said : 'Sad indeed is it that I was not slain at Magh Rath
rather than that I should encounter this hardship'; whereupon
he uttered this lay :

21 'Cold is the snow to-night,
lasting now is my poverty,
there is no strength in me for fight,
famine has wounded me, madman as I am.

Atchid cach nidom chuchtach,
as lom i snáth mo cheirteach,
Suibhne mh'ainm o Ros Ercain,
as misi an gealtán gealtach.

Nidom fois o .thig aghaidh,²
ni thaidlenn³ mo chois conair,
nocha bíu sonna a ccíana,
domeccad ialla omhain.⁴

Mo bháire tar muir mbarcláin⁵
ar ndol tar sáile soclán,⁶
⁷rogab time⁷ mo nertan,
as me gealtán Ghlinne Bolcáin.

Gaoth an reoidh ag mo rébadh,
sneachta romleón⁸ go leige,
an tsíon dom breith a n-éccuibh
do géccuibh gacha geicce. [85a]

Romgonsat géga glasa
co rorébsat mo bossa,
ni fargaibhset na dreasa
damna creasa dom chossa.

Ata crioth ar mo lámha
tar gach mbioth fatha mbúaidre,
do Slíabh Mis ar Sliabh Cuillenn,
do Sléibh Cuillenn co Cuailgne.

As trúagh mo nuallán ⁹ choidhche
i mullach Cruachán Oighle,
do Ghlinn Bolcain for Íle,
do C[h]inn Tíre for Boirche.

21—2 adhaigh K   3 *sic* K ; is ni thaighlenn B   4 domeccadh ialla omhain B ; domechad ialla omhon K, but domfhochaid has been written in the margin by Peter O'Connell, who used the K text for his Dictionary 5 barcglan K   6 *sic* K ; sochlán B   7-7 *sic* K ; rotimi B   8 romlean K 9 nual K

All men see that I am not shapely,
bare of thread is my tattered garment,
Suibhne of Ros Earcain is my name,
the crazy madman am I.

I rest not when night comes,
my foot frequents no trodden way,
I bide not here for long,
the bonds of terror come upon me.

My goal lies beyond the teeming main,
voyaging the prow-abounding sea ;
fear has laid hold of my poor strength,
I am the crazy one of Glen Bolcain.

Frosty wind tearing me,
already snow has wounded me,
the storm bearing me to death
from the branches of each tree.

Grey branches have wounded me,
they have torn my hands ;
the briars have not left
the making of a girdle for my feet.

There is a palsy on my hands,
everywhere there is cause of confusion,
from Sliabh Mis to Sliabh Cuillenn,
from Sliabh Cuillenn to Cuailgne.

Sad forever is my cry
on the summit of Cruachan Aighle,
from Glen Bolcain to Islay,
from Cenn Tire to Boirche.

Beg mo chuid o thig laa,
ni thǽt ar scath la noa,
barr biorair Chluana Cille
la gleorán Chille Cua.[10]

An gen [11] fil ag Ros Earcach
ni thair imn*edh* na olcach,
as *edh* dombeir gan nertach[12]
beith re sneachta go nochtach.'   Anocht.

22 Tainic Suibhne roimhe iarumh co riacht an chill ag
Snamh dha Én for Sionainn, dían comainm [1] Cluain Boirenn
an tan sa; día ṇa haoine dídine an tsainridh rainic-siumh
annsin. As ann iarumh bádar cleirigh na cille ag dénamh
an uird nóna 7 mná ag túargain lín 7 ben ag breth[2] leinb.
'Nior bhó coir eimh,' ar Suibhne, 'don mhnáoi aoine an
Choimdedh do mhill*edh*. Feibh thúairges an ben an líon,'
ar sé, 'as amhlaidh sin rotúairgeadh[3] mo muinter-sa isin
chath a Maigh Rath.' Rochúal*aidh*-sion iarum clog an
esparta[4] aga bhúain, conadh ann adbert: 'Ba binne lem-sa
éimh,' ar sé, 'guth na ccúach do chloinsin ar[5] bruach na
Banna do gach leith inás grig-gráig an chluig si atchl*ui*nim
anocht,' co n-eb*ert* an laoidh:

23 ' Binne lem im na tonna
mh' ingne anocht cidh it cranna
na gricc-graicc chlogáin chille
an chú do[gní] cúi Banna.[1]

21—10 gleour Glinne Coa K   11 gein K   12 *leg.* nerta
22—1 dia na hainm K   2 toirb*ert* K   3 rothuairgitt K   4 *sic* BK.
5 chloisteacht um K
23—1 For this stanza and the following K has:
Binni leam im na tonna
m' adhbha anocht ciodhat crannda,
la nach loingenn Suibhne Geilt
ar seirc righ na firinde.

Small is my portion when day comes,
it comes not as a new day's right (?),
a tuft of watercress of Cluain Cille
with Cell Cua's cuckoo flower.

He who is at Ros Earcach,
neither trouble nor evil shall come to him ;
that which makes me strengthless
is being in snow in nakedness.'

22 So Suibhne fared forth until he reached the church at Snamh dha En on the Shannon, which is now called Cluain Boirenn ; he arrived there on a Friday, to speak precisely. The clerics of the church were then fulfilling the office of nones ; women were beating flax, and one was giving birth to a child. 'It is not meet, in sooth,' said Suibhne, 'for the women to violate the Lord's fast-day ; even as the woman beats the flax,' said he, 'so were my folk beaten in the battle of Magh Rath.' He heard then the vesper-bell pealing, whereupon he said : 'Sweeter indeed were it to me to hear the voices of the cuckoos on the banks of the Bann from every side than the *grig-graig* of this bell which I hear to-night'; and he uttered the lay :

23 'Sweeter to me about the waves—
though my talons to-night are feeble[1]—
than the *grig-graig* of the church-bell,
is the cooing of the cuckoo of the Bann.

A bhen na tairbhir do mhac
dia na haeini didine
na gricc gracc chlogáin cille
an cú doghni cui banna.

---

[1] throughout the story he speaks as though he imagined himself a bird ; see the Notes as to this stanza.

D

A bhen, na tairbhir do mac
día na háoine dídine,
lá nach luingenn³ Suibhne Geilt
ar⁴ seirc⁵ righ na fírinne.

Amail tuairgitt⁶ na mna an líon,
is fior ge nomc[h]luin*ter*-sa,
amlaidh rothuairgit 'san chath
for Maigh Rath mo mhuinter-sa.

O Loch Diolair an aille
go Doire Coluim Chille
nocha deab*aidh* rochúala⁷
ó ealaib búadha binne.

Dord daimh dhíthreibhe ós aille
bios a Siodhmhuine Glinne,
noc[h]an fuil ceol ar talmain
im anmuin acht a bhinne.

A Chriost, a Chriost romc[h]luine,
a Chriost, a Chriost gan bine,
a Chriost, a Chriost romc[h]ara,
na romscara red binne.'   Binne.

24 Rosiecht im*morro* Suibhne arnabhárach go [Cill]
Derfil*e*¹ gur chaith biorar na tiobraidi² 7 an t-uisge robhúi
isin chill 7 tainic doinenn dermhair isin oidchi go rosgab
athtuirsi adhbhalmor 7 snímhche Suibhne tria olcus a beathad
7 bheós rob imsniomhach athtuirseach leis bheith a n-ègm*uis*
Dhál Araidhe ; conadh ann adbert na randa sae :

25 ' Mh'agh*aidh* a cCill Der ffile¹
as í robris mo chroidhe,
dursan damh, a mic mo Dhé,
sgaradh re Dal nAraidhé.

23—3 loingenn K   4 *sic* K a B   5 shearc B ; sc̄ K   6 *sic* K ;
rothurrgid B   7 rocualae K
24—1 go derbhfil ᴗ B ; go derffil ᴗ K   2 tioprat K
25—1 *sic* K ; derffil ᴗ B.

O woman, do not bring forth thy son
on a Friday,
the day whereon Suibhne Geilt eats not
out of love for the King of righteousness.

As the women scutch the flax—
'tis true though 'tis I be heard—
even so were beaten my folk
in the battle of Magh Rath.

From Loch Diolair of the cliff
to Derry Coluim Cille
it was not strife that I heard
from splendid, melodious swans.

The belling of the stag of the desert above the cliffs
in Siodhmuine Glinne—
there is no music on earth
in my soul but its sweetness.

O Christ, O Christ, hear me !
O Christ, O Christ, without sin !
O Christ, O Christ, love me !
sever me not from thy sweetness ! '

24 On the morrow Suibhne went to Cell Derfile where he
fared on watercress of the well and the water which was in
the church ; there came a great storm in the night, and
exceeding sorrow and grief took hold of Suibhne because of
the wretchedness of his life ; and moreover it was a cause of
grief and sorrow to him to be absent from Dal Araidhe,
whereupcn he uttered these staves :

> **25** ' My night in Cell Derfile
> 'tis it has broken my heart ;
> sad for me, O Son of my God,
> is parting from Dal Araidhe.

D 2

Deichneamhar is deich cet laóch
rob é mo slúagh ag Druim‚Fraoch,
ge beó gan treisi, a mic Dé,
ba misi a ccenn comairlé.

Muichn*idh*e mh'aghaidh anocht
gan giolla is gan longphort,
niorbh í mh'aghaidh ag Druim Damh,
meisi is Faolchú is Conghal. [85b]

Mairg ro[m]fuirg*edh* risin dáil,
a mo ruire an ríchid² ráin,
gen go bfhaghainn-si d'ulc dhe
go brath acht an oidhchi-se.'　　　　M'aghaidh.

26 Seacht mbliadhna comhlána do Suibhne ar fud Erenn
as gach aird go aroile go ttoiracht¹ aon na oidhche² ann
co Glenn Bolcáin, fobith is ann robhaoi a dhaingen 7 a
dhunárus comhnaidhe-siumh 7 ba haoibhne leis oirisiumh
7 aittreabadh ann inás i ngach ionadh a nErinn ina égmuis,
úair doṡoich*edh*³ chuige as gach aird d'Eirinn 7 ni theighadh
úadh acht re huaman 7 re huiregla mhóir. Roairbhir bhith
Suibhne ann an aghaidh sin co ttoirracht Loingseachán fora
iarraidh isin maidin arnamhárach. Adberat furenn ann
gurbho mac mathar dho-sumh Loingseachán, adberat furenn
eile ba comhalta, acht cena cibe dhibh sin é roba mór a
dheithidin uime-siumh, uair dochuaidh-siumh fo thrí for
gealtacht 7 dusfug-sumh fo thrí for cculaibh. Robhaoi
Loingseachán aga iarraidh-siomh don dul sin isin ghlionn, co
bfuair sliocht bharr a throigh*edh* a mbruach na glaisi isa biorar
noith*edh* 7 fos fuair na craobha nomheabhtaís fó a chosaibh
ag altherrach do bharr an c[h]roind tor aroile. Ni bfuair-
siumh do*no* an gheilt an lá sin co ndeachaidh a faisteach
folamh isin glinn gur tuit a ṡúan toirrchim codalta fair ann

25—2 richith K ; righthigh B.
26—1 ttoracht K　　　2 noidhche K　　　3 nosoich*edh* K

Ten hundred and ten warriors,
that was my host at Druim Fraoch,
though I am without strength, O Son of God,
'twas I who was their leader in counsel.

Gloomy is my night to-night
without serving-man, without camp ;
not so was my night at Druim Damh,
I and Faolchu and Congal.

Alas ! that I was detained for the tryst,
O my Prince of the glorious Kingdom !
though I should not get any harm therefrom
forever except this night.'

26 For seven whole years Suibhne wandered over Ireland
from one point to another until one night he arrived at Glen
Bolcain ; for it is there stood his fortress and his dwelling-
place, and more delightful was it to him to tarry and abide
there than in any other place in Ireland ; for thither would
he go from every part of Ireland, nor would he leave it except
through fear and terror. Suibhne dwelt there that night, and
on the morrow morning Loingseachan came seeking him.
Some say that Loingseachan was Suibhne's mother's son,
others that he was a foster-brother, but, whichever he was, his
concern for Suibhne was great, for he (Suibhne) went off three
times in madness and thrice he brought him back. This time
Loingseachan was seeking him in the glen, and he found the
track of his feet by the brink of the stream of which he was
wont to eat the watercress. He found also the branches that
used to break under his feet as he changed from the top of
one tree to another. That day, however, he did not find the
madman, so he went into a deserted house in the glen, and
there he fell into deep sleep after the great labour of the

iar morṡaothar luirg Suibhni forsa raibhe³ iarair. Doluidh
iaromh Suibhne fora ṡliocht-somh go mbúi forsan teach co
ccúalaidh iarum srainn Loingseacháin ann ; conadh iarsin
adbert an láoiḋh-si :

27 ‘ An fer ag froig focherd srainn,
      súan mar soin nocha lamhaim,
      seacht mbliadhna on mhairt a Muigh Rath
      nochar chotlus tinneabr*adh*.

   Do chath rod,
   a Dhé [nime], ni ma lott,
   ba Suibhne Geilt m’ainm iar sin,
   mh’aonar dhamh a mbarr eidhin.¹

   Biorar thiobrad Droma Cirb,
   as e mo ṡásadh im theirt,
   as aithn*idh* orm² gnúis a ghné,
   as fíor is mé Suibhne Geilt.

   Dearbh as misi³ Suibhne Geilt
   fer contuil fo choemhna⁴ ceirt,
   im Ṡlíabh Líag ma do cló
   domseannad⁵ na fiora so.

   Antan ba-sum Suibhne sruith
   arbhirinn bith a n-úarbhuith
   i seisg, a sesgonn,⁶ i sléibh :
   rorer m’eol ar⁷ eidirchéin.

   Atloc[h]ar don righ-si thúas
   las nach gnáth an t-iomarchrúas,
   as edh romucc as mo riocht
   a mhéd robhá for ecciort.

26—3 ca added above B
27—1 K has :
          Do chath rot a Dhe nimhe
          ni ma lott ba Suibhne
          geilt m’ainm iarsin
          m’aonar i mbarraibh eidhinn.

pursuit of Suibhne whom he was seeking. Then Suibhne
came upon his track so that he reached the house, and there
he heard Loingseachan's snore; whereupon he uttered this
lay:

27 'The man by the wall snores,
    slumber like that I dare not;
    for seven years from the Tuesday at Magh Rath
    I have not slept a wink.

    O God of Heaven! would that I had not gone
    to the fierce battle!
    thereafter Suibhne Geilt was my name,
    alone in the top of the ivy.

    Watercress of the well of Druim Cirb
    is my meal at terce;
    on my face may be recognized its hue,
    'tis true I am Suibhne Geilt.

    For certain am I Suibhne Geilt,
    one who sleeps under shelter of a rag,
    about Sliabh Liag if . . .
    these men pursue me.

    When I was Suibhne the sage,
    I used to dwell in a lonely shieling,
    on sedgy land, on a morass, on a mountain-side;
    I have bartered my home for a far-off land.

    I give thanks to the King above
    with whom great harshness is not usual;
    'tis the extent of my injustice
    that has changed my guise.

As fuit, fuit damh o nach mair
mo chollan i n-eidhnechaibh,
fer*aidh* mor do śíonaibh air
agus mor do thoirneachaibh.

Gidh im beó o gach dinn do dhinn
isin sliobh os iubairghlinn,
ait i fargb*adh* Congal Claón
monúar na romfar[g]b*adh* faon.[8]

Meinic m' ong
cian om relic mo theach toll,
nidom nía acht im geilt ghann,
Dia romc[h]lann i cceirt gan chonn.

As mor báos
a Glinn Bolcain acht ce tǽs,
fil mor do abhlaibh a nGlinn
Bolcáin do éimh*edh* (?)[9] mo chinn.

Biorar glas
agus deogh d'uisge glain,
nosibhim, ni thibim gen,
ni hionann sa[n] fer ag froigh.

Eidir corraibh Cúailghne saimh,[10]
eitir chúanaibh[11] o thig gaimh,
fo chéibh chaille gach re seal,
ni hionann sa[n] fer ag fraigh.   [86a]

Glenn mBolcáin mbil bél re gaóith
ima ngairid geilte[12] glinne,
ni chodlaim ann, monuar dhamh,
am trúaighe na an fer a[g] fraigh.'[13]   An fer.

27—8 fhargb*ad* i cein K   9 eimh ⌣ K   10 sáimh B ; isnam K
11 conaiph K   12 *sic* B ; geilt ⌣ K   13 srainn K

Cold, cold for me is it
since my body lives not in the ivy-bushes,
much rain comes upon it
and much thunder.

Though I live from hill to hill
in the mountain above the yew glen ;
in the place where Congal Claon was left
alas that I was not left there on my back !

Frequent is my groan,
far from my churchyard is my gaping house ;
I am no champion but a needy madman,
God has thrust me in rags, without sense.

'Tis great folly
for me to come out of Glen Bolcain,
there are many apple-trees in Glen Bolcain
for . . . of my head.

Green watercress
and a draft of pure water,
I fare on them, I smile not,
not so the man by the wall.

In summer amid the herons of Cuailgne,
among packs of wolves when winter comes,
at other times under the crown of a wood ;
not so the man by the wall.

Happy Glen Bolcain, fronting the wind,
around which madmen of the glen call,
woe is me! I sleep not there ;
more wretched am I than the man by the wall.'

28 A haithle na laidhe sin doluidh-siumh isin oidhche
ar ccionn co muilenn Loingseacháin ; aonc[h]ailleach ag a
choimhéd-sidhi .i. Lonnog inghenDui bh Dhit[h]ribh mathair
mhná Loingseacháin.   Tainic Suibhne isin teach cuice 7
tuc si mírenna beca dhó 7 robhúi fri re chían ag aithighidh
an mhuilinn amhlaidh sin.   Luid Loingseachán for a ṡliocht-
somh lá n-ann conusfaca for taidhin an mhuilinn é 7 téit
d'agallamh na caillighi .i. co Lonnóig mathair a mhná.
'An ttainic Suibhne 'san muilenn, a chaillech?' ar Loingseachán.   'Robúi areir co déidhenach sunn,' ar an chaillech.
Rogabh iarum Loingseachán ceirt na caillighe uime 7 roan
isin muilenn tar éis na caillighe 7 tainic Suibhne an oidhche
sin don mhuilinn co ttug aithne ar Loingseachán.   O'dchonn-
arc a ṡúile co·ling[1] úadha focedóir dar forlés an tighe amach 7
adbert : ' A Loingseacháin,' ar sé, ' as trúagh th'amus orm-sa
arim thafann as mh'ionadh 7 as gach ionadh[2] is diule[3] lium
i nErinn 7 o nach leig Rón[án] damh-sa taobh do thabhairt
friot as liosda lenamhnach dhuit ueith dom lenmhuin'; 7
dorinne an laoidh so ann :

> **29** ' A Loingseacháin, liosda sin,
> nochan úain damh t'agalloimh,
> ni léig dhamh Rónán taobh friot,
> as e domrad a n-ainriocht.
>
> Doradus urchar gan ágh
> a lar an chatha ar Ronán,
> co robhen isin chlog chain
> robhaoi for ucht an chléirigh.
>
> Mar dotheilgius urchar n-án
> do lár an chatha ar Ronán,
> ' ced duit,' ar an cleireach cain,
> ' dul aræn risna hénaibh.'

28—1 roling K   2 as truag thangus agam thofann as gach ionad K
3 diliu K

28 After that lay he came the next night to Loingseachan's mill which was being watched over by one old woman, Lonnog, daughter of Dubh Dithribh, mother of Loingseachan's wife. Suibhne went into the house to her and she gave him small morsels, and for a long time in that manner he kept visiting the mill. One day Loingseachan set out after him, when he saw him by the mill-stream, and he went to speak to the old woman, that is, his wife's mother, Lonnog. ' Has Suibhne come to the mill, woman ? ' said Loingseachan. ' He was last here last night,' said the woman. Loingseachan then put on the woman's garment and remained in the mill after her ; that night Suibhne came to the mill and he recognised Loingseachan. When he saw his eyes, he sprang away from him at once out through the skylight of the house, saying : ' Pitiful is your pursuit of me, Loingseachan, chasing me from my place and from each spot dearest to me in Ireland ; and as Ronan does not allow me to trust you, it is tiresome and importunate of you to be following me " ; and he made this lay :

29 ' O Loingseachan, thou art irksome,
I have not leisure to speak with thee,
Ronan does not let me trust thee ;
'tis he who has put me in a sorry plight.

I made the luckless cast
from the midst of the battle at Ronan ;
it pierced the precious bell
which was on the cleric's breast.

As I hurled the splendid cast
from the midst of the battle at Ronan,
said the fair cleric : ' Thou hast leave
to go with the birds.'

Iarsin rolinges-[s]a súas
isin æér eadarbhúas,
ni rolinges o 'tú[1] beó
æinleim badh hettromó.

Da madh isin maidin múaidh,
isin Mairt a haithle an Lúain,
nochar úallcha neach anu[2]
a leith re hóglách m' aosú.

As iongnadh lem inní atchiú,
a fhir rodhealbh an lá aniu,
ceirt na caillighi ar an clár,
dá śúil lúatha Loingsecháin.'   A.

30 'As trúagh an mheabail rob áil duit do dhénamh orm-sa, a Loingsecháin,' ar sé '7 na bí ag mo t[h]oc[h]rádh ni as sía, acht eirg dot thoigh 7 raghat-sa róm[1] gonige an baile itá Eorann.

31 As amhlaidh éimh robhúi Eorann an tan sin ar ffeis le Guaire mac Congail mic Sgannláin, ar rob i Eorann fa ben do Suibhne, uair robhattar dá bhrathair isin tír 7 ba comhdhúthaigh dhoibh an righe rofagaibh Suibhne .i. Guaire mac Congail, mic Sgannnláin, 7 Eochaidh mac Condlo,[1] mic Sgannláin. Rosiacht tra Suibne gonige an baile ina[1a] raibhe Eorann. Dodheachaidh Gúaire do śeilg an lá sin 7 ba sí conair dochúaidh co muinchinn Sleibe Fuaid[2] 7 im Sgirig Chinn Ghlinne 7 im Ettan Tairb. As ann robaoi[3] a longport im Glenn Bolcáin risa raiter Glenn Chíach aniu i machaire chineoil Ainmirech. Deisidh iarumh an gheilt for fordhorus na boithe i raibhe Eorann, conadh ann itbert: 'An cumhain let a ingen,' ar sé, 'an grádh romor dorad cach uainn dá chéle an ionbaidh robhámar imaraon? Agus

29—1 taoi K   2 aniu K
30—1 om. K
31—1 condo K   1a i K   2 sic K om. B, but there is a blank space
following sleibe.   3 sic K ; roúi (?) B

Thereafter I sprang up
into the air above ;
in life I have never leaped
a single leap that was lighter.

Were it in the glorious morning,
on the Tuesday following the Monday,
none would be prouder than I am
by the side of a warrior of my folk.

A marvel to me is that which I see,
O Thou that hast shaped this day ;
the woman's garment on the floor,
two piercing [1] eyes of Loingseachan.'

30 ' Sad is the disgrace you would fain put upon me,
Loingseachan,' said he ; ' and do not continue annoying me
further, but go to your house and I will go on to where
Eorann is.'

31 Now, Eorann at the time was dwelling with Guaire,
son of Congal, son of Scannlan, for it was Eorann who was
Suibhne's wife, for there were two kinsmen in the country,
and they had equal title to the sovereignty which Suibhne
had abandoned, viz.: Guaire, son of Congal, son of Scannlan,
and Eochaidh, son of Condlo, son of Scannlan.   Suibhne
proceeded to the place in which Eorann was.   Guaire had
gone to the chase that day, and the route he took was to the
pass of Sliabh Fuaid and by Sgirig Cinn Glinne and Ettan
Tairbh.   His camp was beside Glen Bolcain — which is
called Glenn Chiach to-day—in the plain of Cinel Ainmirech.
Then the madman sat down upon the lintel of the hut in
which Eorann was, whereupon he said : ' Do you remember,
lady, the great iove we gave to each other what time
we were together ?   Easy and pleasant it is for you now,

29—1 lit. ' swift ', perhaps ' furtive '.

is suanach sadail duit-si,' ar sé, '7 ni headh dhamh-sa';
conadh an adbert Suibhne 7 rofhregair Eorann é :   [86b]

32 [Suibhne:] 'Súanach sin, a Eorann án,
          i leith leaptha red lennán,
          ni hionann is misi ibhus,
          cian o atu-sa ar anbfhorus.

          Roraidhis, a Eorann oll,
          ait[h]esg al*ainn* iméttrom
          co na beithea it bheathaidh dhe
          sgaradh énla re Suibhne.

          Aniú is suaithn*idh* co prab,
          beg let brigh do śencharad,
          te duit ar chluimh cholcaidh cain,
          úar damh-sa amuigh co madain.

[Eorann :] As mochen duit, a gheilt ghlan,
          tú is tocha d' feruibh talman,
          gidh súanach is suaill mo chlí
          on la itcuala tú[1] ar neimhni.[2]

[Suibhne:] As tocha let mac in righ,
          b*erius*[3] tú d'ól gan imśníomh,
          as é do thochmarc togha,
          ní íarr sibh bhar senchara.

[Eorann:] Ce nomber*adh* m*a*c an righ
          do t[h]oig*ibh* oil gan imśniomh,
          ferr liom feis i ccuas cháol c*hr*oinn
          let, a f*hir*, día notcaomhsoinn.

          Dá ttuctha mo rogha dhamh
          d' feruibh Eirenn is Alban,
          ferr lem it chom*air*[4] gan chol
          ar uisge *agus* ar bhiorar.

<hr>

32— 1 otchuala thu K   2 neim*hs*hni B   3 beir*us* K   4 cum⁔ K

but not so for me;' whereupon Suibhne said, and Eorann answered him (as follows):

32 Suibhne: 'At ease art thou, bright Eorann,
               at the bedside with thy lover;
               not so with me here,
               long have I been restless.

               Once thou didst utter, O great Eorann,
               a saying pleasing and light,
               that thou wouldst not survive
               parted one day from Suibhne.

               To-day, it is readily manifest,
               thou thinkest little of thy old friend;
               warm for thee on the down of a pleasant bed,
               cold for me abroad till morn.

Eorann: Welcome to thee, thou guileless mad one!
               thou art most welcome of the men ot the earth;
               though at ease am I, my body is wasted
               since the day I heard of thy ruin.

Suibhne: More welcome to thee is the king's son
               who takes thee to feast without sorrow;
               he is thy chosen wooer;
               you seek not your old friend.

Eorann: Though the king's son were to lead me
               to blithe banqueting-halls,
               I had liefer sleep in a tree's narrow hollow
               beside thee, my husband, could I do so.

               If my choice were given me
               of the men of Erin and Alba,
               I had liefer bide sinless with thee
               on water and on watercress.

[Suibhne:] Ni conair do[5] d*egh*mhnáoi dhil,
S*uibhne* sunn ar sliocht imnidh
fuar mo leaptha ag Ard Abhla,
nidot[6] terctha[7] m' fhúaradhbha.

Córa duit serc *agus* gradh
don fhior 'gá táoi th'ǽnaran
ina do gheilt ghairbh ghort*aigh*
uath*aigh*, omhnaigh, urnochtaigh.

[Eorann:] Monúar amh, a gheilt ghniomhach,
do ueth eitt*igh* imṡniomhach,
saoth lem do chnes rochlói d*a*th,
dreasa is droighin gut[8] réb*adh*.

[Suibhne:] Ni *dá* chairiug*hadh* dhamh ort,
a mháothaind*er* mháothéttrocht,
Críst mac Muire, mor da cacht,
é domrad a n-éccomhnart.

[Eorann:] Robadh maith lem ar mbeth arǽn
co ttig*eadh* clumh ar ar ttaobh,
co sirfinn soirchi is doirchi
let gach lá is gach énoidhche.

[Suibhne:] Ad*aigh* dhamh-sa a mBoirchi bhinn,
ran*a*c Túath Inbhir aloinn,
rosirius Magh Fáil co fraigh,
taïrlius do Cill Ui Súan*aigh*.'   S.

33 Ni thairnic dhó acht sin do radh an uair rolion[1] an
slúagh an longp*hor*t as gach aird. T*éid*-siumh iarumh ina reim
romhadhma for teichedh amail ba[2] minic leis.   Ni roan-somh
don reim sin co rainic ría n-oidhchi co Ros mBeraigh .i. an
c*ét*-cill ag ar oiris a haithle catha Muighe Rath 7 dochóidh
isin iobar robhúidh[3] isin chill.   Muireadach mac Earca da*no*,

_____

Suibhne :   No path for a beloved lady
             is that of Suibhne here on the track of care ;
             cold are my beds at Ard Abhla,
             my cold dwellings are not few.

             More meet for thee to bestow love and affection
             on the man with whom thou art alone
             than on an uncouth and famished madman,
             horrible, fearful, stark-naked.

Eorann :   O toiling madman, 'tis my grief
             that thou art uncomely and dejected ;
             I sorrow that thy skin has lost its colour,
             briars and thorns rending thee.

Suibhne :   I blame thee not for it,
             thou gentle, radiant woman ;
             Christ, Son of Mary—great bondage—
             He has caused my feebleness.

Eorann :   I would fain that we were together,
             and that feathers might grow on our bodies ;[1]
             in light and darkness I would wander
             with thee each day and night.

Suibhne :   One night I was in pleasant Boirche,
             I have reached lovely Tuath Inbhir,
             I have wandered throughout Magh Fail,
             I have happened on Cell Ui Suanaigh.'

33 No sooner had he finished than the army swarmed into the camp from every quarter, whereupon he set off in his headlong flight, as he had often done. He halted not in his career until before the fall of night he arrived at Ros Bearaigh—the first church at which he tarried after the battle of Magh Rath—and he went into the yew-tree which was in the church.

---

as e ba hairchinneach isin cill an tan sin. Dorala iarum ben
an oirchinnigh ag gab*áil* secha⁴ an iub*har* co bfaca⁵ an gheilt
ann 7 tuc aithne fair guruó é Suibhne robhúi ann, co n-éb*er*t sí
fris : ' Táir asin iub*har*, a rí Dhál Araidhe,' ar sí, ' ata baeghal
áonmhná sunna agad.' Do ghab*áil* na geilti 7 dá brégadh
7 cealg*adh* atrubhairt si ind sin. ' Nocha ragha eimh,' ar
Suibhne, ' ar nachamtáir Loingseachán 7 a bhen, ar robhúi
tan ba husa dhuit aithni form-sa inás aniú'; conadh ann atbert
na runna sa sios ann :

> 34 ' A bhen dobheir¹ aithne² form
> do rennuibh do rosg roghorm,
> robhúi tan ba ferr mo gné
> i n-airecht Dal Araidhé.
>
> Rochláoch*aighe*s dealbh is dath
> on úair tanag asin chath,
> rob*o* misi an Suibhne seng
> atchúaladar fir Eireand.
>
> Bí-si gut fhior is gut thoigh,
> nocha biu-sa a Ros mBeraigh,
> ni chomhracfem go bráth mbán,
> misi agus tusa, a bhenaccan.'   A bhen.

35 Doluidh-siomh iarumh asin iubhar co hettrom æerdha
7 tóet roimhe co rainic isin mbile ag Ros Earcáin, úair
dobhadar tri dúnáruis aigi-siumh ina cclecht*adh* comn*aidh*e
do dhenamh ina thír feisin .i. Teach mic Ninnedha 7 Cluain
Creamha 7 Ros Earcáin. Robháoi-siumh iarum co cenn
cáocáoisi ar mhís isin iub*har* sin gan airiughudh, co frith ann
a ionadh 7 a adhbha [87 a] fo dheóidh, co ndernadh comairle
ag maithibh Dhál Araidhe cia durachadh da gab*áil co*
*n*derb*er*tatar uili ba hé Loingseachán robadh cóir do c*hur*¹

33—4 seach K   5 bfac⌣ B
34—1 *sic* K ; na ber⌣ B   2 aithgni K
35—1 dul K

Muireadach mac Earca was erenach of the church at the time, and his wife happened to be going past the yew when she saw the madman in it; she recognized that it was Suibhne was there and said to him : 'Come out of the yew, king of Dal Araidhe ; there is but one woman before you here.' She said so in order to seize the madman, and to deceive and beguile him. 'I will not go indeed,' said Suibhne, 'lest Loingseachan and his wife come to me, for there was a time when it would have been easier for you to recognize me than it is to-day' ; whereupon he uttered these staves :

34   'O woman, who dost recognize me
        with the points of thy blue eyes,
        there was a time when my aspect was better
        in the assembly of Dal Araidhe.

      I have changed in shape and hue
        since the hour I came out of the battle ;
        I was the slender Suibhne
        of whom the men of Erin had heard.

      Bide thou with thy husband and in thy house,
        I shall not tarry in Ros Bearaigh ;
        until holy Judgment we shall not foregather,
        I and thou, O woman.'

35 He emerged then from the tree lightly and nimbly, and went on his way until he reached the old tree at Ros Earcain. (For he had three dwellings in his own country in which he was wont to reside, viz.: Teach mic Ninnedha, Cluain Creamha, and Ros Earcain). Thereafter for a fortnight and a month he tarried in the yew-tree without being perceived ; but at length his place and dwelling were discovered, and the nobles of Dal Araidhe took counsel as to who should go to seize him. Everyone said that it was Loingseachan who

ann. Rogab Loingseachán im*morro* do laimh teacht frisin toisg sin 7 luidh roimhe co ttainic dochum an iub*hair* ina mbáoi Suibhne, conusfacaidh² an gheilt ar an ccráoibh úasa. 'Truagh sin, a Suibhne,' ar sé, 'conadh é th'*í*erdr*aighe* bheith amhlaidh sin gan bhíadh, gan digh, gan edach amail gach n-ethaid n-ǽerdha, ier mbeith a n-étt*aighi*bh sroldae³ siregdha ar each*aibh* ana⁴ allmurdha co sríanaibh soinemhla dhuit, 7 mná málla maisecha let 7 iomad macaomh 7 miolchon 7 degháos gacha dana, iomad sl*úagh*, iomdha iolarrdha d'urr*adh*uibh 7 do tháoisechuibh 7 d'óigthighernaidhibh, do brughadhuibh 7 do bhiatachaibh dot réir. Iomad cúach 7 copán 7 benn mbreacegair mbúabhaill im lennuibh somblasda so-ola let bhéos. Dursan duit bheith fon ionnus sin amail gach n-en ttr*ua*g⁵ ttarimtheachtach ó dhithribh do dhithribh.' 'Leig as a le, a Loingseácháin,' ar Suibhne, 'as *edh* sin robhúi i ttoici dhuinn, 7 in bfhuilid sgéla mo thíri leat-sa dhamh?' 'Atád eimh,⁶' ar Loingseachan, 'anuair⁷ roég th'athair.' 'Domgaibh dom fhorm*adh* on,' ar sé. 'Do m*áthair* do*no* dh' ég,' ar an giolla. 'Rohan*adh* dom oirchisecht a ufecht sa,' ar se. 'Marbh do bráthair,' ar Loingseachán. 'Toll mo thaobh don leith sin,' ar Suibhne. 'Marbh th' ingen,' ar Loingseachán. 'Sn*áth*ad c*h*roidhe da*no* eini*ngen*,' ar Suibhne. 'Marbh do mac atbeir*edh* a phopa friot,' ar Loingseachán. 'Fíor ón,' ar sé, 'as é. sin an banna dobheir an fer co lár'; conadh ann atbertsat an laoidh etarra .i. Loingseachán 7 Suibhne:

36 [Loingseachán:] 'A Suibhne¹ a Sleibh na nEach n-ard,
robsat fuileach faobharghargc,
ar Chriost rodchuir a ccarcra
dámh comhradh red chomhalta.

34—2 *sic* B ; -faca K   **3** sroldaibh K   4 anaibh K   5 ttairisi (?) *add.* B   6 ale *add.* K   ⁊ uair K
36—1 Suibhniu K

should be sent. Loingseachan undertook the task, and he
went along until he came to the yew in which Suibhne was,
whereupon he beheld the madman on the branch above him.
' Sad is it, Suibhne,' said he, ' that your last plight should be
thus, without food, without drink, without raiment, like any
bird of the air, after having been in garments of silk and satin
on splendid steeds from foreign lands with matchless bridles ;
with you were women gentle and comely, likewise many
youths and hounds and goodly folk of every art ; many hosts,
many and diverse nobles and chiefs, and young lords, and
landholders and hospitallers were at your command. Many
cups and goblets and carved buffalo horns for pleasant-
flavoured and enjoyable liquors were yours also. Sad is it for
you to be in that wise like unto any miserable bird going
from wilderness to wilderness.' ' Cease now, Loingseachan,'
said Suibhne ; ' that is what was destined for us ; but
have you tidings for me of my country ? ' ' I have in
sooth,' said Loingseachan, ' for your father is dead.' ' That
has seized me . . .', said he. ' Your mother is also dead,' said
the young man. ' Now all pity for me is at an end,' said
he. ' Dead is your brother,' said Loingseachan. ' Gaping is
my side on that account,' said Suibhne. ' Dead is your
daughter,' said Loingseachan. ' The heart's needle is an only
daughter,' said Suibhne. ' Dead is your son who used to
call you ' daddy ',' said Loingseachan. ' True,' said he, ' that
is the drop (?) which brings a man to the ground ;' whereupon they, even Loingseachan and Suibhne, uttered this lay
between them:

36 Loingseachan: 'O Suibhne from lofty Sliabh na nEach,
                 thou of the rough blade wert given to
                     wounding ;
                 for Christ's sake, who hath put thee in
                     bondage,
                 grant converse with thy foster-brother.

Eist rium-sa ma romc[h]luini,
a rí rán, a righ-ruire,
co n-innisinn tre mhíne
sgéla dhuit do dheighthire.

Ni marthain at thír tar th'eis,
as dó tánag² da aisneis,
marbh do bhrathair ann co mbl*aidh*,
marbh th'athair is do mhathair.

[Suibhne :]   Mása mharbh mo mháthair mhín
deacraidi damh dol dom thir,
cían o rochair si mo chorp
roscair si friom oirchisecht.

Baoth comairle gach mic mhir
ag nach mairid a sinnsir,
amail as c*r*om c*r*aobh fo chnoibh,
toll taobh o bheith gan bhráthair.

[Loingseachán:]   Ata urb*aidh*³ oile ann
cáoint*er* ag feruibh Eireann
cidh garbh do thaobh is do throigh,
marbh do bhen chaomh d*o*t chum*aidh*.

[Suibhne :]   Tig*edhus* do bheith gan mnáoi,
as iomramh luinge gan láoi,
as cad*adh* clúimhe re cnes,
as adudh re hénoires.⁴

[Loingseachán:]   Atchúala sgél n-uathmar n-ard
ima raibhe gul glégharg,
as dorn im⁵ dhíaidh cia bé dhe,
atáoi gan tsiair, a Suibhne.

36—2 thanag K   3 urb*aidh*e K   4 haenaires K   5 na K

Hearken to me if thou hearest me,
O splendid king, O great prince,
so that I may relate gently
to thee tidings of thy good land.

There is life for none in thy land after thee ;
it is to tell of it that I have come ;
dead is thy renowned brother there,
dead thy father and thy mother.

Suibhne: If my gentle mother be dead,
harder is it for me to go to my land ;
'tis long since she has loved my body ;
she has ceased to pity me.

Foolish the counsel of each wild youth
whose elders live not ;
like unto a branch bowed under nuts ;
whoso is brotherless has a gaping side.

Loingseachan: There is another calamity there
which is bewailed by the men of Erin,
though uncouth be thy side and thy foot,
dead is thy fair wife of grief for thee.

Suibhne: For a household to be without a wife
is rowing a rudderless boat,
'tis a garb of feathers to the skin,
'tis kindling a single fire.

Loingseachan: I have heard a fearful and loud tale
around which was a clear, fierce wail,
'tis a fist round smoke, however,
thou art without sister, O Suibhne.

[Suibhne :]　　　　Seinbhríathar so, serb an snomh,⁶
nocha lium-sa as airfidiudh,⁷
an*aidh* grian chíúin in gach cladh,
car*aidh* siúr cen co·ccarthar.

[Loingseachán :]　Nocha legar laoigh co búaibh
agoinn i nAruidhe uair,
os marbh th'ingen chaomh rodc[h]ar
maráon is mac do⁸ seathar.

[Suibhne :]　　　　Mac mo sethar is mo chú,
nocham ttreigfittís ar bhú,
as táthacht⁹ uilc re himnedh,
snáthad c*hr*oidhe éninghen.

[Loingseachán :]　Ata sgél eile co mbl*oidh*,
as leasg lem a innisin,
fir Aradh go ngaoineimh¹⁰ nglic
atád ag cáoineadh th'énmhic. [87 b]

[Suibhne :]　　　　As e sin an banna¹¹ co mbloidh
dob*heir* an fer co talmain,
mac beg adber*edh* popa¹²
do ueith og*a* gan anm*ain*.

Romfrithail chugad don chraoibh,
súaill nacha nderna anmáoin,¹³
nocha nfuil[n]ghim¹⁴ thúas don beirt
o rochuala tásg mh'¹⁵ éinmhic.

[Loingseachán :]　O doriachtais, a laoich láin,
eidir di láimh Loingseacháin
mairidh do mhuintir uile
a Ua¹⁶ Each*ach* Sálbhuidhe.

36—6 an snomh B ; asnomh altered later to asniomh K　　7 airfid*edh* B ;
nu airfithiodh K　　8 *sic* K ; mo B　　9 táthacht B ; tathacht K, *an leg.*
táthad?　　10 ngaoineimh altered later to ngaoineamh K　　11 ase
sin bannae K　　12 popae K ; papa B　　13 nacham derna annmein K
14 nfuilingim K　　15 *sic* K ; *om.* B　　16 *sic* K ; uadh B

Suibhne : A proverb this, bitter the . . . —
    it has no delight for me—
    the mild sun rests on every ditch,
    a sister loves though she be not loved.

Loingseachan: Calves are not let to cows
    amongst us in cold Araidhe
    since thy gentle daughter, who has loved thee died,
    likewise thy sister's son.

Suibhne : My sister's son and my hound,
    they would not forsake me for wealth,
    'tis adding loss to sorrow ;
    the heart's needle is an only daughter.

Loingseachan: There is another famous story—
    loth am I to tell it—
    meetly[2] are the men of the Arada
    bewailing thy only son.

Suibhne: That is the renowned drop (?)
    which brings a man to the ground,[3]
    that his little son who used to say 'daddy'
    should be without life.

    It has called me to thee from the tree,
    scarce have I caused enmity,
    I cannot bear up against the blow
    since I heard the tidings of my only son.

Loingseachan: Since thou hast come, O splendid warrior,
    within Loingseachan's hands,
    all thy folk are alive,
    O scion of Eochu Salbuidhe.

36—1 lit. 'kine.'   2 lit. ' with clever fancy ' (?)
3 see p. 52 l. 24 and Notes.

Bi it tocht, tigeadh do chiall,
thoir ata do theach is ni thiar,
fada od thír tangais a lle,
as é so a fhíor, a Suibhne.

Aoibhne leat eitir dhamaibh
i feadhuibh i fidbhadhaibh,
ina codladh it dhún thoir,
ar c[h]luimh[17] 7 ar cholcaidh.

Ferr let bheth ar chraoibh chuilinn
i ttaoibh linni an lúathmhuilinn
ina bheith a ngrinne ghlan,
is gille óga it fharradh.

Da ccodailteá i ccigibh cnoc
re tédaibh míne mennchrot,
binni leat fo bharr doiri
cronán dhaimh dhuinn[18] dhamhghoiri.

At lúaithe na[19] gaoth tar glenn,
as tú éingheilt na hEirenn,
glédonn th' aobh,[20] tasci a lle,
bat[21] ségonn[22] saor, a Suibhne.'　　　A.S.

37 Atróchair eimh Suibhni asin iubhar o rochuala tasg a
éinmhic, gur ro-iadh Loingseachán a dhá láimh thairis 7
rochuir cuibhreach fora lámhaibh. Ro-innis dó iaromh a
muinter do mharthain uile 7 rug leis é gusin ionadh i
rabhadar maithe Dhál Araidhe. Tucaid dono[1] glais 7

36—17 chlum K　　　18 om. K　　　19 luaithi ina K　　　20 gledonn do
thaob K　　　21 sic K ; b⌣ B　　　22 séghuinn B ; segonn K
37—1 om. K

Be still, let thy sense come,
in the east is thy house, not in the west,
far from thy land thou hast come hither,
this is the truth, O Suibhne.

More delightful deemest thou to be amongst deer
in woods and forests
than sleeping in thy stronghold in the east
on a bed of down.

Better deemest thou to be on a holly-branch
beside the swift mill's pond
than to be in choice company
with young fellows about thee.

If thou wert to sleep in the bosom of hills
to the soft strings of lutes,
more sweet wouldst thou deem under the oak-wood
the belling of the brown stag of the herd.

Thou art fleeter than the wind across the valley,
thou art the famous madman of Erin,
brilliant in thy beauty, come hither,
O Suibhne, thou wast a noble champion.'

37 When Suibhne heard tidings of his only son, he fell
from the yew, whereupon Loingseachan closed his arms around
him and put manacles on him. He then told him that all his
people lived ; and he took him to the place in which the nobles
of Dal Araidhe were. They brought with them locks and fetters

gebheṇna eaturra² aca-somh faoi Suibhne² 7 roherb*adh* do
Loingseachan ạ breith leis co ceṇn caocaoisi ar mhís. Ruc-
sumh iarum Suibhne leis 7 robhadar maithe an chuig*edh*
chuigi 7 úadha frisin re sin. Tainic trá a chiall 7 a chuimhne
dhó a ffoircenn na ree sin. Tainic bheos a chruth 7 a
dhealbh budhdhein dó. Robhenaid a chuibhrighe de 7
rosamhlaidh*edh*²ᵃ [a ríghe]³ fris. Tainic ionbaidh fhoghamhair
ann fáoi sin 7 luidh Loingseachán cona muinter [do bhuain]³
lá n-ann. Ro*cuiredh* eision a ttuilg Loingseacháin iar mbéin
a glais de 7 ar ttecht a cheille dhó. Rohíadh*adh* an tuilg
fair 7 nior fágb*adh* neach ina fharradh acht an⁴ chailleach
namá .i. cailleach an mhuilinn 7 rohaithnidhedh dhi gan
comhr*adh* do ṡoighin ar Suibhne. Ara áoi sin roṡoigh sí cóir
chomhr*aidh* air-siomh co rofhiafraigh ní día imthechtuibh
dhe oiread robhaoi ar gealtacht. ' Mallacht for do bhél, a
chaill*ech,* ar Suibhne, ' as olc a n-abra,⁵ ni léigfi Día mo
bheith-si for gealtacht doridhisi.' ' Maith a fios agum-sa,' ar
an c[h]ailleach, ' gurab é sárugudh Rónáin fodera duit dul for
gealtacht.' ' A bhen,' ar sé, ' is granna duit beth gom b*rath*
7 gom bíat*hadh.*' ' Nocha brat[h] edir,' ar sí, ' acht fírinne ' ;
7 adubairt Suibhne :

38 [Suibhne:]   ' A chaill*ech*¹ an mhuilinn thall,
              cid duit mo chor ar imrall ?
              nach meabhail deit tre bháigh² mban
              mo brath agus mo biathadh ?

[An chailleach :] Nocha misi dobhraith thú,³
              a Ṡuiune, cidh caomh do chlú,
              acht ferta Rónáin do nimh
              rolá it gheilt eidir ghealtuibh.

37—2 *om.* K   2ᵃ rosaml⌣ K   3 *sic* K ; *om.* B   4 en K   5 nabrae K
38—1 chailliuch K   2 *sic* K ;· bháidh B   3 robhraith tu K

to put on Suibhne, and he was entrusted to Loingseachan to
take him with him for a fortnight and a month. He took
Suibhne away, and the nobles of the province were coming
and going during that time; and at the end of it his sense
and memory came to him, likewise his own shape and guise.
They took his bonds off him, and his kingship was manifest.'
Harvest-time came then, and one day Loingseachan went
with his people to reap. Suibhne was put in Loingseachan's
bed-room after his bonds were taken off him, and his sense
had come back to him. The bed-room was shut on him and
nobody was left with him but the mill-hag, and she was
enjoined not to attempt to speak to him. Nevertheless she
spoke to him, asking him to tell some of his adventures while
he was in a state of madness. 'A curse on your mouth, hag!'
said Suibhne; 'ill is what you say; God will not suffer me to
go mad again.' 'I know well,' said the hag, 'that it was
the outrage done to Ronan that drove you to madness.'
'O woman,' said he, 'it is hateful that you should be betraying
and luring me.' 'It is not betrayal at all but truth'; and
Suibhne said :

38 Suibhne :   'O hag of yonder mill,
            why shouldst thou set me astray ?
            is it not deceitful of thee that, through
                women,
            I should be betrayed and lured ?

  The hag :   'Tis not I who betrayed thee,
            O Suibhne, though fair thy fame,
            but the miracles of Ronan from Heaven
            which drove thee to madness among mad-
                men.

37—1 lit. 'his kingship was likened to him.' (?)

[Suibhne :] Da madh misi is go madh mé
      badh righ ar Dhál Araidhé,
      robudh mana duirn tar smech,⁴
      nochatfia cuirm, a chaill*ech*.'⁵   A chaillech.

39 A chaill*ech*,' ar sé, 'is mor do dheacraibh fuarus-sa dá
ufestá-sa é, mor leim ndoiligh rolinges-[s]a o gach diongna 7
o gach dionn, o gach fuithir 7 o gach fáinghlenn di aroile.'
'Ar Día friot,' ar an chaillech, 'ling duinn leim dona
leimennuibh sin anois rolingthea it ghealtacht.' Rolincc-
siomh iarumh leim tar colbha na tuilgi co rainic cenn
na hairidhni síos. 'Mo chubhuis éimh,' ar an chaillech,
'rolingfinn-si féin an léim sin.' Roling sí ón fón ccuma
cedna.¹ [88 a] Roling-siomh leim eile dar forles na bruighniu
amach. 'Rolin[g]finn-si do*no* sin,' ar an chaillech, 7 roling
fo cedóir. Acht chena ba *sedh* a chumair. Roŝir Suibhne
cuig triocha ched Dhal Araidhe roimpe an lá sin co rainic
Glenn na nEachtach i Fidh Gaibhle 7 rolen sí é frisin ré sin.
O rothairis Suibhne ar barr c*r*aoibhe urairde eidhn*igh*e
annsin, rothairis an chaillech ar c*r*ann eile ina fharradh ; a
nderedh an fhoghamhair do sunnradh ind sin, conadh ann
atchuala Suibhne gair ŝealga na soch*aidh*e ind-imeal an
fheadha. 'Gair mo*r*ŝlu*aig* so,' ar sé, '7 as iad Úi Faeláin
failet ann ag techt dom mharbadh-sa a ndioghail Oiliolla
Cédaigh .i. righ Ua bF*æ*láin romharbhus-[s]a i ccath Muighe
Rath.' Atchúala*ï*dh-siomh búir*iudh* an doimh alla, 7 dorinni
an laoidh 7 tuc testmolta² c*r*ann Eirenn ós aird innte 7
ag foraithmheadh araill dia dheacruibh 7 dia imŝniomh
budhdhéin ; go ndébairt annso :

40 'A bhennáin, a bhuir*e*dháin,
      a bhéiceadháin bintt,
      is binn linn an cuic*her*án
      do[g]ni tú 'san ghlintt.

38—4 *sic* K ; smeich B   5 chailliuch K
    39—1 The following note occurs here in B :—' Ar mo Dhia go mbrister cosa
na caillighe '; ' by my God, may the hag's feet be broken.'   2 tesmholta K

Suibhne :   Were it myself, and would it were I,
            that were king of Dal Araidhe
            it were a reason for a blow across a chin ;
            thou shalt not have a feast, O hag.'

39 'O hag,' said he, 'great are the hardships I have
encountered if you but knew ; many a dreadful leap have
I leaped from hill to hill, from fortress to fortress, from
land to land, from valley to valley.' 'For God's sake,' said
the hag, 'leap for us now one of the leaps you used to leap
when you were mad.' Thereupon he bounded over the
bed-rail so that he reached the end of the bench. 'My
conscience!' said the hag, 'I could leap that myself,' and in
the same manner she did so. He took another leap out
through the skylight of the hostel. 'I could leap that too,'
said the hag, and straightway she leaped. This, however, is
a summary of it : Suibhne travelled through five cantreds
of Dal Araidhe that day until he arrived at Glenn na
nEachtach in Fiodh Gaibhle, and she followed him all that
time. When Suibhne rested there on the summit of a tall
ivy-branch, the hag rested on another tree beside him. It was
then the end of harvest-time precisely. Thereupon Suibhne
heard a hunting-call of a multitude in the verge of the wood.
'This,' said he, 'is the cry of a great host, and they are the
Ui Faelain coming to kill me to avenge Oilill Cedach,
king of the Ui Faelain, whom I slew in the battle of Magh
Rath.' He heard the bellowing of the stag, and he made a
lay wherein he eulogized aloud the trees of Ireland, and,
recalling some of his own hardships and sorrows, he
said :

40 'O little stag, thou little bleating one,
       O melodious little clamourer,
       sweet to us is the music
       thou makest in the glen.

Eolchaire mo mhendatain
dorala ar mo chéill,
na lois isin machaire,
na hois isin tsléibh.

A dhair dhosach dhuill*edh*ach,
at ard os cionn c*r*oinn ;
a c[h]olláin, a chraobhach*áin*,
a chomhra cnó cuill.

A fhern, nidot naimhdidhe,
as aloinn do lí,
nidat cuma sceó sceanb*aidh*i
ar an mbeirn a mbí.

A d*hr*oighnéin, a dhealgnach*h*áin,
a áirneacháin duibh,
a bhiorair, a bharrghlasáin,
do bhrú thobair luin.

A mhinen[1] na conaire
at millsi gach luibh,
a ghlasáin, a adhghlasáin,
a lus forsa mbi in t-ṡuibh.

A abhall, a abhlachóg,
tren rotc*hr*aithenn cách,
a chaerthainn, a chaeirecháin,
as aloinn do bhláth.

A dhriseog, a dhruimnechog,
ni damha cert cuir,
ni ana gum leadradh-sa
g*ur*s*a*t lomlán d'fuil.

Longing for my little home
has come on my senses—
the flocks in the plain,
the deer on the mountain.

Thou oak, bushy, leafy,
thou art high beyond trees ;
O hazlet, little branching one,
O fragrance of hazel-nuts.

O alder, thou art not hostile,
delightful is thy hue,
thou art not rending and prickling
in the gap wherein thou art.

O little blackthorn, little thorny one ;
O little black sloe-tree ;
O watercress, little green-topped one,
from the brink of the ousel (?) spring.

O *minen* of the pathway,
thou art sweet beyond herbs,
O little green one,[1] very green one,
O herb on which grows the strawberry.

O apple-tree, little apple-tree,
much art thou shaken ;
O quicken, little berried one,
delightful is thy bloom.

O briar, little arched one,
thou grantest no fair terms,
thou ceasest not to tear me,
till thou hast thy fill of blood.

40—1 Perhaps *glasán* is the name of a plant ; see Dinneen, ' watercress,
salad, oyster-grass.'

A iubhair, a iubhracháin,
i rei[l]gibh² bat reil,
a eidhinn, a eidhneacháin,
at gnáth a ccoill cheir.

A chuilinn, a chlithmharáin,
a c[h]omhla re gáoith,
a uinnes, a urbhadach,
a arm lámha láoich.

A bheithi blaith bennachtach,
a bhorrfadaigh bhinn,
aluinn gach craobh cengailteach
i mullach do chinn.

Crith*ach* ara c*r*iothug*udh*,
atchluinim ma seach
a duille for riothug*udh*,
dar leam as í an chreach.

Mo mhioscais i fidhbadhuibh,
ni cheilim ar chách,
gamhnach dharach d*ui*lleadhach
ar siub*al* go gnáth.

As olc sén ar mhilles-[s]a
oineach Rónáin Fhinn,
a fherta rombúaidhretar,
a chlogáin ón chill.

As olc sén a fúarus-sa
eairadh Cong*hail* chóir,
a ionar caomh cumhdachtghl*an*
co ccorthar*aibh* óir.

O yew-tree, little yew-tree,
in churchyards thou art conspicuous ;
O ivy, little ivy,
thou art familiar in the dusky wood.

O holly, little sheltering one,
thou door against the wind ;
O ash-tree, thou baleful one,
hand-weapon of a warrior.

O birch, smooth and blessed,
thou melodious, proud one,
delightful each entwining branch
in the top of thy crown.

The aspen a-trembling ;
by turns I hear
its leaves a-racing—
meseems 'tis the foray !

My aversion in woods—
I conceal it not from anyone—
is the leafy stirk of an oak
swaying evermore. (?)

Ill-hap by which I outraged
the honour of Ronan Finn,
nis miracles have troubled me,
his little bells from the church.

Ill-omened I found
the armour of upright Congai,
his sheltering, bright tunic
with selvages of gold.

F 2

Rob é guth gach aenduine
don t-slóg dhédla daith,
na tegh uaibh fán ccaelmhuine
fer an ionair mhaith.

Gon*aidh*, marb*aidh*, airlig*idh*,
gabhaid uile a eill,[3]
cuir*idh* é, cidh lór do chion,
ar bior is ar beinn.[4]

Na marcaigh dom tharrachtain
dar Magh Cobha c*ru*inn,
ní roich úaidhibh aenurc*har*
dhamh-sa dar mo d*hru*im.

Ag dula dar eidhneachuibh,
ni cheilim, a láoich,
degurchar na gothn*aid*e
dhamh-sa resan ngáoith.

A ellteóg, a luirgnechóg,
fuarus-[s]a do g*hr*eim,
misi ort ag marcaighecht
as gach beinn a mbeinn.

O Chárn Cornáin comhramh*ach*
co beinn Slébhe Níadh,
o bheinn Slebhi Uillinne[5]
rigim Crota Clíach.

O Chrotaibh Clíach comhdhála
co Carn Lifthi Luirc
rigim re trath iarnóna
co Beinn Ghulbain ghuirt.

It was a saying of each one
of the valiant, active host :
'Let not escape from you through the narrow copse
the man of the goodly tunic.'

'Wound, kill, slaughter,
let all of you take advantage of him ;
put him, though it is great guilt,
on spit and on spike.'

The horsemen pursuing me
across round Magh Cobha,
no cast from them reaches
me through my back.

Going through the ivy-trees—
I conceal it not, O warrior—
like good cast of a spear
I went with the wind.

O little fawn, O little long-legged one,
I was able to catch thee
riding upon thee
from one peak to another.

From Carn Cornan of the contests
to the summit of Sliabh Niadh,
from the summit of Sliabh Uillinne
I reach Crota Cliach.

From Crota Cliach of assemblies
to Carn Liffi of Leinster,
I arrive before eventide
in bitter Benn Gulbain.

M'adhaigh[6] ría ccath *Conghaile*,
roba siorsan[7] lem,
síu nobheinn for udmhaille
ag sir*edh* na mbenn.

Glenn mBolcáin mo bhithárus,
fior fuarus a greim,
mor n-oidhchi rofriothálus
rioth roit*hr*én re beinn.

Da sirinn am aonaidhe[8]
sléibhti domhain duinn,
ferr liom ionadh aonboithe
i nGlionn Bolcain buirr.

Maith a uisci iodhanghlas,
maith a ghaoth ghlan gharg,
maith a bhiorar biorurglass,[9]
ferr a fhothlacht ard.

Maith a eidhn*ech* iodhn*aidhe*,
maith a ṡoil ghlan g*r*inn,
maith a iub*har* iubraidhe,
ferr a bheithe binnd.

Da ttiosta-sa, a Loingseacháin,
chugum in gach riocht,
gach n-oidhche dom agallaimh
bes ni anfainn friot.

Ni anfainn re t' agallaimh
munbadh sgél rom*g*ett,
athair, máthair, ingen, mhac,
bráthair, ben balc d'écc.   [88 b]

My night before the battle of Congal,
I deemed it fortunate,
before I restlessly
wandered over the mountain-peaks.

Glen Bolcain, my constant abode,
'twas a boon to me,
many a night have I attempted
a stern race against the peak.

If I were to wander alone
the mountains of the brown world,
better would I deem the site of a single hut
in the Glen of mighty Bolcan.

Good its water pure-green,
good its clean, fierce wind,
good its cress-green watercress,
best its tall brooklime.

Good its enduring ivy-trees,
good its bright, cheerful sallow,
good its yewy yews,
best its melodious birch.

If thou shouldst come, O Loingseachan,
to me in every guise,
each night to talk to me,
perchance I would not tarry for thee.

I would not have tarried to speak to thee
were it not for the tale which has wounded me—
father, mother, daughter, son,
brother, strong wife dead.

Da ttístea dom agallaimh
ni budh fer[r]de leam,
rosirfinn ria madanr*aidh*
sleibhti Boirchi benn.

Do mhuilenn an mheanmaráin
domheilte do th*uaith*,
a thrúagháin, a thuirseacháin,
a Luingseacháin lúaith.

A chailleach an mhuílinn-si,
cidh 'mongeibhe mh' eill?
mh' égnach d*ui*t itchluinim-si,
is tú amuigh ar an mbeinn.

A chailleach, a chuirrchennach,
an ragha for each?
[An chailleach:] Noraghainn, a thuirrchennach,
munam faicinn neach.

Dá ndeachar, a Suibhneacháin,
rob sor*aidh* mo léim.
[Suibhne :] Da ttora-sa, a chaillcheacháin,[10a]
ní ris sís slán céill.

[An chailleach:] Ni cóir éimh a n-abraidh-si,[10]
a mhic Colmáin Chais,
nach ferrdi mo mharcachus[11]
gan tuitim tar mh'ais?

[Suibhne :] As cóir eimh a n-abraim-si,
a chailleach gan chéill,
demhan agat th'aidhmill*iudh*,
romillis[12] fadhéin.

40– 10ᵃ *sic* B; chailliuchain K   10 abra-si K   11 marcachsa K   12 rodmillis K

If thou shouldst come to speak to me,
no better would I deem it ;
I would wander before morn
the mountains of Boirche of peaks.

By the mill of the little floury one (?)
thy folk has been ground, (?)
O wretched one, O weary one,
O swift Loingseachan.

O hag of this mill,
why dost thou take advantage of me ?
I hear thee revile me
even when thou art out on the mountain.

O hag, O round-headed one, (?)
wilt thou go on a steed ?'
The hag : ' I would go, O fool-head (?)
if no one were to see me.

O Suibhne, if I go,
may my leap be successful.'
Suibhne : ' If thou shouldst come, O hag,
mayst thou not dismount full of sense !' (?)

The hag : ' In sooth, not just is what thou sayest,
thou son of Colman Cas ;
is not my riding better
without falling back ?'

Suibhne : ' Just, in sooth, is what I say,
O hag without sense ;
a demon is ruining thee,
thou hast ruined thyself.'

[An chailleach:] Nach ferrde let mh'ealadhain,
                 a ghelt saerrdha seng,
                 mo beth agat lenam*ain*[13]
                 a mullaighibh na[14] mbenn ?

[Suibhne :]   Dosán eidhinn iomúall*ach*
                 fasas tre chrann chas,
                 da mbeinn-si 'na c*er*tmhull*ach*
                 noaghsainn techt ass.

                 Teichim riasna huiseóga,
                 as é an t*r*enr*i*oth tenn,
                 lingim tar na guiseóga
                 a mullaighibh benn.

                 Fer[a]n eidhinn iomuall*ach*
                 an tan eirghi*us* duinn,
                 goirid bhim da ttarrachtain
                 o rofas mo chluimh.

                 Creabhar oscc*ar* antuiccseach
                 an tan eirghius damh,
                 indar liom as dergnamha
                 an lon do[g]ní an sgal.[15]

                 Gach áonúair rolinginn-si
                 co mbinn ar an lár,
                 co fhaicinn an creamhthannán
                 thios[16] ag creim na gcnámh.

                 Seach gach coin a n-aidhnechuibh
                 luath noghcibh*adh* m'eill,
                 as é luas nolinginn-si
                 co mbinn ar an mbeinn.

40—13 re anmhain K   14 *om.* K   15 sgál K   16 *sic* K ;
om. B

The hag : ' Dost thou not deem my arts better,
        thou noble, slender madman,
        that I should be following thee
        from the tops of the mountains ?'

Suibhne : ' A proud ivy-bush
        which grows through a twisted tree—
        if I were right on its summit,
        I would fear to come out.

        I flee before the skylarks—
        'tis a stern, great race—
        I leap over the stumps
        on the tops of the mountains.

        When the proud turtle-dove
        rises for us,
        quickly do I overtake it
        since my feathers have grown.

        The silly, foolish woodcock
        when it rises for me
        methinks 'tis a bitter foe,
        the blackbird (too) that gives the cry of alarm.

        Every time I would bound
        till I was on the ground
        so that I might see the little fox
        below a-gnawing the bones.

        Beyond every wolf (?) among the ivy-trees
        swiftly would he get the advantage of me,
        so nimbly would I leap
        till I was on the mountain-peak.

Sionn*aigh* beca ag bregairecht
chugum agus úaim,
mic thíri ara leg*air*echt (?),[16a]
teichim-si re a ffúaim.

Rothriallsat mo tharrachtain
ag tocht 'na rioth thenn,
gur teiches-[s]a reampa-somh
a mullaighibh beann.

Tainic friom mo thairmthechta
gibé conair théis,
as leir dhamh ar mh'a[i]rchisecht
am caora gan léis.

Bile Chille Lughaidhe
i tuilim súan sáimh,
ba haoibne i ré Chong*aile*
aenach[17] Line láin.

Doraghae an reodh realtán*ach*
ferfas ar gach linn,
asam suairreach, seachránach,
misi fáoi ar an mbinn.

Na corra go ccorrghaire
i nGlionn Aighle úair,
ealta d'énuibh[18] iomlúatha
chugum agus úaim.

Ni charaim an sibheanr*adh*
do[g]niad fir i૩ mna,
binne liom a ceileabradh
luin 'san aird ittá.

40—16[a] leḡés B ; leḡes K, ? leg. ledairecht, which has been translated
17 *sic* K ; aena B   18 dena K

Little foxes yelping
to me and from me,
wolves at their rending,
I flee at their sound.

They have striven to reach me,
coming in their swift course,
so that I fled before them
to the tops of the mountains.

My transgression has come against me
whatsoever way I flee;
'tis manifest to me from the pity shown me
that I am a sheep without a fold.

The old tree of Cell Lughaidhe
wherein I sleep a sound sleep;
more delightful in the time of Congal
was the fair of plenteous Line.

There will come the starry frost
which will fall on every pool;
I am wretched, straying
exposed to it on the mountain-peak.

The herons a-calling
in chilly Glenn Aighle,
swift flocks of birds
coming and going.

I love not the merry prattle
that men and women make:
sweeter to me is the warbling
of the blackbirds in the quarter in which it is.

Ni charaim in stocairecht
atcluinim go moch,
binne lium a crocairecht[19]
bruic a mBennuibh Broc.

Ni charuim an chornairecht
atchluinim go tenn,
binni lium ag damhghairecht
damh dá fhiched benn.

Ata adhbur seisr*igh*e
as gach glionn i nglenn,
gach damh ina freislighe
a mullach na mbenn.

Cidh iomdha dom dhamr*aidh*-si
as gach glinn i nglenn,
ni minic lámh oirem*han*
ag dún*adh* a[20] mbenn.

Damh Sléibhi aird Eibhlinne,
damh Sléibhe Fúaid feigh,
damh Ella, damh Orbhraidhe,
damh lonn Locha Léin.

Damh Seimhne, damh Latharna,
damh Line na lenn,
damh Cúailghni, damh *Con*achla,
damh Bairni dá bhenn.

A m*atha*ir na g*r*oidhi-si
rolíath*adh* do lenn,
ni fhuil damh at dheag*aidh*-si
g*an* dá fhichead benn.

I love not the trumpeting
I hear at early morn :
sweeter to me the squeal
of the badgers in Benna Broc.

I love not the horn-blowing
so boldly I hear :
sweeter to me the belling of a stag
of twice twenty peaks.

There is the material of a plough-team
from glen to glen :
each stag at rest
on the summit of the peaks.

Though many are my stags
from glen to glen,
not often is a ploughman's hand
closing round their horns. (?)

The stag of lofty Sliabh Eibhlinne,
the stag of sharp Sliabh Fuaid,
the stag of Ealla, the stag of Orrery,
the fierce stag of Loch Lein.

The stag of Seimhne, Larne's stag,
the stag of Line of the mantles,
the stag of Cuailgne, the stag of Conachail,
the stag of Bairenn of two peaks.

O mother of this herd,
thy coat has become grey,
there is no stag after thee
without two score antler-points.

Mó ná[21] adhb*hur* leinnine
roliath*adh* dot chenn,[22]
da mbeinn ar gach beinnine
beinnini ar gach mbenn.

A dhoimh do[g]ni an fogharán
chugum tar an nglenn,
maith an t-ionadh foradh*án* (?)
i mullach do bhenn.

As mé Suibhni sirtheachán,
luath reithim tar glenn,
nocha n-é mh'ainm dl*igh*theachán,
mó is[23] ainm damh fer benn.

Tioprata is ferr fúarus-sa,
tiopra Leith*i*d Láin,
tiopra is aille ionnuaire,
úarán Dhúine Máil.

Gidhat iomdha mh'imeirce
mh'édach aniú is gerr,
me féin do[g]ní m'*for*faire[24]
i mullach na mbend.

A raithnech, a rúadhfhada,
rorúadh*adh* do lenn,
ní hosair fir fuag*ar*ta
a ngabhl*aibh* do bhenn.[25]

Bidh ann bhias mo bhithlighi
tes ag Tuidhin tenn,[26]
ag Tegh Moling bíothaingl*igh*i
taotus[27] do bheind.

Greater than the material for a little cloak
thy head has turned grey ;
if I were on each little point,
there would be a pointlet on every point.

Thou stag that comest lowing
to me across the glen,
pleasant is the place for seats
on the top of thy antler-points.

I am Suibhne, a poor suppliant,
swiftly do I race across the glen ;
that is not my lawful name,
rather is it Fer benn.[1]

The springs I found best :
the well of Leithead Lan,
the well most beautiful and cool,
the fountain of Dun Mail.

Though many are my wanderings,
my raiment to-day is scanty ;
I myself keep my watch
on the top of the mountains.

O tall, russet fern,
thy mantle has been made red ;
there is no bed for an outlaw
in the branches of thy crests.

At ever-angelic Tech Moling,
at puissant Toidhen in the south,
'tis there my eternal resting-place will be,
I shall fall by a [spear]-point.

40—1 i.e. man of the peaks.

G

Dorad misi it chumann-sa
mallacht Ronáin Finn,
a bhennáin, a bhúireadháin
a bhéiceadáin binn.'   A beannain.

41 [89 a] A haithle na laidhe sin tainic Suibhne a Fidh
Gaibhle co Beinn mBóghaine, assein co Beind Fhaibhne,
aisséin co Raith Murbuilg 7 ni ffuair a dhíon ar an ccaill*igh*
co rainig co Dun Sobairce i nUlt*aibh*. Roling Suibhne
iarumh do bheinn an dúine síos cach ndíriuch riasan ccaill*igh*.
Roling sí co hiomhathlomh ina dheaghaidh co ttorchair do
aill Dhúine Sobharci co ndernadh mionbhrúar 7 minchomairt
di ann co ttorchair isin bhfairrge, conadh amhlaidh sin fúair
bás i ndedhaidh Suibhne.

42 Atbert Suibhne iarsin : ' Ni bhíu-sa i nDal Araidhe
fesda úair nommhuir*fedh* Loingseachán i ndiogail a chaillighi
mé día mbeinn ara chumus.' Luid Suibhne iarumh co Ros
Chcmáin i Connachtuibh 7 rothoirinn for s*rai*th an top*uir*
co rochaith bior*ar* 7 uisgi ann. Tainic ben a tigh an
oircinnigh dochum an tobair. *For*bhas*ach* mac Fordhal*aigh*
an t-oirchinneach sin. Rob í an bhean tainic ann, Finnseng
ingen Fhíndeal*aigh*. Rotheich iarumh an gheilt reimpe 7
tuc sisi lamh tar an mbior*ar* báoi for an s*ru*th. As ann
robhúi Suibhne forsan mbili ina fiadhnuisi 7 robhúi ag
eccáoine moir fa na chuid bior*air* dobhreth uadha conadh
edh atbert : ' A bhen,' ar sé, ' as trúagh duit mo bhiorar do
ureith[1] úaim 7 da festá mar atú úair ni dhénann fer túaithe
na fine mh'oirchisecht ; ni theighim for aeidh*id*eacht do
thigh duine ar druim dhomain. As é mo búar mo bhiorar,
as e mo mhiodh mh'uisci, as iad mo chairde mo chroinn
crúadhloma cliothardhlúithe 7 cén co mberthá-sa mo biorar,'
ar sé, ' as derb nocha beitheá gan ní anocht mar atú-sa tar
éis mo bhiorair do breith úaim '; 7 dorinne a[n] laoidh so :

The curse of Ronan Finn
has thrown me in thy company,
O little stag, little bleating one,
O melodious little clamourer.'

41 After that lay Suibhne came from Fiodh Gaibhle to Benn Boghaine, thence to Benn Faibhne, thence to Rath Murbuilg, but he found no refuge from the hag until he reached Dun Sobairce in Ulster. Suibhne leaped from the summit of the fort sheer down in front of the hag. She leaped quickly after him, but dropped on the cliff of Dun Sobairce, where she was broken to pieces, and fell into the sea. In that manner she found death in the wake of Suibhne.

42 Thereafter Suibhne said : ' Henceforth I shall not be in Dal Araidhe, for Loingseachan, to avenge his hag, would kill me if I were in his power.' Suibhne then went to Ros Comain in Connacht, and he alighted at the brink of the well, where he fared on watercress and water. A woman came from the erenach's house to the well ; Forbhasach son of Fordhalach was the erenach. Finnsheng daughter of Findealach (?) was the name of the woman who came. The madman fled from her and she laid hold of the watercress which was in the stream. Suibhne on the tree in front of her was bemoaning greatly that his portion of watercress was taken away. Whereupon he said: 'O woman,' said he, ' sad is it that you should take my watercress from me, if you but knew the plight in which I am, for neither tribesman nor kinsman pities me, nor do I visit as a guest the house of anyone on the ridge of the world. For kine I have my watercress, my water is my mead, my trees hard and bare or close-sheltering are my friends. And even if you did not take away my watercress,' said he, ' certain is it that you would not be without something else to-night as I am after my watercress has been taken from me': and he made this lay :

G 2

43 'A bhen bhenus an biorar
agus bher*us* in uisci,
nocha betheá gan ní anocht
gén co mbertheá mo chuid-si.

Monúaran, a bhenagán,
nocha ragha an leth raghad,
misi amuigh a mbarraibh c*r*ann,
tusa tall a tigh charad.

Monúarán, a bhenagán,
as fúar an ghaeth domanuig,
nimoirchis mathair na mac,
ni fuil brat ar mo braghuid.

Da festá-sa, a bhenagan,¹
mar atá² sunna Suibhne,
seach ni fhag*aidh* cuibhdhe neich,
ni fhag*aidh* nech³ a⁴ chuibhdhe.

Ni theighim a n-oirechtus
edir oguibh mo thíre,
ni déntar dam oin*ech*treas,⁵
ni théit mh'aire re righe.

Ni theighim ar aeidh*idh*eacht
do thigh mic duine a nÉire,
fa m*ein*ce liom b*ǽ*ithgeltacht
ar bennuibh corra sl*ébh*e.

Ni tegar dom airfidedh
ath*aigh* re ndul im lighi,
nocha nfhaghuim oirchisecht
o f*er* túaithe na fini.

43-- 1 *sic* K ; bhenagain B   2 *sic* K ; tá B   3 *sic* K neich B   4 *om.* K
5 an. leg. enechras, which has been translated.

43 'O woman who pluckest the watercress
and takest the water,
thou wouldst not be without something to-night
even though thou didst not take my portion.

Alas, O woman!
thou wilt not go the way that I shall go ;
I abroad in the tree-tops,
thou yonder in a friend's house.

Alas, O woman!
cold is the wind that has come to me ;
nor mother nor son has pity on me,
no cloak is on my breast.

If thou but knewest, O woman,
how Suibhne here is :
he does not get friendship from anyone,
nor does anyone get his friendship.

I go not to a gathering
among warriors of my country,
no safeguard is granted me,
my thought is not on kingship

I go not as a guest
to the house of any man's son in Erin,
more often am I straying madly
on the pointed mountain-peaks.

None cometh to make music to me
for a while before going to rest,
no pity do I get
from tribesman or kinsman.

Antan robsom Suibhni-si
agus théighinn ar each*aibh*,
antan tig im c[h]uimh[n]i-si[5]
mairg[6] romfuirg*edh* a mbeth*aidh*.

As mé Suibhne sæirchend*aidh*,
as úar anaoibinn mh'ionadh,
ge béo anocht ar bhaithbend*aibh*
a b*hen* b*hen*us mo bhiorar.

As é mo mhiodh mh'uisci fúar,
as é mo bhúar mo bhiorar,
as íad mo charaid mo chroinn,
ge 'tú gan leann, gan ionar.

As úar anocht an adhaigh,
gidh im[7] bhocht ar áoi mbiorair,
atchúala guth an ghioghruinn
ós Iml*igh* iomluim Iobhair.

Atú gan brat, gan ionar,
fada a ulc úair romlean*adh*,
teichim re guth na cuirre
m*ar* b*udh* buille romben*adh*.

Rigim co[8] Dairbre ndaing*en*
isna láibh aidhbhlibh earr*aigh*,
agus teichim re n-oidhche
síar co Boirche[9] mbenn*aigh*.

Diamsat eolach, a fionnghág,
mo ghort ni t*r*eorach tenngharg,
ata nech dianad sgeile
an t-eiri be*r*i, a bhengág.

When I was Suibhne indeed
and used to go on steeds—
when that comes to my memory
alas that I was detained in life!

I am Suibhne, noble leader (?),
cold and joyless is my abode,
though I be to-night on wild peaks,
O woman who pluckest my watercress.

My mead is my cold water,
my kine are my cresses,
my friends are my trees,
though I am without mantle or smock.

Cold is the night to-night,
though I am poor as regards watercress,
I have heard the cry of the wild-goose
over bare Imlech Iobhair.

I am without mantle or smock,
the evil hour has long clung to me (?),
I flee at the cry of the heron
as though it were a blow that struck me.

I reach firm Dairbre
in the wondrous days of Spring,
and before night I flee
westward to Benn Boirche.

If thou art learned, O fair, crabbed one,
my field . . .
there is one to whom the burden thou takest
is a grievous matter, O hag.

At úara dotachuisi*n*
ar brú tobair ghlais grean*aigh*,
deogh ghleórdha d'uisci iodhan
agus an biorar bhenaidh.

Mo chuid-si an[10] biorar bheanaidh,
cuid gheilte sáoire singi,[11]
sging*idh* gǽth úar mam reand*aibh*
do bend*aibh* gacha binni.

As úar gǽth an mhadanr*aidh*,
doicc etrom is mh'ionar,
nacha nfhétoim t'agalloimh,
a bhen bhenus an mbiorar.

[An bhean:] Fágaibh mo chuid don Choimdhi,
rium-sa na déna duilghe,
móide foghebha cennacht,
is b*eir* bennacht, a Suibhne.

[Suibhne :] Denam cennach cert cubhaidh
ge 'tú a mullach an iubhair,
b*eir* mh'ionar is mo chertín,
fágaibh an mbertín mbiorair.

As terc n*ech* las am ionm*uin*,
ni fhuil mo theach ar talmain,
uaim o bh*ere*[12] mo bhiorar
mo chuid chion*adh* ar th'anmain.

Ni ris a[13] n*ech* rocharuis,
meisdi don[13a] tí rolenuis,
rofhágbhuis neach co daidbhir
imon airb*ir* robhenais.

It is cold they are
at the brink of a clear, pebbly spring—
a bright quaff of pure water
and the watercress you pluck.

My meal is the watercress you pluck,
the meal of a noble, emaciated madman ;
cold wind springs around my loins
from the peaks of each mountain.

Chilly is the wind of morn,
It comes between me and my smock,
I am unable to speak to thee,
O woman who pluckest the watercress.

The woman : Leave my portion to the Lord,
be not harsh to me ;
the more wilt thou attain supremacy,
and take a blessing, O Suibhne.

Suibhne : Let us make a bargain just and fitting
though I am on the top of the yew ;
take thou my smock and my tatters,
leave the little bunch of cress.

There is scarce one by whom I am beloved,
I have no house on earth ;
since thou takest from me my watercress
my sins to be on thy soul !

Mayest thou not reach him whom thou has
loved,
the worse for him whom thou hast followed ;
thou hast left one in poverty
because of the bunch thou hast plucked.

Creach na nGall ngorm dot gabháil,
orm nocha dernais deghdháil,
co bfaghbha on Choimdhe a chionaidh
mo chuid biorair do bhenail.¹⁴ [89 b]

A bhen, chugud da ttóra
Loingseachan ata rún¹⁵ reabha
tabhair-si dhó trem chion*aidh*
a leth an bhiorair bhena.'   A bhen.

44 Robáoi-siomh i Ros Chomáin an oidhche sin, luid
aissein arnamhárach co Slíabh n-uráoibhinn nEachtghe,
aissein co Slíabh mínaluinn Mis, aissein co Slíabh bennard
Bladhma, aissein co hInis Muread*haigh*; coecáois ar mhís do
inti-sein i n-uaimh Dhon*n*áin Eghæ, aissidhein co Carraic
Alustair.¹ Gabh*aidh* aite 7 ionadh ainsidhe 7 báoi cæcaois
ar mhís eile innti. Fagbhais i iarsin agus ceileabhraidh dhi ;
gonadh ann adbert ag tabhairt a dhocra fein os aird annso :

45 'Duairc an bhetha-sa
bheith gan m*aei*thleaptha,¹
adhbha úairseaca,
garbha gáoithsnechta.

Gaoth uar oighreata,
sgáth fann fainng*hr*éine,
fosgadh einbhile,
a mullach maighsléibhe.

Fulang fraissíne,
ceim dar aisseola,
imthecht glaismhíne,
madain ghlaisreódha.

43—14 The following note occurs at the foot of the page in B do choimh-
lionadh an bháinn ' to fill up the blank space '.   15 run K
44—1 *sic* K ; *om*. B
45—1 *sic* K ; maithleaptha B

May a raid of the blue-coated Norsemen take thee!
thine has not been a fortunate meeting for me,
mayest thou get from the Lord the blame
for cutting my portion of watercress.

O woman, if there should come to thee
Loingseachan whose delight is sport,
do thou give him on my behalf
half the watercress thou pluckest.'

44 That night he remained in Ros Comain and went
thence on the morrow to delightful Sliabh Aughty, thence to
smooth, beautiful Sliabh Mis, thence to lofty-peaked Sliabh
Bloom, thence to Inis Murray.   For a fortnight and a
month he tarried in the cave of Donnan of Eig, and went
thence to Carrick Alastair where he took up his abode and
remained another fortnight and a month.   He left it
afterwards and bade it farewell, and, proclaiming aloud his
own woes, said :

> **45** 'Gloomy this life,
>   to be without a soft bed,
>   abode of cold frost,
>   roughness of wind-driven snow.
>
> Cold, icy wind,
>   faint shadow of a feeble sun,
>   shelter of a single tree,
>   on the summit of a table-land.
>
> Enduring the rain-storm,
>   stepping over deer-paths, (?)
>   faring through greensward
>   on a morn of grey frost.

Gair na damhraidhe
ar fhud fidhbhuidhe,
dreim re hoisbherna,
fogar fionnmhuire.

Maith, a morChoimdhe,
mor an meirbhnéll-sa,[2]
duilghe an duibhlén-sa,
Suibhne an[3] seingbhlén-sa.

Rith dar breicbhernaibh
Boirche boithleaptha,
osnadh geamhoidhche,
coss i ccloichsneachta.

Luighe[4] fliuchleapthach
learga LoichÉirne,
menma ar mhuichimthecht
madan mhuicheirghe.

Rith tar tuinnbennaibh
Duine Sobhairce,
clúas re tromthonnaibh
Dhúine Rodairce.[5]

Rith on rathuinn-si
co tuinn mbǽithBerbha,
feis ar crúadhcholbha
Dhúine cǽimhC[h]ermna.

O Dhún caoimhChearmna
co Beinn mbláthmBoirne,
clúas re clochadhart
Crúacháin ghargOighle.

The bellowing of the stags
throughout the wood,
the climb to the deer-pass,
the voice of white seas.

Yea, O great Lord,
great this weakness,
more grievous this black sorrow,
Suibhne the slender-groined.

Racing over many-hued gaps
of Boirche of hut couches,
the sough of the winter night,
footing it in hailstones.

Lying on a wet bed
on the slopes of Loch Erne,
mind on early departure,
morn of early rising.

Racing over the wave-tops
of Dun Sobairce,
ear to the billows
of Dun Rodairce.

Running from this great wave
to the wave of the rushing Barrow,
sleeping on a hard couch
of fair Dun Cermna.

From fair Dun Cermna
to flowery Benn Boirne,
ear against a stone pillow
of rough Cruachan Oighle.

Utmhall mh'imirce
a muigh na Bóruime,
o Bheinn Iughoine[6]
go Beinn mBóghoine.[7]

Tainic chugum-sa
neach romlámhaigh-si,
ní romsiodhaigh-si
bean romsáraigh-si.

Rug mo chuidigh-si
d'eis na cionadh-sa,
truagh an monar-sa,
adúas mo bhiorar-sa.

Biorar bhuingim-si,
biadha fionndlochtán,
ceithre *cr*onnghlacáin
Glinne fionnBholcáin.

Sásadh saicchim-si,
suairc an monarán,
deoch don uisgi-si,
thiobrad fhionnRonán.

Corra mh'ingni-si,
maeth mo chreasa-sa,
toll mo chosa-sa,
lom mo leasa-sa.

Béraitt oram-sa
fian co talchuraibh,
cían o Ultachaibh,
triall a nAlban*ch*aibh.

Restless my wandering
in the plain of the Boroma,
from Benn Iughoine
to Benn Boghaine.

There has come to me
one who has laid hands on me,
she has brought no peace to me,
the woman who has dishonoured me.

She has taken my portion
on account of my sins,
wretched the work—
my watercress has been eaten.

Watercress I pluck,
food in a fair bunch,
four round handfuls
of fair Glen Bolcain.

A meal I seek—
pleasant the bogberry,
a drink of water here
from the well of Ronan Finn.

Bent are my nails,
feeble my loins,
pierced my feet,
bare my thighs.

There will overtake me
a warrior-band stubbornly,
far from Ulster,
faring in Alba.

D'éis an astair-si
truagh mo *ṡanuslaidh*,
bith a ccrúadhchom*aidh*
Chairrge Alastoir.

C*n*rraig Alastair,
adhbha d' fáoilennaibh,
truagh a Dhúilemhain,
uar dha háoidheadhaibh.

Carraig Alastair,
cloc na cruthailde,
lór a leathairde,
srón re s*ru*thḟairrge.

Truagh ar ccomhraic-ne,
días chorr crúadhluirgnech,
misi crúaidhleadhbach,
sisi crúaidhghuilbnech.

Fliuch na leaptha-sa
itá mh'áras-[s]a,
beg doṡaoiles-[s]a
gur chreg chádhasa.

Olc do chláonChong*al*
cath do thárrachtain,
mar chuing n-imeachtair
rothuill mallachtain.

A cath RathM*uigh*e
tráth do rúachtas-[s]a
re nguin mh'échta-sa
nimdluigh dúarcus-[s]a.   D.

After this journey—
sad is my secret song—
to be in the hard company
of Carraig Alastair.

Carraig Alastair,
abode of sea-gulls,
sad, O Creator,
chilly for its guests.

Carraig Alastair,
bell-shaped rock,[1]
sufficient were it half the height,
nose to the main.

Sad our meeting;
a couple of cranes hard-shanked—
I hard and ragged,
she hard-beaked.

Wet these beds
wherein is my dwelling,
little did I think
it was a rock of holiness.

Bad was it for Congal Claon
that he arrived at the battle;
like an outer yoke[2]
he has earned a curse.

When I fled
from the battle of Magh Rath
before my undoing,
I deserved not harshness.

Truagh an turus-[s]a,
ni ma tánag-sa,
cían om eólus-sa,
crioch gusa ránag-sa.[8]

Tiucfaidh Loingseachán,
truagh a thurusa,
ge romlena-sa
ni ba hurusa.

Caille comhfhada,
cladh na cúarta-sa,
tír gus ránag-sa,
ni gniomh dúarcusa.   D.

Duibhlinn dúnBhoirche,
tren romfúasnaidh-si,
aidhbhle a hiochtair-si,
daingne a húachtair-si.

As ferr fúarus-[s]a
coillte cosmhuile,
roighni ruisMhidhe,
aidhbhle Osraighe.

Ulaidh fhoghamhair
im Loch Cúan critheólaigh,
tadhall samhrata
Cheineóil mbithEóghain.

Imthecht lughnasaidh
Taillten tiobraidhe,
iasgach earrchaidhe
Sionna siobhlaighe.

Sad this expedition;
would that I had not come!
far from my home
is the country I have reached.

Loingseachan will come,
sad his journeys;
though he follow me,
it will not be easy.

Far-stretching woods
are the rampart of this circuit—
the land to which I have come—
not a deed of sadness.

The black lake of fortressed Boirche
greatly has it perturbed me;
the vastness of its depths,
the strength of its wave-crests.

Better found I
pleasant woods,
choice places of wooded Meath,
the vastness of Ossory.

Ulaidh in harvest-time
about quivering Loch Cuan,
a summer visit
to the race of enduring Eoghan.

A journey at Lammastide
to Taillten of fountains,
fishing in springtime
the meandering Shannon.

Minig riccim-si
tír conúachtus-[s]a,
buidhni bar[r]chasa,
druimni dúarcusa.'   Dúairc.

46 [90 a] Rofhágaibh Suibhne an charraicc iarsin 7
dochúaidh tar an muir ccráosfhairsing, ccithainbhthenaigh
co ráinic Crioch Bhreatan.   Dorad a láimh[1] ndeis re dúnadh
righ Bretan co ttarla dochum feadha moir é 7 an chonair
tainic fon fidh atchualaidh[2] an uchbhadach[3] 7 an eccaoini 7
an mhairgneach mor 7 an osnadhach éccalma.   As edh
robhui annsin, geilt eile robhoi ar fhud an fhedha.   Tainic-
siomh iaromh dha ionnsaighe. 'Cía thu? a dhuine,' ar
Suibhne. 'Geilt misi,' ar sé.   'Másat[4] geilt,' ar Suibhne,
'tair ale co n[d]ernom comann, ar isam[5] geilt-si bheos.'
'Doragainn,' ar an gheilt oili, 'muna bheith egla thighe no
theglaigh an righ dom tharrachtain 7 ni fhetar nach diobh
duit-si.' 'Ni diobh éiccin,' ar Suibhne, '7 sloinn-si t'ainm
bunaidh dhamh o nac[h] diobh.' 'Fer Cailli mh'ainm,' ar
an gheilt; conadh ann itbert Suibhne an rann sa 7 rofreagair
Fear Caille é, mar so síos :

47 [Suibhne :] 'A Fhir Chaille, cidh dotharraidh ?
                truagh do ghuth,
            abair damh-sa cidh rodmannair[1]
            ceill no[2] cruth ?

     [Fer Caille :] Ro-innisfinn duit mo sgéla,
                sceo mo ghniomh,
            muna bheith eaglach Inn slúagh seghdha[3]
            thoighe an righ.

46—1 lámh K   2 atchuala K   3 uchtbadhach K   4 masae K
5 *sic* K ; isim B

Often do I reach
the land I have set in order,
curly-haired hosts,
stern ridges.'

46 Suibhne then left Carraig Alastair and went over the
wide-mouthed, storm-swept sea until he reached the land of
the Britons. He left the fortress of the king of the Britons
on his right hand and came on a great wood. As he passed
along the wood he heard lamenting and wailing, a great moan
of anguish and feeble sighing. It was another madman who
was wandering through the wood. Suibhne went up to him.
' Who are you, my man ? ' said Suibhne. ' I am a madman,'
said he. ' If you are a madman,' said Suibhne, ' come hither
so that we may be friends, for I too am a madman.' ' I
would,' said the other, ' were it not for fear of the king's house
or household seizing me, and I do not know that you are not
one of them.' ' I am not indeed,' said Suibhne, ' and since I
am not, tell me your family name.' ' Fer Caille (Man of the
Wood) is my name,' said the madman ; whereupon Suibhne
uttered this stave and Fer Caille answered him as
follows :

47 Suibhne : ' O Fer Cailli, what has befallen thee ?
sad is thy voice ;
tell me what has marred thee
in sense or form.

Fer Caille: I would tell thee my story,
likewise my deeds,
were it not for fear of the proud host
of the king's household.

47—1 riotmannuair K   2 do K   3 muna eagla leam sluaigh seghdha K

As mé Ealadhan⁴ noroich*edh*
iolar ndreann,
as diom-sa la cách dogoirt*idh*i
lúam⁵-gheilt ghlenn.

[Suibhne ·] As misi Suibhne mac Colmáin
o Bhúais bhil,
as usaidi dhuinn ar ccomhradh
sunn, a fhir.'   A fhir.

48 Tug cách dhiobh taobh re 'roile iersin gur fhiafraigh-
eddar fe[i]n sgéla da chéle. Atbert Suibhne risin ngeilt:
' Dén-sa do slondadh dhamh-sa,' ar sé. ' Mac brughaidh mé,'
ar an gheilt Breathnach, ' 7 is don tír-si ittám mo bhunadhus
7 Alladhán mh'ainm.' ' Innis dam,' ar Suibhne, ' cidh rottuc
ar gealtacht thú.' ' Ni *hansa.* Dhá righ robhádar ag
imchosnamh im righe na crÍche-si fecht n-aill .i. Eochaidh
Aincheas mac Guaire Mat*hra*(?) 7 Cúgúa mac Gúaire ; ba do
muint*ir* Each*aidh* damh-sa,' ar sé, ' uair as é dobudh ferr
don días sin. Dorónadh iarumh moirthionól do c*hur* c*hatha*
fria aroile imon tír-si. Roc*uir*es-[s]a gesa ar gach aon do
muint*ir* mo thigherna cona tigs*edh* neach dhiobh gan édach
sroil uime dochum an chatha ar go mbudh suaithenta seach
cách íet la huaill 7 diumus. Tucsat im*morro* na slúaigh tri
gairthi mallacht form-sa, co ttucsat-sidhe misi ar fáoineal 7
ar foluamhuin amail atchíthi-si.'

49 Rofhiarfaidh-siomh mar an cetna do Suibhne cidh
dusfug for gealtacht. ' Briath*ra* Rónáin,' ar Suibhne, ' uair
roesccáoin-siomh misi re hucht c*atha* Muighe Rath, co
roeirghes a n-airde asin ccath sin co ufuilim ar faoinneal 7
ar foluamain osin ale.' ' A S̀uiune,' ar Alladhán, ' coimhed*adh*
cach uainn a chéile co maith o doratsom taobh¹ fria aroile .i.
antí úain as luaithe chluinfes glǽdh cuirre do loch linnghlas
linnúaine no guth gléghlan gaircce, no leim creabhair do

47—4 Alladhan K, and so throughout.   5 luaith K
49—1 *sic* K ; *om.* B

Ealadhan am I
who used to go to many combats,
1 am known to all
as the leading[1] madman of the glens.

Suibhne :   Suibhne son of Colman am I
from the pleasant Bush;
the easier for us is converse
here, O man.'

48 After that each confided in the other and they asked
tidings of each other.   Said Suibhne to the madman : ' Give
an account of yourself.'   ' I am son of a landholder,' said the
madman of Britain, ' and I am a native of this country in
which we are, and Ealladhan is my name.'   ' Tell me,' said
Suibhne, ' what caused your madness.'   ' Not difficult to
say.   Once upon a time two kings were contending for the
sovereignty of this country, viz., Eochaidh Aincheas, son of
Guaire Mathra, and Cugua, son of Guaire.   Of the people of
Eochaidh am I,' said he, ' for he was the better of the two.
There was then convened a great assembly to give battle to
each other concerning the country.   I put *geasa* on each
one of my lord's people that none of them should come to
the battle except they were clothed in silk, so that they might
be conspicuous beyond all for pomp and pride.   The hosts
gave three shouts of malediction on me, which sent me
wandering and fleeing as you see.'

49 In the same way he asked Suibhne what drove him
to madness.   ' The words of Ronan,' said Suibhne, ' for he
cursed me in front of the battle of Magh Rath, so that I rose
on high out of the battle, and I have been wandering and
fleeing ever since.'   ' O Suibhne,' said Ealladhan, ' let each of
us keep good watch over the other since we have placed trust
in each other ; that is, he who shall soonest hear the cry of a
heron from a blue-watered, green-watered lough or the clear

---

1 ' swift ' K.

chraoibh, fedghaire no guth feadóige ar na fiordhús*gadh* no
fuaim crionaigh aga choimhbris*edh*, no fosgadh eóin ós
fiodhb*aidh*, erfhúagradh 7 innisedh antí atchluinfe é ar tús
don fior oile, biodh ead dhá *crann*[2] eatrainn 7 da ráthaigh*edh*
neach uainn ní dona neithibh réimráitiu sin no a n-ionnsamail
oile dentar teichedh maith linn iaromh.'

50 Dogniat samhlaidh 7 badar bliadhain lán i ufarradh
aroili. Hi cinn na bliadhna sin adbert Alladhan fri Suibhne :
' As mithidh duinn sgaradh aniú,' ar sé, ' uair tainic forcheann
mo ṡoeghail-si 7 nocha nfhéduim gan dul gusin ion*adh* in
rocinn*edh* dhamh ég d'fhagháil.' ' Cidh ón, gá bás fogébha ? '
ar Suibhne. ' Ní *hansa*,' ar Alladhán, ' .i. rachad anois go
hEs nDubhthaigh 7 cuirfidhther ath*ach* gaeithe fum ann 7
romc[h]uirther[1] 'san es mé[2] go rombait*er* ann 7 nomadh-
naict*her* iarsin i relic fhíreóin 7 foghebh nemh, conadh í sin
crioch mo bheathadh-sa, 7, a Ṡuiune,' ar Alladhán, ' innis
damh-sa cia haidh*edh* notbéra fadhéin ? ' Ro-innis Suibhne
dhó iarum febh atféd an sgél síosana. Rosgarsat lasodhain 7
rotriall an Breathnach go hEs nDubhthaigh 7 o rainic an t-es
robaid*edh* ann é.

51 [90 b] Tainic iarumh Suibhne reimhe dochum nErenn
co ttarla i ndíuidh laoi é go Magh Line i nUltaibh 7 o tuc
aithne ar an magh atbert: Maith éimh cách aga rabhadus-[s]a
ar an magh sa,' ar sé, ' .i. Congal Cláon mac Sgannláin 7
fos,' ar se, ' ropudh maith an magh sa ina rabham*ar* ann.
Robhadhus-[s]a 7 Congal la forsan magh sa ; co n-ébart-sa
fris : ' Rob áil damh dol dochum tigerna eile,' ar laghad mo
thuarastail aigi-siomh, conadh annsin dorad-som dhamh-sa
ar oirisiumh aicci tri choega each n-aluinn n-allmhardha
imon each donn robhói aigi budhdhein 7 tri chaoga calg ndéd
ndreachṡolus, caoca feinḋogh 7 caoca banmhogh 7 ionar go
n-or 7 fúathrog bhuilidh bhreacṡróil.' Conadh ann atbert
Suibhne an dán so ann go léig :

49—2 no tri crainn *add* K   **50**— 1 romcuirfidhther K   2 *om.* K

note of a cormorant, or the flight of a woodcock from a branch, the whistle or sound of a plover on being woke from its sleep, or the sound of withered branches being broken, or shall see the shadow of a bird above the wood, let him who shall first hear warn and tell the other ; let there be the distance of two trees between us ; and if one of us should hear any of the before-mentioned things or anything resembling them, let us fly quickly away thereafter.'

50 They do so, and they were a whole year together. At the end of the year Ealladhan said to Suibhne : ' It is time that we part to-day, for the end of my life has come, and I must go to the place where it has been destined for me to die.' ' What death shall you die ?' said Suibhne. ' Not difficult to say,' said Ealladhan ; ' I go now to Eas Dubhthaigh, and a blast of wind will get under me and cast me into the waterfall so that I shall be drowned, and I shall be buried afterwards in a churchyard of a saint, and I shall obtain Heaven ; and that is the end of my life. And, O Suibhne,' said Ealladhan, ' tell me what your own fate will be.' Suibhne then told him as the story relates below. At that they parted and the Briton set out for Eas Dubhthaigh, and when he reached the waterfall he was drowned in it.

51 Suibhne then came to Ireland and at the close of day he arrived at Magh Line in Ulster. When he recognized the plain he said : ' Good in sooth was he with whom I sojourned on the plain, even Congal Claon, son of Scannlan, and good moreover was the plain on which we were. One day Congal and I were there and I said to him : ' I would fain go to another master,' because of the meagre recompense I received from him. Whereat, in order that I might stay with him, he gave me thrice fifty beautiful, foreign steeds together with his own brown steed, and thrice fifty gleaming, tusk-hilted swords, fifty bondsmen, and fifty bondsmaids, a tunic with gold and a splendid girdle of chequered silk. Thereupon Suibhne recited this poem :

52 ' I Muigh Line itu-sa anocht,
atgeóghuinn[1] mo chroidhe taobhnocht,
is atgeoin misi an magh
i mbidh mo ṡeisi Conghal.

Feacht rombá-sa[2] is Congal Claon
sunn ar an muigh-si maráon,
ag dul a nDruim Lorgan láin
doronsamar sist chomhráidh.

Adubhart-sa ris an righ,
ba tal*ach* (?) ar thairisi,[3]
as ail damh dul ar astar,
as beg lem mo thúarastal.

Rugus-[s]a úadh mar asgaidh
tri cháoga each n-adhastair,
tri chaoga claideamh tren tailc,
caoga gall, caoga ionnailt.

Rugus-[s]a úadh an t-each donn
as ferr dosir fér is fonn,
rucus a ionar go n-ór
is a fuathrog do breacsról.

Ga magh is fiú Magh Lini
acht in magh ata i Midhe,
no Magh Femhin co lion cros,
no an mag itá i nAirgeadros?

No Magh Feadha, no Magh Luirg,
no Magh nAoi co n-áille uird,
no Magh Life, no Magh Lí,
no an magh ita i Muirtheimhní?

52—1 atgheoin K   2 rombadhusa K   3 thairsi K

52 ' In Magh Line I am to-night,
my bare breast knows it ;
I know too the plain
wherein dwelt my mate Congal.

Once upon a time Congal Claon and I
were here in the plain together ;
as we were going to plenteous Druim Lurgain,
we made converse for a while.

Said I to the king—

    .   .   .   —

' I am fain to depart
too little do I deem my recompense.'

I got from him as a gift
thrice fifty bridled steeds,
thrice fifty strong swords,
fifty foreigners and fifty handmaidens.

I got from him the brown steed,
the best that sped over meadow and sward ;
I got his golden tunic
and his girdle of chequered silk.

What plain is a match for Magh Line,
unless it be the plain that is in Meath,
or Magh Femin of many crosses,
or the plain that is in Airgeadros ?

Or Magh Feadha, or Magh Luirg,
or Magh Aei with beauty of rank,
or Magh Life, or Magh Li,
or the plain that is in Murthemne ?

Do neoch atchonnarc-sa riamh
edir thúaidh, thes is thíar,
nocha nfaca-sa[4] go se
a macsamhla an muigi-se.'   A magh.

53 A haithle na laoidhi sin tainic Suibhne roime co
Glenn mBolcáin 7 robhúi aga chúartugudh co ttarla bengheilt
dó ann. Teich*idh*-siumh roimpi 7 ara áoi sin tuigedh gurab
ar gealtacht robháoi an bhen 7 iomp*aigh*is ría. Teich*idh*
sisi reimhi-sium ainnsein. 'Uchán a Dhé,' ar Suibhne, 'as
trúagh an bhetha sa .i. misi ag teich*edh* ríasan ngealtóig 7
sisi ag teich*edh* róm-sa ar lar Ghlinne Bolcáin ; [1]is ionmuin
eim an t-ion*ad* eisidhen ';[1] co n-ebairt :

> **54** 'Misgais, mairg duine dobheir,
> ni má cin 's ni má roghein,
> cidh ben dobéra, cidh fer,
> ni rois*et* an dís naoimhneamh.
>
> Ni minic bhíos cumann trír
> gan duine fo[1] fhodhord dibh,
> droigni is drisi romc[h]oirb
> conadh misi an fer fodhoird.
>
> Gealtóg ar[2] teich*edh* a fir,
> gidhedh as sgél n-anaithnidh,
> fer gan meither is gan bhróig
> ag teich*edh* ríasan ngealtóig.
>
> Ar mían o thigid cadhain
> gusan mbealltine ar samhuin,
> in gach coill cheir gan tacha
> bheith i ccrannuibh eidhneacha.

52—4 nfaca K

53—1–1 *sic* K ; 7 is ionmhuin eimh eisidhéin 7 in t-ionad gealtachta B

Of all that I have ever seen
both north and south and west,
I have not yet beheld
the peer of this plain.'

53 After that lay Suibhne came on to Glen Bolcain, and
he was wandering through it when he encountered a mad
woman. He fled before her and yet he divined that she
was in a state of madness, and he turned towards her. At
that she fled before him. 'Alas, O God!' said Suibhne,
'wretched is this life; here am I fleeing from the crazy
woman and she fleeing from me in the midst of Glen
Bolcain; dear in sooth is that place'; whereupon he
said :

54 ' Woe to him who bears enmity,
would that he had not been born or brought forth!
whether it be a woman or a man that bear it,
may the two not reach holy Heaven!

Seldom is there a league of three
without one of them murmuring;
blackthorns and briars have torn me
so that I am the murmurer.

A crazy woman fleeing from her man—
however, it is a strange tale—
a man without clothes, without shoes,
fleeing before the woman.

Our desire when the wild ducks come
at Samhuin, up to May-day,
in each brown wood without scarcity
to be in ivy-branches.

54—1 *om.* K   2 ag K

Uisge Ghlinne Bolcáin báin,
éistecht re a énlaith n-iomláin,
a ṡrotha millsi nach mall,³
a innsi agus a abhann.

A chuilenn cliuthar 's a choill,
a duille, a dreasa, a dercoinn,
a sméra áille uagha,
a chna, a airne ionnúara.

Iomad a chúan fo c*hra*nnuibh,
búir*edh*ach a dhamh n-all*aidh*,⁴
a uisci iodhan gan gheis,
ni liom-sa roba miosgais.'   M.

55 Luidh iarum Suibhne gusin bhail ina raibhi Eorann
co rothoiris ar fordhorus in tighe i mbói an riogan cona
banntracht, conadh ann adbert : 'Sádhal sin, a Eorann,' ar
sé, 'cidh anṡádhal damh-sa.' 'As fíor,' ar Eorann, '⁊ táir-si¹
asteach,' ar sí. 'Ni raghatt éimh,' ar Suibhne, 'ar nach gabat²
in sluagh imchumhang an toighi form.' 'Dar liom,' ar an
inghen, 'nocha nferr do chiall [91 a] ar gach ló da ttig dhuit ⁊
ó nach áil duit anadh aguinn,' ar sí, 'dena imtecht ⁊ na háitigh
chugainn idir, doigh is nar³ linn t'fhaicsin fon deilbh sin dona
dáoinibh atchonn*catar* thú fod dheilbh fé[i]n.' 'Truagh éimh
sin,' air Suibhne, 'as mairg dob*heir* taobh re mnáoi tar eis
na mbriathar sin. Uair ba maith mo chummaoin-si ar an
mnáoi romfúag*ra*nn samhlaidh, dóigh tucus inn-aonló dhi tri
chaoga bó ⁊ caoga each, ⁊ da madh é an la romhaiblius
Oilill Cédach, rí Ua fFhaoláin, robadh maith lé mh'fhaicsin-si';
gonadh ann adbert annso síos :

Water of bright Glen Bolcain,
listening to its many birds ;
its melodious, rushing streams,
its islands and its rivers.

Its sheltering holly and its hazels,
its leaves, its brambles, its acorns,
its delicious, fresh berries,
its nuts, its refreshing sloes.

The number of its packs of hounds in woods,
the bellowing of its stags,
its pure water without prohibition ;
'tis not I that hated it.'

55 Thereafter Suibhne went to the place where Eorann
was and stood at the outer door of the house wherein
were the queen and her womenfolk, and then he said: ' At
ease art thou, Eorann, though ease is not for me.' ' True,'
said Eorann, ' but come in,' said she. ' In sooth I will not,'
said Suibhne, ' lest the army pen me in the house.'
' Methinks,' said the woman, ' no better is your reason from
day to day, and since you do not wish to stay with us,'
said she, ' go away and do not visit us at all, for we are
ashamed that you should be seen in that guise by people
who have seen you in your true guise.' ' Wretched in sooth
is that,' said Suibhne, ' woe to him who trusts a woman
after these words. For great was my kindness to the woman
who dismisses me thus, seeing that on one day I gave her
thrice fifty cows and fifty steeds ; and if it were the day I
slew Oilill Cedach, king of the Ui Faolain, she would have
been glad to see me '; whereupon he said :

55—1 tairis*edh* K   2 gabhaid K   3 nair K

56 ' Mairg fa ttabhr*ai*d mna menma
cia bheith d'feabhus a ndealbha,
an tan as e Suibne Geilt
na fuair cuibhdhe dá cheidśeirc.

As mairg dobheir taobh re mnáibh
cidh a n-oidhchibh, cidh i lláibh,
cidh bed bhes ina n-in*n*e
d'aithle meabhla Eorainne.[1]

Maith mo chummáoin ar an mnáoi,
gan fordal, gan iomargháoi,
tarr*aidh* diom tri cháoga bò
la cáoga each a n-áonló.

Antan dobhinn isin bfeidhm
nocha n-iomghabhainn ceitheirn,
ait ina mbiodh treas no troid
robsam comhlann do t*hr*iochaid.

Rofhíarfaidh Congal, céim nglan,
din inar n-óccaibh Uladh,
cuich úaibh dhiongbhus isin chath
Oilill Cédach comhromhach ?

Allata, fergach an fer,
adhbhal a sgíath is a śleagh,
dorat i socht seal an slógh,
an fer dífreagra, dímhór.

Adubhart-sa ar láimh *Chongail*,
noc[h]arbh áithesg fir omhnaigh,
dingébhad-sa Oilill oll
gidh tren tar çhách a chomhlonn.

56—1 This stanza is taken from K, it does not occur in B   2 ngal K

56 ' Woe to those who strike women's fancy,
    however excellent their form,
    since Suibhne Geilt
    has got no sympathy from his first love.

    And woe to him who trusts in women
    whether by night or by day,
    whatever be in their minds,
    after the treachery of Eorann.

    Good was my kindness to the woman—
    without guile, without deceit—
    she got from me thrice fifty cows
    and fifty steeds in one day.

    When I was in the conflict
    I would not avoid an armed band ;
    where there was a fight or a tussle
    I was a match for thirty.

    Rightly did Congal ask
    of us Ulster warriors :
  ' which of you will repel in battle
    Oilill Cedach the combative ?'

    Wild and angry the man,
    huge his shield and his spear,
    he stilled for a time the host,
    the matchless, huge man.

    Said I at Congal's side—
    it was not the response of a timid man—
  ' I will ward off mighty Oilill,
    though hard beyond all is it to encounter him.'

I

Rofhágbhus Oilill gan chenn
agus robudh lánmhaith leam,
torchradar leam imalle
cuig mic righ Muige Mairge.'   Mairg.

57 Rothógaibh Suibhne uimi lasodhain co hétrom imísiol
ǽerdha do[1] ind gach aird 7 do tulmhoing gacha tulchi for
araill co riacht Benna Boirche fodhes. Roghabh fós isin
maighin sin, co n-ebairt: ' Maith in t-ionadh geilte so,' ar
sé, ' acht namá ni hionadh eatha, blechta no bídh é, acht is
ionadh anforusta anṡocair 7 ni díon ar dhoininn na ar
dherthan bheith ann, gidh ionadh urartt aoibhinn é '; gonadh
and adbert na briathra so sios cco léig :

> **58** ' Fuar anocht Benna Boirche,
> as ionadh fhir anfhoirfe,
> ni hionadh bidh na blechta,
> re sín is re sírṡnechta.
>
> As fuar mo leabaidh oidche
> a mullach Bheinne Boirche,
> am fann, nimfulaing édach
> ar chrann chuilinn crúaidhghégach.
>
> O romgeibh fúacht isind aigh[1]
> tigim go háith 'na agh*aidh*,
> beirim daig*er* don gháoith ghle
> dar leirg Laig*en* Laogha[i]re.
>
> Glenn Bolcáin an tobair gloin,
> as e mh'árus re hanmoin,
> o thicc lá Samhna, o teid sam,
> as é mh'árus re han*adh*.

57—1 *sic* K dhó B

58—1 aig B

Headless I left Oilill,
and right glad was I thereat ;
by me also there fell
five sons of the king of Magh Mairge.'

57 Thereupon Suibhne rose lightly, stealthily, airily, from
the point of every height and from the summit of one hill to
another until he reached Benn Boirche in the south. In that
place he rested saying : ' This is a spot for a madman, but
yet no place is it for corn or milk or food ; it is an uncom-
fortable, unquiet place, nor has it shelter against storm or
shower, though it is a lofty, beautiful place,' whereupon he
uttered these words :

58 ' Cold to-night is Benn Boirche,
       'tis the abode of a blighted man ;
       no place is it for food or milk,
       nor in storm and endless snow.

       Cold is my bed at night
       on the summit of Benn Boirche ;
       I am weak, no raiment covers me
       on a sharp-branching holly-tree.

       When cold has gripped me in the ice
       I move sharply against it,
       i give fire to the glinting wind
       blowing over the plain of Laoghaire's Leinster.

       Glen Bolcain of the clear spring,
       it is my dwelling to abide in ;
       when Samhuin comes, when summer goes,
       it is my dwelling where I abide.

Gacha sirinn thíar is toir
seachnóin ghlenntadh Glanamhr*aigh*,
bidh sion cruaidhṡnechta im cheann,
i ndion úairghealta Eirenn.

As é sin mo ghlenn grádha,
as é m'ferann comhdhála,
as é mo dún riogh re roinn,
as é mo dion ar dhoininn.

As é sin m'fulang oidhche :
cnúasach mo da *chr*obh choidhche,
benoim a ndoiribh doirch*ibh*
do luib*ibh*, do lántoirth*ibh*.

Mian lium na mó[n]ain*n* co mbl*oidh*,
at millsi na maothnatoin
fothlac[h]t, femar, as mían damh,
an lus bian is an biorar.

Ubhla, caora, cna cuill chain,
sméra, dercain do dhar*aigh*,
subha craobh, is fíach féile,
sgeachóra scíach scenbhg*é*re.

Siomsán, samhadh, creamhlus cain
agus bior[o]ráin bharrghlain,
benuidh dhiom géire malle,
dercain sléibhe, bu*n* melle.

Meisi i *fer*ann ghlas n*ach* glenn,
a Christ, ni rochomhraceam,
ni fhuil mo dual-sa re a dul
acht² gidhim fúar-sa, is fúar-s*u*m.'   Fuar anocht.

58—2 *om.* K.

Wheresoever I might wander west and east
throughout Glanamhrach's glens
the biting snowstorm is in my face,
for shelter of the chilly madman of Erin.

That is my beloved glen,
my land of foregathering,
my royal fortress that has fallen to my share,
my shelter against storm.

For my sustenance at night
I have all that my hands glean
in dark oak-woods
of herbs and plenteous fruit.

I love the precious bog-berries,
they are sweeter than . . .
brooklime, sea-weed, they are my desire,
the *lus bian* and the watercress.

Apples, berries, beautiful hazel-nuts,
blackberries, acorns from the oak-tree,
raspberries, they are the due of generosity,
haws of the prickly-sharp hawthorn.

wood-sorrels, goodly wild garlic,
and clean-topped cress,
together they drive hunger from me,
mountain acorns, *melle* root.

I in a green land that is not a glen,
O Christ, may I never reach it!
it is not my due to be there;
but though I am cold, it also is cold.[1]

---

1 See Notes.

59 [91 b] Tainic-siumh roimhe isin maidin arnamhárach
co Magh Feimhin, luid aisséin co Sionainn *sru*thghlain
sriobhúaine, asséin co hEchtge n-aird n-uraoibhinn, aisséin co
feronn mionghlas móirédrocht Maenmhuighe, aisséin co
*sru*th sáoraluinn Suca, aissein go himlibh Locha soileathain
Ríbh. Gab*haidh* iaromh fos 7 comhnaidhe i nglaic Bhile
Tiobradáin[1] i cCrích Gháille i n-oirther Connacht in oidhche
sin. Dá mhennat*aibh* disli-siom i nErinn an t-ionadh sin.
Rogabh tuirsi mor 7 muichneachus é, conadh ann adbert :
' As mor eimh,' ar sé, ' do imn*edh* 7 do dhocomhul roché*sus*
conuige so, ba fúar mh'ionadh aréir.i.i mullach Bheinne Boirche
7 ní nemhfhúaire mh'ionadh anocht a nglaic Bhile Tiobradáin.'

60 Úair is amhlaidh robhói an oidhchi sin, ag *cur* śnechta
7 an mhéd nocuredh noreod*adh* fa*che*toir a haithli a chuir,
conadh ann adbert-somh : ' Mo chubhais éimh,' ar sé, ' as
mor do dhocruibh rofhuilnges-[s]a, o rofhás mo chluimh
gus anocht. Rofheadar,' ar sé, ' cidh bás foghebhainn de,
robadh ferr dhamh taóbh do thabhairt re dáoinibh ina na
docra-sa do fhulang do ghrés ;' gonadh ann adbert an laoidh
ag tabairt a dhocra os áird :

61 ' Mor múich attú-sa anocht,
　　rot*r*eaghd mo chorp an gháoth ghlan,
　　toll mo throighthiu, glas mo ghrúadh,
　　a Dhé mhóir, atá a dhúal damh.

　　I mBeinn Bhoirche dhamh aréir,
　　romt[h]uairg bráoin in Echtga úair,
　　anocht robhretait[1] mo bhoill
　　i nglaic chroinn i nGaille ghlúair.

　　Rofhuilnges mor ttreas gan tlás
　　o rofhás clúmh ar mo chorp,
　　ar gach n-oidhche is ar gach ló
　　as mó sa mhó fhuilghim d'olc.

59—ı tioprata K　　**61**—ı K *has* rochreathait *above* robhreatait

59 On the morning of the morrow Suibhne came on to Magh Femhin, thence he fared to the limpid, green-streamed Shannon, thence to lofty, beautiful Aughty, thence to the smooth-green, bright land of Maenmagh, thence to the noble and delightful river Suck, thence to the shores of spreading Lough Ree. That night he made his resting-place in the fork of Bile Tiobradain in Crich Gaille in the east of Connaught. That was one of his beloved places in Ireland. Great sorrow and misery came upon him, whereupon he said : ' Great in sooth is the trouble and anxiety I have suffered hitherto ; cold was my dwelling-place last night on the summit of Benn Boirche, nor less cold is my dwelling-place to-night in the fork of Bile Tiobradain.'

60 For it was snowing that night and as fast as the snow fell it was frozen, whereupon he said : 'My conscience ! great is the suffering I have endured from the time my feathers have grown until to-night. I know,' said he, 'that though I might meet my death therefrom, it were better that I should trust people than suffer these woes forever.' Thereupon he recited the poem proclaiming aloud his woes :

61 ' I am in great grief to-night,
        the pure wind has pierced my body ;
        wounded are my feet, my cheek is wan,
        O great God ! it is my due.

        Last night I was in Benn Boirche,
        the rain of chilly Aughty beat on me ;
        to-night my limbs are racked
        in the fork of a tree in pleasant Gaille.

        I have borne many a fight without cowardice
        since feathers have grown on my body ;
        each night and each day
        more and more do I endure ill.

Romc[h]raidh sioc, sion nach súairc,
romt[h]uairg snechta ar Sleibh mhic Sin,
anocht romgeoghain an ghǽth
gan fraech Ghlenna Bolcáin bil.

Utmhall mh'imirce in gach íath,
domríacht bheith gan chéill gan chonn,
do Muigh Line for Muigh Lí,
do Muigh Lí for Life lonn

Saighim dar seghais Sleibhi Fúaid,
rigim im rúaig co Raith Móir,
dar Magh nAoi, dar Magh Luirg luinn
rigim co cuirr Chruacháin chóir.

O Sliabh Cúa, ni turus tais,
riccim go Glais Gháille ghrinn,
o Ghlais Gháille, gidh céim cían,
riccim soir go Slíabh mBreagh mbinn.

Dúairc an bhetha bheith gan teach,
as truagh an bhetha, a Chriosd chain,
sásadh biorair bairrghlais búain,
deogh uisge fhúair a glais ghlain.

Tuisledh do bharraibh chraobh ccrion,
imthecht aitin, gniom gan gháoi,
seachna daoine, cumann cúan,
coimhrith re damh rúadh dar rǽi.

Feis oidhche gan chluimh a ccoill
i mullach croinn dosaigh dhlúith,
gan coisteacht re guth ná glór,
a mhic Dé, is mór an mhúich.

Frost and foul storm have wrung my heart,
snow has beaten on me on Sliabh mic Sin;
to-night the wind has wounded me,
without the heather of happy Glen Bolcain.

Unsettled is my faring through each land,
it has befallen me that I am without sense or reason,
from Magh Line to Magh Li,
from Magh Li to the impetuous Liffey.

I pass over the wooded brow of Sliabh Fuaid,
in my flight I reach Rathmor,
across Magh Aoi, across bright Magh Luirg,
I reach the border of fair Cruachan.

From Sliabh Cua—no easy expedition—
I reach pleasant Glais Gaille;
from Glais Gaille, though a long step,
I arrive at sweet Sliabh Breagh to the east.

Wretched is the life of one homeless,
sad is the life, O fair Christ!
a meal of fresh, green-tufted watercress,
a drink of cold water from a clear stream.

Stumbling from withered tree-tops,
faring through furze—deed without falsehood—
shunning mankind, keeping company with wolves,
racing with the red stag over the field.

Sleeping of nights without covering in a wood
in the top of a thick, bushy tree,
without hearing voice or speech;
O Son of God, great is the misery!

Reithim rúaig re beinn co báoth,
uath*adh* rotráoth a los lu,[2]
dosgarus rem c[h]ruth gan clodh,
a mhic Dé, is mór an mhúich.'   Mór.

62 'Cidh fil ann atrá,'[1] ar sé, 'acht cidh é Domhnall
mac Aodha nommhuirf*edh* raghad dochum Dál Araidhe 7
dobhér taobh rem dháoin*ibh* fodhéin 7 m*un* beith[2] caill*each*
an mhuilinn d'atach Christ frim im ṡist leimennd*aigh* do
dhenumh dhi [92 a] ni rachainn ar an aithghealtacht.'

63 Tainic taom da cheill do annsin 7 doluidh roime ar
amus a thíre do thabairt taobha re a muint*ir* 7 do anmhuin
aca. Rofoillsig*edh* do Ronán an tan sin a chiall do tuidhecht
do Suibhne 7 a bheith ag dul chum a thíre d'anadh eiter a
mhuint*ir*, co n-ebairt Ronán : 'Aitchim-si an Righ uasal
uilechumhachtach nar fféde[1] se an t-ingrinnt*idh* sin do
ionnsaighe na heagailsi dia hingreim doridhisi amail dorighni
fecht n-aill 7 an t-inneach*adh* tuc Día fair a ndiogail a
dhimhiadha-somh for a mhuint*ir* na raibe furtacht na
fóiridhin dhó dhe co roscara a anam fri a chorp, ar dháigh na
tiobhra a aithghin oil*e* do ingrinnt*idh* dia éis sár no dimigin
for an ccoimdigh nach for a mhuint*ir* itir.'

64 Roéisd Dia itchi Rónáin, uair antan tánic Suibhne co
medhón Sléibhe Fúaid rochobhs*aidh* a cheim annsin co
ttárfás taidhbhsi n-iongnadh dhó annsin a medhónoidhchi
.i. méidh*edh*a maoilderga 7 cinn gan cholla 7 cúig cinn
gaoisidecha, gairbhlíatha, gan c*hor*p, gan chol*ainn* etarra, ag
sianghail 7 ag leimn*igh*[1] imon slig*idh* anond 7 anall. Antan
rosiacht-somh eatarra rochúalaidh ag comhradh iad 7 is edh
adberdís : 'Geilt é,' ar an cétchenn. 'Gelt Ultach,' ar an
dara cenn. 'Λ lemm*huin* co maith,' ar an treas cenn. 'Gurab
fada an lenm*hain*,' ar an cethramadh cenn. 'Nogo ría

Foolishly I race up a mountain-peak
alone, exhausted by dint of vigour;
I have parted from my faultless shape ;
O Son of God, great is the misery !'

62 'Howbeit,' said he, 'even if Domhnall son of Aodh were to slay me, I will go to Dal Araidhe and I will entrust myself to my own people, and if the mill-hag had not invoked Christ against me so that I might perform leaps for her awhile, I would not have gone again into madness.'

63 A gleam of reason came to him then, and he set out towards his country to entrust himself to his people and abide with them. At that time it was revealed to Ronan that Suibhne had recovered his reason and that he was going to his country to abide among his folk ; whereupon Ronan said : ' I entreat the noble, almighty King that that persecutor may not be able to approach the church to persecute it again as he once did, and, until his soul has parted from his body, may there be no help or relief to him from the vengeance which God inflicted on him in revenge for the dishonour done to His people, so that no other like tyrant after him may inflict outrage or dishonour on the Lord or on His people.'

64 God heard Ronan's prayer, for when Suibhne came to the centre of Sliabh Fuaid he stopped still there, and a strange apparition appeared to him at midnight; even trunks, headless and red, and heads without bodies, and five bristling, rough-grey heads without body or trunk among them, screaming and leaping this way and that about the road. When he came among them he heard them talking to each other, and this is what they were saying: 'He is a madman, said the first head; 'a madman of Ulster,' said the second head ; 'follow him well,' said the third head ; 'may the pursuit be long,' said the fourth head ; 'until he reaches the

fairrge,' ar an cuig*edh* cenn. Noseirgheatt a n-áoinfeacht chuige. Rostóg*aibh*-siumh uime rempa tar gach muine día aroile 7 geruó mor an glenn nobhiodh roimhe ni thaidhledhsomh é, acht noling*edh* don bhord co aroile de 7 do bheinn na tulchi for araill.

65 Ba lór im*morro* d'úathbhás, do grec[h]ach 7 golfort*ach*, sianghal 7 sioréighemh, sestán 7 seiseilbhe na ccenn ina dhiaidh-siumh ga tharrachtain 7 ga t*hr*entograim. Ba hé treisi 7 tinnesn*aigh*e na togroma sin co lingdís na cinn da oircnibh 7 da iosgad*aibh* 7 da lesrach 7 da slinnén*ibh* 7 do chlais a chuil, co mba samhalta leisiumh 7 bloisgbheim buinne[1] dilionn do ucht airdślé*ibh*e seisbheimneach gach cinn for aroile dhiobh 7 comhthuairgnech uile fri sleas*aibh* crann 7 fria cennuibh carrag le lar 7 re lántalm*ain*, co nár ansat de co ndeach*aidh* re néll*aibh* uretroma æieoir uatha.[2]

66 Roscarsat ris iarsin edir chenn ghabhair 7 cenn *chon*, uair andar lais bádar sidhe a ttréchumusc na ccenn n-oile ina lenmhuin. Ba neimhthni[1] faoinneal no folúamhuin da raibhi fair-siumh ina haithfhegh*adh* riamh roimhe sin, uair ni thairisedh eadh lasa n-iobhadh digh co cenn trí choicthidhisi ina dhíaidh sin, go ttarla aen na n-oidhche[2] é i mullach Sléibhe Eidhneach,[3] *gur* ro-oiris i mbárr *ch*roinn ann eadh na hoidhche sin co madain. Roghabh ag eccaoine móir annsin ; conadh *edh* roráidh : 'Olc eimh atáthar agom anocht a haithle na caillighe 7 na ccenn ar Slíabh Fúaid,' ar se, ' acht chena as cóir mo ueth amail atú, uair soch*aidh*e risa ndernus fe[i]n olc ; ' conadh ann adbert :

67 ' Eccáointeach atú-sa anocht,
am tuirseach truagh, am taobhnocht,
da bfcsdáois fuim na dáolne
fil damh damhna eccáoine.

65—1 baindi K   2 uathadh BK
66—1 tra *add.* K   2 aen do n-oidchibh K   3 Aidneach K

sea,' said the fifth head. They rose forth together towards
him. He soared aloft in front of them (passing) from
thicket to thicket, and no matter how vast was the glen
before him he would not touch it, but would leap from one
edge of it to another, and from the summit of one hill to the
summit of another.

65 Great in sooth was the terror, the crying and wailing,
the screaming and crying aloud, the din and tumult of the
heads after him as they were clutching and eagerly pursuing
him. Such were the force and swiftness of that pursuit that
the heads leaped on his calves, his houghs, his thighs, his
shoulders, and the nape of his neck, so that the impact of
head against head, and the clashing of all against the sides
of trees and the heads of rocks, against the surface and the
earth, seemed to him like the rush of a wild torrent from the
breast of a high mountain ; nor did they cease until he escaped
from them into the filmy clouds of the sky.

66 Then they parted from him, both goat-heads and dog-
heads—for it seemed to him that these were all intermingled
with the other heads pursuing him. The wandering and flying
which he had ever before done were as nothing in comparison
with this, for he would not rest long enough to take a drink
to the end of three fortnights after that until he came one
night to the summit of Sliabh Eidhneach ; that night he
rested there on the top of a tree until morning. He then
began lamenting grievously; whereupon he said : 'Wretched
indeed is it with me to-night after the hag and the heads on
Sliabh Fuaid, and yet it is right that I should be as I am,
because of the many to whom I myself have done harm';
whereupon he said :

67 ' Mournful am I to-night,
          I am sad and wretched, my side is naked,
          if folk but knew me
          I have cause for lament.

Reod, sioc, sneachta agus síon
agum thúargain tre bhith síor,
mo beith gan teini, gan tech
a mullach Sléibhe Eidhneach.

Teach mór agum is ben mhaith,
adeir*edh* cách robsum flaith,
as é a[s] ruire 'sas rí
antí domrad¹ i neimhthní.   [92 b]

Cidh 'ma ttuc Dia me asan ccath
nach bfrith ann neach dom mharbadh,
suil dobheinn eing a n-eing
agus cailleach an mhuilinn ?

Cailleach an mhuilinn 'ga toigh,
mallacht Crist ar a hanmoin,
mairg dorad taobh risin ccrín,
mairg da ttaratt a choinmhír.

Robhaoi Loingseachán ar m'eing
tre gach díthreabh² a nÉirinn,
go romchealg chuigi don chraoibh
tan adfett ég mo m*a*cáoimh.

Domrad-sa leis 'san teach mor,
ait a mbáoi an slúagh ac comhól,
as romc[h]eng*al* thiar 'san t*s*eit
ag*haidh* d'ag*haidh* rem chét*s*eirc.

Sluagh an toighe gan táire
ag cluithe is ag gáire,
meisi *com* muint*ir* is toigh
ag surdl*aigh*, ag lemendoigh.

Frost, ice, snow, and storm,
forever scourging me,
I without fire, without house,
on the summit of Sliabh Eidhneach.

I have a mansion and a good wife,
everyone would say that I was a prince ;
'tis He who is Lord and King
has wrought my downfall.

Wherefore did God rescue me from the battle
that no one was found there to slay me,
rather than that I should go step by step
with the hag of the mill ?

The hag of the mill at her house,
Christ's curse on her soul !
woe whosoever has trusted the hag !
woe to whom she has given his dog's portion !

Loingseachan was on my track
throughout every wilderness in Erin,
until he lured me from the tree
what time he related my son's death.

He carried me into the great house
wherein the host was feasting,
and bound me behind in the house (?)
face to face with my first love.

The people of the house without reproach
playing games and laughing ;
I and my folk in the house
leaping and jumping.

Munbadh caillech in tighi
ni rachainn ar aithmhire,
ro-ataigh rium³ Crist do nimh
ar šíst mbig do léimeand*aigh*.

Roling*ius* leim no dhá leim
ar an athair nemhdha féin,
adbert an chaillech 'ga toigh
co ling*fedh* fé[i]n léim amhlaidh.

Rolinges leim oile amach
dar fíormhullach na cathrach,
lúaithi ina deathach tre theach
an teath*adh* rug an chailleach.

Roširsium Éire uile
o Thigh Duinn co Tráigh Ruire,
otá an T*r*aig co B*e*nna mBrain,
nir c*h*uires diom an chailleach.

Eiter mhagh is mhóin is leirg
dhiom nír chuires an crúaidhleidhb,
gur ling*edh* lem an leim ngle
do bheinn Dúine Sobhairce.

Ar sin rolinges fon dún
agus nochar ceim ar ccúl,
rugus isin bfairrge amach,
rosfágbhus thall an chailleach.

Iarsin tangadar 'san t*r*áigh
mu*i*nt*er* dhiabhail 'na comhdháil
agus roluaidhset a corp,
mairg tír nErenn 'nar hadnocht.

Were it not for the hag of the house,
I would not have gone again into madness ;
she besought me by Christ of Heaven
to leap for her a little while.

I leaped a leap or two
for the sake of the Heavenly Father Himself ;
the hag at her house said
that even so could she herself leap.

Once more I leaped out
over the top of the fortress ;
swifter than smoke through a house
was the flight of the hag.

We wandered through all Erin,
from Teach Duinn to Traigh Ruire,
from Traigh Ruire to Benna Brain,
but the hag I did not elude.

Through plain and bog and hillside
I escaped not from the slattern
until she leaped with me the famous leap
to the summit of Dun Sobairce.

Thereafter I leaped down the *dun*,
nor did I step back,
I went out into the sea,
yonder I left the hag.

There came then to the strand
the devil's crew to meet her,
and they bore away her body ;
woe to the land of Erin in which it was buried !

K

Feacht roluighes ar⁴ Slíabh Fúaid
i n-oidhchi duib dhorchi dhuairc,
co bfaca coig cinn 'san ccnoc
arna n-oirleach inn-áonport.⁵

Adubhairt cenn dibh 'na ruth,
rium-sa roba garb an guth,
'geilt Ultach, lentar libh dhe,
co ría romhaibh i bfairrge.'

Rorethus rompa an ród
is nír fuirmhess troig ar fód,⁶
eiter chenn gabhair is con,
ann roghabhsat malloghadh.

Cóir cía rogheibhinn-si olc,
mor n-oidhchi rolinges loch,
mór do rosgaibh ban mbáidhe
doradus fo eccaoine.'   Ecc.

68 Aroile aimsir do Suibhne i Luachair Dheadhadh for a
bhaeithreimennaibh baoisi; luid assidhén ina réimimh roi-
ghealtachta go ranic Fiodh glansrot[h]ach gégáloinn Gaible.
Báoi bliadhain an du sin 7 as edh fa bíadh dhó frisiu
mbliadhoin sin .i. caor[a] croiderga crúandatha cuilinn 7
dercoin darach dubhdhuinne 7 deogh d'uisci na Gabhla, .i. an
abhann on ainmnighthir an fiodh, conadh ann roghabh tuirsi
trom 7 dobrón derbháir antí Suibhni i bforcenn na ré sin tre
olcus a bhethadh, conadh ann adbert an laoidh mbig si:

69 'Ochán, as meisi Suibhne,
mo chorpán as lor mairbhe,
gan ceol, gan codladh choidhche
acht osnadh ghaoit[h]e gairbe.

Once as I passed over Sliabh Fuaid
on a dark, black, gloomy night,
on the hill I beheld five heads,
having been cut off in one place.

Said one of them of a sudden—
harsh was the voice to me—
' a madman of Ulster, follow him
so that you drive him before you to the sea.'

I sped before them along the path
and I set not foot on ground ;
both goat-head and dog-head
then began to curse.

'Tis right that I should get harm ;
many a night have I leaped a lake,
many eyes of fond women
have I made weep.'

68 On a certain occasion Suibhne happened to be in
Luachair Deaghaidh on his wild career of folly; he went
thence in his course of madness until he reached Fiodh
Gaibhle of clear streams and beautiful branches. In that
place he remained a year and during that year his food
consisted of blood-red, saffron holly-berries and dark-brown
acorns, and a drink of water from the Gabhal, that is, the
river from which the wood is named. At the end of that
time deep grief and heavy sorrow took hold of Suibhne there
because of the wretchedness of his life ; whereupon he uttered
this little poem :

69 ' I am Suibhne, alas !
my wretched body is utterly dead,
evermore without music, without sleep,
save the soughing of the rude gale.

Tanacc o Luachair Dheaghadh
co bruachaibh Feadha Gaibhle,
as í mo chuid, ni cheilim,
caora eidhinn, mes dairbhre.

Bliadhain dhamh isin mbeinn-si
isin deilbh-si ina bfuilim
gan biadh do dhul 'san corp-sa
acht caora corcra cuilinn.

As me geilt Glinni Bolcáin,
ni bhíu-sa ag ceilt mo dhochnáidh,[1]
tairnicc anocht mo láthar,
ni damh nach ádhbhar ocháin.   Ochán.

70 [93 a] Dorala dho-somh laithe n-áon techt co Druim
Iaroinn i Connachtaibh co rochaith biorar barrghlas na cilli
ar brú na tiobratta tonnghlaisi 7 ro-ibh ni dia huisge ina
dheghaidh. Ro-eirigh cleirech amach asin ecclais 7 roghabh
tnúth 7 trenformud frisin ngeilt é im thomhailt an tuara
rothoimhleadh feisin 7 adbert gurbho socair sadal robhaoi
Suibhne isin iubardhos íar mbuing[1] a phroinne de budhdhéin.
' Truagh eimh sin, a chléirigh,' ar Suibhne, ' uair as meisi dúil
as anšádhaile 7 anšocra dogheibh a betha isin domun daigh
ni thig tinneabhradh na toirrchim ar mo šuilibh ar úaman
mo mharbhtha ; deithbhir són, dáigh is cuma noraghainn ar
gealtacht ría slógaib na cruinne d'fhaicsin dom fhobairt a
n-aoinfecht 7 re folúamain an dreolláin a áonar ; et a Dhé
neimhe, a chleirigh,' ar Suibhne, 'nach bfuili-si im riocht-sa
7 meisi isin chongaibh crabaidh ittáoi-si, noco n-aithnicchedh
th'aigneadh 7 th'inntinn nach gnáth dom aithghin-si no dom
ionnšamail bheith co soinmech febh adbeiri-si'; conadh annsin
roghabh an cléirech tosach na laoidhe 7 rofhreagair Šuibhne
a deiredh, mar so :

69—1 dhochnaidh, altered later to dochráidh K
70—1 muing K

I have come from Luachair Deaghaidh
to the border of Fiodh Gaibhle,
this is my fare—I hide it not—
ivy-berries, oak-mast.

A year have I been on the mountain
in this form in which I am,
without food going into my body
save crimson holly-berries.

The madman of Glen Bolcain am I,
I shall not hide my gnawing grief;
to-night my vigour has come to an end,
not to me is there no cause for grief.'

70 One day it happened that he went to Druim Iarainn in
Connacht where he eat green-topped watercress of the church
by the brink of the green-flecked well and he drank some of
its water after. A cleric came out of the church and he was
indignant and resentful towards the madman for eating the
food which he himself used to eat, and he said that it was
happy and contented Suibhne was in the yew-tree after
taking his meal from himself. ' Sad in sooth is that (saying),
O cleric,' said Suibhne, ' for I am the most discontented and
unhappy creature in the world, for neither rest nor slumber
comes on my eyes for fear of my being slain. That is natural,
because I would equally go into madness at seeing the united
hosts of the universe threatening me as at the flight of
a single wren ; and, O God of Heaven ! cleric,' said Suibhne,
' that you are not in my place and I in the state of devotion
in which you are, so that your mind and understanding
might recognise that it is not usual for the like of me or for
my counterpart to be happy as you say '; whereupon the
cleric recited the beginning of the poem and Suibhne
responded (by reciting) the end, as follows :

71 [An clerech:] 'Sadha[i]l sin, a gealtagáin,
a mbarr na geige iubair
do leathtáobh mo mennatáin,[1]
docait[h]is mo c[h]uid biolair.

[Suibhne:] Ni sadha[i]l mo bhetha-sa,
a chléirigh Droma hIaroind,
ata do mhéd m'eagla-sa
suil dom śúilibh nach íadhaim.

Fir[2] domhain da bfaicinn-si
chugum, a fhir an cheóláin,
is comhmór dotheithfinn-si[3]
ríu is re heitil an dreolláin.

Truagh gan tusa im inmhe-si,
is meisi im chléirech chrába*idh*,
no co ttuig*edh* th'inntinn-si
nach c*e*rd geilte b*ei*th sáda[i]l.' Sádail.

72 Aroile laithe do Suibhne ag cúartugudh criche *Con*nacht
go hudmhall anbhsaidh go ttarla é fo dheoidh go hAll
[Fh]arannáin a tTír Fhíachrach Mhúaidhe; glenn aloinn eisi-
dhén, sruth aloinn sriobhúaine ag teibersain[1] co tinnesnach
frisin all[2] anúas 7 bennach*adh* ann ina rabadar sénadh náomh 7
fíreó[i]n co hiomdha iolarrdha, et ba hiomdha ann ámh c*r*ann
caomhaloinn co ttoirth*ibh* troma tóthachtacha isin all hisin.
Ba hiomda ann eimh eidheann fiorchluthmar 7 aball cenntrom
ag cromadh co talmain le troma a tor*aidh*, ba cuma nobhíttís
isin allt sin ois allta 7 miola muighe 7 muca mórthroma,
ba hiomdha im*morro* rón roiremhar rochodl*adh* ann tar éis
techt o muir móir anall isin all[2] sin. Roŝannt*aigh* Suibhne
co mor an t-ionadh sin, go roghabh for adhmoladh 7 ag
tabhairt a thúarusgbhála os aird ; go ndébairt an laoidh-si :

71—1 bennatáin BK   2 an *add* K   3 doteichfinn-si K
72—-1 tepersin K   2 aill K

71 The cleric: 'Thou art at ease, madman,
            on the top of the yew-branch
            beside my little abode,
            thou hast eaten my watercress.

   Suibhne :   My life is not one of ease,
            O cleric of Druim Iarainn,
            such is my fear
            that I do not close an eye.

            If I were to see the men of the world
            coming to me, O man of the bell,
            I would flee from them as fast
            as at the flight of a wren.

            Alas ! that thou art not in my place
            and I a devout cleric,
            so that thy mind might grasp
            that it is not the accomplishment of a madman
                to be at ease.'

72 One day as Suibhne was wandering aimlessly and restlessly through Connacht he came at last to All Fharannain in Tir Fhiachrach Mhuaide ; a delightful valley with a beautiful green-streamed river dropping swiftly down the cliff and a blessed place there wherein was a synod of saints and multitudes of righteous folk. Numerous too on that cliff were the beautiful trees, heavy and rich with fruits ; numerous also the well-sheltered ivy-trees and heavy-topped apple-trees bending to the ground with the weight of their fruit ; wild deer and hares and great, heavy swine were there also, likewise many fat seals that used to sleep on that cliff, after coming from the main beyond. Suibhne greatly coveted that place and he began praising and describing it aloud ; whereupon he uttered this lay :

73 ' All [Fh]arannain, adhbha náomh,
co n-iomad call[1] caomh is cnúas,
uisge tinnesnach can tess
ag snige[2] re a chness anúas.

As iomdha ann eidhnech ghlass
agus meass re mberar[3] geall
agus abhall chenntrom chaomh
ag fill*iudh* a c*r*aobh fa cheann.

Imdha broc ag dol fa a dhíon,
ann is miol muighe nach mall,
is édan rio*nn*tanach[4] róin
ag techt on muir moir anall.

Me Suibhne mac Colmáin chóir,
mor n-oidhchi reoidh bhim co fann,
romt*hru*aill Rónán do D*ru*im Gess,[5]
codlaim fa c*hr*aoibh 'san ess tall.'   All.

74 Tainic Suibhne roime fo dheóidh conuige an baile i
raibhe Moling .i. Teach Moling. Ba hisin tan sin roboi
psaltair Chaoimhghin i ffiadnuise Moling aga dénamh do
lucht an aiceapta. [93 b] Tainic iarumh Suibhne for s*rai*th
na tioprat[1] i fiadhnuisi an chléirigh 7 rogab ag ithe biorair.
' As moch-long*adh* sin, a ghealtagáin,' ar an cléirech ; conadh
ann adbert Moling 7 rofreagair Suibhne é:

75 [Moling:]   Mochthráth[1] sin, a ghealtagáin,
                   re ceileabhradh cóir.
    [Suibhne :] Gidh moch[2] leat-sa, a chlérecháin,[3]
                   tanic tert ag Róimh.

73—1 crann K   2 snaoidhe K   3 le a mberar K   4 roinnteach K
5 do D*ru*im Gess K ; domhuin B

73 'Cliff of Farannan, abode of saints,
with many fair hazels and nuts,
swift cold water
rushing down its side.

Many green ivy-trees are there
and mast such as is prized,
and fair, heavy-topped apple-trees
bending their branches.

Many badgers going under its shelter
and fleet hares too,
and . . . brows of seals
coming hither from the main.

I am Suibhne son of upright Colman,
many a frosty night have I been feeble ;
Ronan of Druim Gess has outraged me,
I sleep 'neath a tree at yonder waterfall.'

74 At length Suibhne came along to the place where
Moling was, even Teach Moling. The psalter of Kevin
was at the time in front of Moling as he was reading it to
the students. In the cleric's presence Suibhne then came
to the brink of the fountain and began to eat watercress.
'O mad one, that is eating early,' said the cleric ; whereupon
Moling spoke and Suibhne answered him :

75 Moling : 'An early hour is it, thou madman,
for due celebration.
Suibhne : Though to thee, cleric, it may seem early,
terce has come in Rome.

74—1 *sic* K ; tioprait B
75—1 *sic* K ; Muchthrath B   2 *sic* K ; much B   3 cleirigain K

[Moling:]   Ga fios duit-si, a ghealtagáin,
              cuin tig tert ag Róimh?
[Suibhne:] Fios tig dhamh om Thigerna
              gach madain 's gach nóin.

[Moling:]   Innis tre rún ráitsighe
              sgela Fíadhat finn.
[Suibhne:] Agut-sa ata an fháitsine
              masa thú Moling.

[Moling:]   Cidh tuc duit-si mh'aithni-si,
              a gheilt ghníomach ghér?
[Suibhne:] Minic me ar an fhaith[ch]i¹-si
              o rosaoi mo chéill.

[Moling:]   Cidh na tairni a n-aonbhaili,
              a mhic Colmáin Chúair?
[Suibhne:] Ferr leam bheith a n-áonṡuidhe
              isin mbeathaidh bhúain.

[Moling:]   A thruaigh, an ría t'anam-sa
              ifrinn aidhbhle dos?
[Suibhne:] Ni thabhair Día orum-sa
              pían acht bheith gan fhos.

[Moling:]   Glúais alle go ttormalla
              cuid bhus milis lat.
[Suibhne:] Dá fhestá-sa, a chléirecháin,
              doilghe bheith gan bhrat.

[Moling:]   Béra-sa mo chochlán-sa
              no béra mo leann.
[Suibhne:] Aniú gidh im c[h]rochbán⁵-sa
              robá uair budh ferr.

75—4 faithi B ; faitche K   5 cróchban B

Moling: How dost thou know, mad one,
when terce comes in Rome?

Suibhne: Knowledge comes to me from my Lord
each morn and each eve.

Moling: Relate through the mystery of speech
tidings of the fair Lord.

Suibhne: With thee is the (gift of) prophecy
if thou art Moling.

Moling: How dost thou know me,
thou toiling, cunning madman?

Suibhne: Often have I been upon this green
since my reason was overthrown.

Moling: Why dost thou not settle in one place,
thou son of Colman Cuar?

Suibhne: I had rather be in one seat
in life everlasting.

Moling: Miserable one, will thy soul reach
hell with vastness of slime?

Suibhne: God inflicts no pain on me
save being without rest.

Moling: Move hither that thou mayest eat
what thou deemest sweet.

Suibhne: If you but knew, cleric,
more grievous is it to be without a cloak.

Moling: Thou shalt take my cowl
or thou shalt take my smock.

Suibhne: Though to-day I am ghastly,
there was a time when it was better.

[Moling :]   An tú an Suibhne sgáthaighthe
          tainic a cath Roth?
[Suibhne :] Mása mé, ní ráthaighthe
          cidh nomheilinn[6] moch.

[Moling :]   Canas tárla mh'aithni-si
          duit, a ghealtáin ghéir?
[Suibhne :] Meinic mé ar an fhaithchi-si[7]
          got fheithemh[8] do chéin.

[Moling :]   Aluinn duille an liubhair-si,
          psaltair Cháoimhghin cháidh.
[Suibhne :] Aille duille mh'iubhair-si
          i nGlinn Bolcáin báin.

[Moling :]   Nach suairc leat-sa an relec-sa
          ba scoil scíomhda dath?
[Suibhne :] Nirbh anśúarca mh'oirecht-sa
          madain ar Muigh Rath.

[Moling :]   Ragat-sa do cheileabhradh
          go Glais Chille Cró.
[Suibhne :] Ling*fet*-sa c*r*ann eidhinnghl*an*,
          lem ard, is badh mó.

[Moling:]   Saothrach dhamh 'san eglais-[s]i
          ar cinn tren is trúagh.
[Suibhne :] Saothr*aighe* mo leab*aidh*-si
          i mBeinn Fhaibhni fhúar.

[Moling :]   Cáit i ttig do[9] śaogal-sa,
          in a ccill no i loch?
[Suibhne :] Aeghaire dot æghairibh[10]
          nommharbhann go moch.'   Muchthrath.

75–-6 nomelinn K   7 *sic* K; faithi-si B   8 go teithemh B; got
fheithiomh K   9 *sic* K; mo B   10 *sic* K; aedhaire dot aedhairibh B

Moling :   Art thou the dreaded Suibhne
            who came from the battle of Rath ?
Suihhne :   If I am, 'tis not to be guaranteed
            what I might eat at early morn.

Moling :   Whence has come my recognition,
            cunning madman, to thee ?
Suibhne :   Often am I upon this green
            watching thee from afar.

Moling :   Delightful is the leaf of this book,
            the psalter of holy Kevin.
Suibhne :   More delightful is a leaf of my yew
            in happy Glen Bolcain.

Moling :   Dost thou not deem this churchyard pleasant
            with its school of beautiful colours ?
Suibhne :   Not more unpleasant was my muster
            the morning at Magh Rath.

Moling :   I will go for celebration
            to Glais Cille Cro.
Suibhne :   I will leap a fresh ivy-bush
            a high leap, and it will be a greater feat.

Moling :   Wearisome is it to me in this church
            waiting on the strong and weak.
Suibhne :   More wearisome is my couch
            in chilly Benn Faibhni.

Moling :   Where comes thy life's end,
            in church or lake ?
Suibhne :   A herd of thine
            will slay me at early morn.'

76 'As mochen éimh do t[h]echt sonn, a Ṡuibhne,' ar
Moling, 'ar atá a ndán duit bheith annso 7 do ṡáogal do
thecht ann, do sgéla 7 th' imthechta d' fhágbáil sunn 7
th' adhnacal[1] i reilicc fíreóin, 7 naisgim-si fort,' ar Moling,
'gidh mor ṡire[2] gach láoi d' Érinn techt gacha hespurtan[3]
chugum-sa go rosgriobh*thar* do sgéla lium.'

77 Iomthúsa na geilte iarsin ; robhaoi risin mbliadhain
sin ag tathaigh*idh* Moling. Roṡoigh*edh* lá n-ann co hInnis
Bó Finni i n-iarthar Chonnacht, lá oile co hEss rocháoin
Rúaidh, lá oile co Slíabh mínáluinn Mis, lá oile go Benda
biothfhúara Boirche ; gidbé diobh sin doṡoigh*edh* gach láoi
nofritháil*edh* a n-espurtain gach n-oidhche co Teach Moling.
Ro-ordaigh Moling proinn mbig dhó frisin ré sin, doigh
adubairt re bhanchoig ni do bhleaghan na mbó do thabairt
dó. Muirghil a hainm-sidhe, as í ba ben do Mhungán do
mhuicidhi Moling. Ba hí méd na proinni sin[1] dobheir*edh*
an bhen dó .i. nodhing*edh* a sáil conuige a hadhbronn isin
mbualtrach fa coimhnesa dhi 7 nofágb*adh* a lán lemnachta
ann do Suibhne. Dothig*edh*-somh co faiteach f*ure*chair i
n-eat*ar*fhásach na búail*edh* do ibhe an bhainne sin.[1]

78 Tarla iomchaineadh adh*aigh* [94 a] ann eitir Mhuirghil
7 mhnáoi oile isin mbúail*idh*, co n-eb*er*t an bhen eile : ' As
mesa duit-si,' ar sí, ' nach tocha leat [1]fer eile 7 fós nach ferr
let[1] th' fer féin dot ríachtain ina an gheilt ata got thath*igh*id
risin mbliaduin-si anall.'[2] Atchúala siúr an bhúachalla anní
sin 7 gidhedh ní ro-innis ní dhe co bfac*aidh* Muirghil isin
mad*ain* arnabhárach ag dul d' iodnacal an bhainne go Suibhne
conuige an mbúaltrach ba comhfhogus don fhál i raibhe.
O'dchonnairc siúr an bhuachalla sin tainic asteach 7 atbert re
a bráthair : 'Atá do bhen isin ffál sin thoir ag fer oile, a
mheath*aigh* mhiodhlaochda,' ar sí. Roghabh éd an búachaill
ag a chloistecht sin, 7 roeirigh go hobonn inníreach 7 tarr*aidh*
a láimh leathga robói for alchuing astigh 7 téit for amus na

76—1 tiodnacal K   2 sirfisi (.i. do ṡiubhal) L   3 tair gach esparta L
77—1 *sic* K ; iṡin B   **78**—1-1 *om.* K   2 all K

76 'Welcome in sooth is your coming here, Suibhne,' said Moling, ' for it is destined for you to be here and to end your life here ; to leave here your history and adventures, and to be buried in a churchyard of righteous folk ; and I bind you,' said Moling, ' that however much of Ireland you may travel each day, you will come to me each evening so. that I may write your history.'

77 Thereafter during that year the madman was visiting Moling. One day he would go to Innis Bo Finne in west Connacht, another day to delightful Eas Ruaidh, another day to smooth, beautiful Sliabh Mis, another day to ever-chilly Benn Boirche, but go where he would each day, he would attend at vespers each night at Teach Moling. Moling ordered a collation for him for that hour, for he told his cook to give him some of each day's milking. Muirghil was her name ; she was wife of Mongan, swineherd to Moling. This was the extent of the meal the woman used to give him: she used to thrust her heel up to her ankle in the cowdung nearest her and leave the full of it of new milk there for Suibhne. He used to come cautiously and carefully into the vacant portion of the milking yard to drink the milk.

78 One night a dispute arose between Muirgil and another woman in the milking enclosure, whereupon the latter said : ' the worse is it for you,' said she, ' that another man is not more welcome to you, and yet that you do not prefer your own husband to come to you than the madman who is visiting you for the past year.' The herd's sister hearkened to that ; nevertheless she mentioned nothing about it until she saw Muirgil on the morrow morning going to leave the milk for Suibhne in the cowdung near the hedge at which he was. The herd's sister seeing that, came in and said to her brother: 'You cowardly creature, your wife is in yonder hedge with another man,' said she. The herd hearing that became jealous, and he rose suddenly and angrily and seized a spear that was within on a rack and made for the

geilte. As amhlaidh robhúi an geilt 7 a tháobh ris 7 é 'na luidhe ag caithemh a phroinne asin mbúaltrach. Tuc *dono* an buachaill sadh*udh* don leathgha asa láimh fair, gur rosgon³ a n-odhar a chighe clé antí Suibhne, gur gabh urrainn trid ar mbrisedh a droma ar dhó ann. Adb*erat*⁴ foirenn conadh benn chongna fíadha ro-innell an búachaill fáoi, áit a n-ibhedh a dhigh⁵ asan mbúalltrach, co tǽth-somh furri, conadh amhlaidh fuair bás.

79 As annsin robhaoi Énna mac B*rac*áin¹ ag búain chluig na prímhi i ndorus na reilge² co bfac*a* an t-eacht dorinnedh³ ann ; go n-ébairt an laoidh :

80 ' Truagh sin, a mhucaidh Moling,
    dorighnis gniomh talchair¹ tinn,
    mairg domharb a los a neirt
    an rígh, an [n]áomh, an náomhgheilt.

    Bidh olc dígeann bhías duit de,
    tocht fo dheóidh gan aithrighe,
    ²biaidh th' anam ar seilbh deamhain,
    biadh do chorp inn-ethannaidh.²

    Bidh ionann ionadh ar nimh
    dhamh-sa is do-somh, a fhir,³
    gebhthar psailm ag lucht áoine
    for anmain an fhíoraoidhe.

    Robadh righ, robadh geilt glan,
    rop fher oirnighe úasal,
    ag sin a lighe, líth ngle,
    dobhris mo chroidhe a thrúaighe.'   Trúagh.

78—3 rosguinn   4 atberat K   5 *sic* K ; dhi B
79—1 Breacain K   2 reilicce K   3 *sic* K ; te*cht* mo*r* (?) bo*cht* do-
dorinnedh B

madman. The madman's side was towards him as he was lying down eating his meal out of the cowdung. The herd made a thrust of the spear out of his hand at Suibhne and wounded him in the nipple of his left breast, so that the point went through him, breaking his back in two. (Some say that it is the point of a deer's horn the herd had placed under him in the spot where he used to take his drink out of the cowdung, that he fell on it and so met his death.)

79 Enna Mac Bracain was then sounding the bell for prime at the door of the churchyard and he saw the deed that was done there ; whereupon he uttered the lay :

80 ' Sad is that, O swineherd of Moling,
    thou hast wrought a wilful, sorry deed,
    woe to him who has slain by dint of his strength
    the king, the saint, the saintly madman.

    Evil to thee will be the outcome therefrom—
    going at last without repentance—
    thy soul will be in the devil's keeping,
    thy body will be . . .

    In Heaven the same will be the place
    for me and for him, O man,
    psalms will be sung by fasting folk
    for the soul of the true guest.

    He was a king, he was a madman,
    a man illustrious, noble, was he ;
    there is his grave—bright festival—
    pity for him has rent my heart.'

80—1 *sic* K ; tulchair B   2–2 *sic* K ; *om.* B, the MS. has ethanntan⤸ but this would be a syllable too long, ? *leg.* ethannaidh or etarnaigh.   3 *sic* K ; ar nimh B

81 Ro-iompo Énna anonn go ro-innis do Mholing Suibhne do mharbadh do Mhongán mucaidhe Moling. Ro-eirigh Moling fo chétóir¹ cona c[h]leirchibh imalle fris co hairm ina raibhe Suibhne 7 ro-adaimh Suibhne a choire 7 a choibhsena² do Mholing 7 rothóchaith corp Crist 7 rofailtigh fri Día a airittin 7 rohongadh iarum lasna cléirchibh.³

82 Tainic an búachaill dia ṡaigid. 'As dúairc an gniomh dorighnis, a bhúachaill,' ar Suibhne, '.i. mo mharbadh-sa gan chionaidh, úair ní fhédaim-si festa teichedh fon ffál dobhithin na gona doradais form.' 'Da ffeasainn-si co mbadh tú nobheth ann,' ar an búachaill, 'nitgonfuinn itir gidh mor dom aimhles doghénta.'¹ 'Dar Criosd, a dhuine,' ar sé, 'ni dhernus-sa th' aimhlessa ²ar áonchor ar bioth² amail ṡaoile ina aimhles duine eile ar druim dhomhain o dochuir Día ar gealtacht mé 7 robadh beg a dhioghbhail duit-si mo bheth a ffal annso 7 bainne beg d' faghail ar Dia dhamh³ on mnaoi ucchat, et ni thiubhrainn taobh frit mnáoi-si ina fri mnáoi n-oile ar talmhain gona thoirthaibh.' [94 b] 'Mallacht Crist ort, a bhúachaill,' ar Moling, 'as olc an gniomh dorighnis, goirde ṡaogail duit abhus 7 ifrenn thall ar dhenamh an gniomha dorónais.'⁴ 'Ni bfuil bá do ṡodhain damh-sa,' ar Suibhne, ' uair tangadar bur ccealga im thimchell 7 bidh im marb-sa don guin doradadh form.' 'Ragaidh éric duit ann,' ar Moling, ' i. comhaitte⁵ frium-sa for nimh dhuit,' 7 roráidhset⁶ an laoidh-si eatura ina ttriur .i. Suibhne, Mongán 7 Moling :

83 [Suibhne :] ' Dorignis gniom, nach súairc sin,
a bhúachaill Moling Lúochair,
nocha nfédoim dul fon fhál
don ghuin romgon do dhubhlámh.

81—1 fochethair B ; focetoir K   2 chomheiccnꝰ K   3 é add. B
82—1 sic K ; dodhénta B   2–2 om. K   3 om. K   4 dorighnis K
5 comfhaide K   6 doraidhset K

81 Enna turned back and told Moling that Suibhne had been slain by his swineherd Mongan. Moling at once set out accompanied by his clerics to the place where Suibhne was, and Suibhne acknowledged his faults and (made) his confession to Moling and he partook of Christ's body and thanked God for having received it, and he was anointed afterwards by the clerics.

82 The herd came up to him. 'Dour is the deed you have done, O herd,' said Suibhne, 'even to slay me, guiltless, for henceforth I cannot escape through the hedge because of the wound you have dealt me.' 'If I had known that it was you were there,' said the herd, 'I would not have wounded you however much you may have injured me.' 'By Christ, man!' said he, 'I have done you no injury whatever as you think, nor injury to anyone else on the ridge of the world since God sent me to madness, and of small account should be the harm to you through my being in the hedge here and getting a little milk for God's sake from yonder woman. And I would not trust myself with your wife nor with any other woman for the earth and its fruits.' 'Christ's curse on you, O herd!' said Moling. 'Evil is the deed you have done, short be your span of life here and hell beyond, because of the deed you have done.' 'There is no good to me therefrom,' said Suibhne, 'for your wiles have compassed me and I shall be dead from the wound that has been dealt me.' 'You will get an *eric* for it,' said Moling, 'even that you be in Heaven as long as I shall be'; and the three uttered this lay between them, that is, Suibhne, Mongan, and Moling:

83 Suibhne: 'Not pleasant is the deed thou hast done,
　　　　　O herd of Moling Luachair,
　　　　　I cannot go through the hedge
　　　　　for the wound thy black hand has dealt me.

[Mongan :] Abair frium mád cluine, a fhir,
cuich thú, a duine, go deimhin?

[Suibhne :] As mé Suibhne Geilt gan oil,
a buac[h]aill Moling Lúachair.

[Mongan :] Da bfessain, a Suibhne ṡeing,
a dhuine, dia nadaithninn[1]
nocha ttiubrainn gái red[2] chnes
ge atchifinn thú dom aimhleas.[3]

[Suibhne :] Nocha dernus thiar na thoir
aimhleas duine ar druim dhomhain
o domrad Crist om thír theinn
ar gealtacht ar fhud Eirinn.

[Mongan :] Ro-innis, nocha beug dhamh,
inghean mh'athar 'smo mháthar
th' fághbháil isin fhál sin thoir
ag mo mhnáoi fein ar madain.

[Suibhne :] Nír chóir dhuit a chreidemh sin
co bfionnta fein a dheimhin,
mairg tainig dom ghuin-si a le
nogo bhfaictís do súile.

Ge nobheinn a fál i ffál,
robadh beag dhuit a dhioghbhal
ge dobhéradh ben damh digh
do bainne bhiucc a n-almsoin.

[Mongan :] Da ffesainn-si 'na bhfuil de,
do ghuin tréd chích, tret chroidhe,
go bráth nitgonfadh mo láimh,
a Ṡuibhne Ghleanna Bolcáin.

83—1 notaithninn K   2 tred K   3 tu ag deanam m'aimhleas K

Mongan :   Speak to me if thou hearest,
           who art thou in truth, man ?
Suibhne : Suibhne Geilt without reproach am I,
           O herd of Moling Luachair.

Mongan :   If I but knew, O slender Suibhne,
           O man, if I could have recognised thee,
           I would not have thrust a spear against thy
               skin
           though I had seen thee harm me.

Suibhne : East or west I have not done
           harm to one on the world's ridge
           since Christ has brought me from my valiant
               land
           in madness throughout Erin.

Mongan :   The daughter of my father and my mother
           related—'twas no trifle to me—
           how she found thee in yonder hedge
           with my own wife at morn.

Suibhne : It was not right of thee to credit that
           until thou hadst learnt its certainty,
           alas that thou shouldst come hither to slay me
           until thine eyes had seen !

           Though I should be from hedge to hedge,
           its harm were a trifle to thee,
           though a woman should give me to drink
           a little milk as alms.

Mongan: If I but knew what comes of it,
           from wounding thee through breast and heart,
           till Doom my hand would not wound thee,
           O Suibhne of Glen Bolcain.

[Suibhne :]   Ge romgonais isin fhál
nocha ndernus do thochrádh,
ni thiubhrainn taobh rét mhnáoi ndil
ar talm*ain* gona thorthaibh.

Mairg tainic at[h]aidh o t[h]oigh
chuccatt, a Mholing Lúachair,
nocha leicc dhamh dol fon choill
an guin romgon do bhúachoill.

[Moling :]   Mallacht Crist docum gach cloinn
ort, ar Moling re a bhúachoil,
tre ed[4] i ccridhe do chnis,
as trúagh an gniomh dorighnis.

O dorighnis gniomh n-úathmar,
atbert Moling re a bhúachuil,
raghaidh dhuit-si dar a chenn
goirde saoghail is ifreann.

[Suibhne :]   Ge dognéi-si dioghal[5] dhe
a Mholing, ni beó meisi,
nochan fhuil mo chabair ann,
tainig bar ccealg im t[h]imcheall.

[Moling :]   Raghaidh éruic dhuit-si ind,
ar Moling Lúachra, lúaidhim,
comhaitte[6] friom-sa for nimh
dhuit-si, a Suibhne, on Ardchoimdidh. [95a]

[Mongan :]   Bidh maith dhuit-si, a Suibhne seing,
thusa ar nemh, ar an búacheill,
ni hionann as meisi sunn,
gan nemh, gan soeghal agum.

83—4 éd K   5 dioghbhail K   6 comaitte K

Suibhne: Though thou hast wounded me in the hedge,
I have not done thee ill ;
I would not trust in thine own wife
for the earth and its fruits.

Alas for him who has come for a while from
    home
to thee, O Moling Luachair,
the wound thy herd has dealt me
stays me from wandering through the woods.

Moling: The curse of Christ who hath created everyone
on thee, said Moling to his herd,
sorry is the deed thou hast done
through envy in thine heart.

Since thou hast done a dread deed,
said Moling to his herd,
thou wilt get in return for it
a short span of life and hell.

Suibhne: Though thou mayest avenge it,
O Moling, I shall be no more ;
no relief for me is it,
your treachery has compassed me.

Moling: Thou shalt get an *eric* for it,
said Moling Luachair, I avow ;
thou shalt be in Heaven as long as I shall be
by the will of the great Lord, O Suibhne.

Mongan : It will be well with thee, O slender Suibhne,
thou in Heaven, said the herd,
not so with me here,
without Heaven, without my life's span.

[Suibhne:] Ba binne lium robháoi tan
           na comhradh ciúin na muintear,
           bheith icc luthmhairecht im linn
           cuchairecht fhéráinn[7]-eidhinn.

           Ba binne lium robháoi tan
           na gut[h] cluigín im fharradh,
           ceileabhradh an luin don bheinn
           is dordán doimh ar doininn.

           Ba binne lium robháoi[8] tan
           na guth mná aille im fharradh,
           guth circe fráoich an tsléibhe
           do cluinsin im iarmhéirghe.

           Ba binne lium robháoi tan
           donálach na gcon alla,
           ina guth cléirigh astoigh
           ag meiligh is ag meigeallaigh.

           Gidh maith libh-si i ttighibh óil
           bhar ccuirm leanna go n-onóir,
           ferr lium-sa deogh d'uisge i ngoid
           d'ol dom bais asin tiopraid.

           Gidh binn libh thall in bhar ccill
           comhradh mín bar mac leighinn,
           binne lium[8a] ceileabhradh án
           doghníad coin Ghlinne Bolcáin.

           Gidh maith libh-si an tsaill 's an fheóil
           caithter a ttighibh comhóil,
           ferr lium-sa gas biorair ghloin
           d' ithe i n-ionadh gan chumaidh.

83—⁊ ferain K   8 robhi K   8ᵃ an *add.* B

Suibhne : There was a time when I deemed more melodious
than the quiet converse of people,
the cooing of the turtle-dove
flitting about a pool.

There was a time when I deemed more melodious
than the sound of a little bell beside me
the warbling of the blackbird to the mountain
and the belling of the stag in a storm.

There was a time when I deemed more melodious
than the voice of a beautiful woman beside me,
to hear at dawn
the cry of the mountain-grouse.

There was a time when I deemed more melodious
the yelping of the wolves
than the voice of a cleric within
a-baaing and a-bleating.

Though goodly you deem in taverns
your ale-feasts with honour,
I had liefer drink a quaff of water in theft
from the palm of my hand out of a well.

Though yonder in your church you deem melodious
the soft converse of your students,
more melodious to me is the splendid chant
of the hounds of Glen Bolcain.

Though goodly ye deem the salt meat and the fresh
that are eaten in banqueting-houses,
I had liefer eat a tuft of fresh watercress
in some place without sorrow.

Romgon an c*ru*adhmhucaidhe corr[9]
go ndeachaidh trem[10] chorp comhtrom,
truag, a Christ rolamh gach breth,
nach ar Mhagh Rath rommarbhadh.

Gidh maith gach leaba gan fheall
dorighnes seachnóin Eirenn,
ferr lem leabaidh ós an loch
i mBeinn Bhoirche gan fholoch.

Gidh maith gach leaba gan fheall
dorighnes sechnoin Eireand,
ferr [lem] leabaidh os an ross
i nGlenn Bolcáin doronoss.

Beirim a bhuidhe friot sin
do chorp, a Christ, do chaithimh,
aithrighe iodhan abhus
in gach olc riamh doronus.'   Do.

84 Tainic iaromh taimhnell do Suibhne 7 ro-eirigh Moling
gona c[h]leirchibh mar áon fris 7 tugsat cloch gach fir i leachtt
Suibhne. 'Ionmhain eimh an fer isa leacht so,' ar Moling,
'meinic bámar inar ndís slán síst ag comhradh fri aroile
seachnóin na conaire so. Rob aobhinn lem faicsin Suibhne
.i. antí isa leachtt so ar an tioprait ud thall .i. Tiupra[1] na Gealta
a hainm, úair is meinic notoimhledh ní dia biorar 7 día huisci
7 úadha[2] ainminighter an tioprat. Ionmhuin bheós gach ionadh
eile no-iomaithighedh antí Suibhne'; conadh ann adbert
Moling:

The herd's sharp spear has wounded me,
so that it has passed clean through my body;
alas, O Christ, who hast launched every judgment,
that I was not slain at Magh Rath!

Though goodly each bed without guile
I have made throughout Erin,
I had liefer a couch above the lake
in Benn Boirche, without concealment.

Though goodly each bed without guile
I have made throughout Erin,
I had liefer the couch above the wood
I have made in Glen Bolcain.

To Thee, O Christ, I give thanks
for partaking of Thy Body;
sincere repentance in this world
for each evil I have ever done.'

84 A death-swoon came on Suibhne then, and Moling, attended by his clerics, rose, and each man placed a stone on Suibhne's tomb. 'Dear in sooth is he whose tomb this is,' said Moling; 'often were we two—happy time!—conversing one with the other along this pathway. Delightful to me was it to behold Suibhne—he whose tomb this is—at yonder well. The Madman's Well is its name, for often would he eat of its watercress and drink its water, and (so) the well is named after him. Dear, too, every other place that Suibhne used to frequent'; whereupon Moling said:

85 ' Leachtán Suibhne sunn imne,
rocráidh mo chroidhe a chuimhne,
ionmuin lium bhós[1] ar a ṡeirc
gach airm i mbiodh an náoimhgheilt.

Ionmuin lium Glenn mBolcáin mbán
ar a ṡerc ag Suibhne slán,
ionmuin gach sruth do-icc ass,
ionmhuin [a] bhior[ar] barrghlass.   [95b].

Tiubra na Gealta[2] súd thall,
ionmuin cách dar bíadh a barr,
ionmuin lium a gainemh glan,
ionmuin a huisge iodhan.

Orm-sa doghnídh a haicill,
fada lium go nosfaicinn,
rothiomghair[3] a breith dom thigh,
ba hionmhuin an eadarnaigh.[4]

Ionmhuin gach sruth go bhfúaire
fors' mbíodh[5] biorar barrúaine,
is[6] gach tobar uisge ghil,
ar Suibhne ag a aithighidh.

Masa chead le[7] Righ na reann
eirigh agus imthigh leam,
tucc dhamh, a c[h]ridhe,[8] do lámh
on lighe agus on leachtán.

Ba binn lium comhrádh Suibhne,
cían bhérus im chlí a chuimhne :
aitchim mo Righ nimhe nár
os a lighe is ar a leachtán.'   Leachtan.

<del>___</del>

85—1 bheos K   2 Tioprat na gealta K ; Tiubra na nGealt B
3 rotromghair K   4 etharnaigh K   5 forsa imbíodh B ; forsmbi an K
6 in K 7 re K   8 chridhe K

85 ' The tomb of Suibhne here !
remembrance of him has wrung my heart !
dear to me too, out of love for him,
each place in which the holy madman used to be.

Dear to me is fair Glen Bolcain
because of perfect Suibhne's love of it ;
dear each stream that flows out of it,
dear its green-topped watercress.

Yonder is the Well of the Madman,
dear was he to whom it gave food,
dear to me its clear sand,
dear its pure water.

On me was imposed his preparation,
it seemed long until I should see him,
he asked that he be taken to my house,
dear was the lying in wait.

Dear each cool stream
wherein the green-topped watercress grew,
each well of bright water too,
because Suibhne used to visit it.

If it be the will of the King of the stars,
arise and come with me,
give me, O heart, thy hand
from the grave and from the tomb !

Melodious to me was the converse of Suibhne,
long shall I keep his memory in my breast :
I entreat my noble King of Heaven
above his grave and on his tomb ! '

86 Ro eirigh Suibhne asa niull iarsin 7 roghabh Moling ar laim é, go rangadar rempa ina ndís co dorus na heglaisi 7 o dorad Suibhne a ghúala risin ursoinn tug a osnadh mór ós aird co rofháoidh a spiorad doc[h]um nimhe 7 rohadhnacht[1] go n-onóir ag Moling é.

87 Gonadh ní do sgélaibh 7 do imthechtuibh Suibhne mic Colmáin Chuair rígh Dhál Aruidhe gonuige sin.   Finis.

86—1 rothadhnacht

86 Thereafter, Suibhne rose out of his swoon and Moling taking him by the hand the two proceeded to the door of the church. When Suibhne placed his shoulders against the door-post he breathed a loud sigh and his spirit fled to Heaven, and he was buried honourably by Moling.

87 So far, some of the tales and adventures of Suibhne son of Colman Cuar, king of Dal Araidhe. *Finis.*

NOTES

§ 1, p. 3. **Rónán Finn.** St. Rónán, son of Bearach, &c., was abbot of Druim Ineascluinn (Drumiskin) in Co. Louth. His death from the plague known as *buidhe conaill* is recorded in the Ann. Four Mast. at the year 664. He is mentioned in the Félire of Aengus at 18 November, where (in the notes) his pedigree is given. A Rónán Finn (son of Saran, son of Colchu, &c.) is mentioned in the Félire of Aengus at 22 May ; he was of Lann Rónáin Finn in Húi Echach of Ulster. It is possible that the two saints are confused in our tale, just as they are in the Martyrology of Donegal. Lann Rónáin Finn was in Magh Rath ; see Hogan's *Onomasticon*.

§ 3, p. 3. **Cell Lainne (Luinne)** ; in Dal Araidhe. I have not succeeded in identifying this place. There are two townlands named Killaney in Co. Down. One of these is in the parish of Killaney, a little to the N. of Lough Henney, and about three miles W. of Saintfield ; it contained an ancient church, see Reeves, *Eccl. Antiq.*, p. 217. The other is in the parish of Garvaghy to the S. of Dromore. It is possible that Cell Lainne may be identical with Lann Rónáin Finn ; see foregoing note.

§ 5, p. 5. **an Otter . . . came to Rónán with the psalter.** A similar miracle is recorded in the Irish Lives of St. Kevin; see Plummer's *Vitae Sanctorum Hiberniae*, Vol. I, p. cxliv, note 5.

§ 5, p. 5. **may it be thus that he will ever be.** Curses of this kind as a result of which the offending person (with his descendants) is always to remain in the state in which he is when cursed are common ; see Plummer's *Vitae Sanctorum Hiberniae*, p. clxxvii. I am indebted to Mr. Plummer for a reference to a very curious case of children cursed always remaining the size of children ; *Le Grand Vie des Saints de la Bretagne Armorigue*, ed. 1835, p. 315 b.

§ 5, p. 5. **death from a spear-point** ; i.e. a violent death as opposed to *éc fri adart* (Plummer) ; cf. *bás re hadart*, Acall. na Senórach, ed. Stokes, 3590.

§ 6, p 6. The metre of this poem is *debide*.[1]

§ 6, p. 8. **is nir mhisdi an breac-bán ;** or should we read *breac bán*, 'white trout,' i.e. the psalter which the otter rescued ? I think it more likely that it means 'the speckled-white (i.e. variegated, ornamented) book '; cf. such titles as Lebor Brec, Lebor na hUidhre, &c.

---

1 For a description of Irish metres see Professor Kuno Meyer's *Primer of Irish Metrics*, Dublin, School of Irish Learning, 1909.

§ 8, p. 11. **likewise the tunic which Congal had given him** ; cf. *Banquet of Dun na nGedh*, p. 39 : ' And they [the saints of Ireland] also cursed Suibhne, the son of Colmán Cuar, son of Cobthach, king of Dál Araidhe, for it was he that had carried away from them by force the many-coloured tunic which Domhnall had given into the hand of St. Rónán Finn, the son of Berach, to be presented to Congal ; but as Congal had refused to accept of the King's tunic, Suibhne took it from the cleric's hand in despite of him.' See also *Battle of Magh Rath*, ed. O'Donovan, p. 235.

§ 9, p. 11. **the bell which was on his breast.** The ancient Irish bell was a small hand-bell ; how small may be inferred from this passage. A great deal of interesting lore about ancient Irish bells is given by Mr. Plummer in the Introduction to his *Vitae Sanctorum Hiberniae.*

§ 9, p. 11. **Uradhran (Furadhran) and Telle.** A Furudrán is mentioned in the Félire of Aengus at 18 June ; son of Moenán of Land Luachar in Bregia. A Telle is mentioned there also, at 25 June ; of Tech Telli near Durrow in Westmeath.

§ 10, p. 12. The metre of this poem is *rindaird*.

§ 11, p. 14. With the description of Suibhne's madness given here cf. *Battle of Magh Rath*, pp. 230-235.

§ 12, p. 15. **Ros Bearaigh in Glenn Earcáin (Arcáin).** I have not been able to identify this place. Hogan (*Onomasticon*) has ' Glenn Archain in Scotland.' It may be that the Gl. Earcáin of our text was situated in the vicinity of Ros Ercain, with which place Suibhne is associated, see p. 31, l. 3. O'Donovan (Four Mast.) identifies Ros Ercain as Rasharkin, a townland and parish in Co. Antrim, about 8 miles S. of Ballymoney ; cf. also Reeves, Eccl. Ant., p. 340.

§ 14, p. 16. The metre of this poem is *debide*.

§ 15, p. 17. **Cell Riagain in Tir Conaill** : Kilrean in p. of Killybegs Lr., Co. Donegal. Whatever we may think of Suibhne, it is scarcely likely that Domnall and his army went so far afield after the battle.

§ 16, p. 18. The metre of this poem is *debide*.

§ 16, p. 20. **Targús-sa do Chongal Chlaon.** With this and the following stanzas cf. *Battle of Magh Rath* :—

(p. 130)
' Targasa do Congal Claen
in tan ro bi ag Dun na naem,
bennacht fear n-Erend uile,
ba momor in t-íc aen uige.

(p. 136)
La na gabai uaim-si sin
a mic Scannlain Sciath-lethain
ca breth beire, mor in modh,
orm-sa, masead, at aenor ?

Gebasa uait, mad maith lat ;
tabair dam-sa, do dag mac,
do lam dít, is do bean maith,
t'ingean is do rosc ro-glas.

Nocha beri acht rind re rind ;
bid me do teine timcill,
not gonfa in gai dreman dubh ;
nocho dlig deman dilgud.

Atai a t'aenar seach cach rig
'gom aimleas o thir do tir,
rod leasaigius tairis sin,
o'n lo rod n-uc do mathair.'

' I offered to Congal Claen,
when he was at Dun na naemh,
the blessing of the men of Erin all,
it was a great mulct for one egg.

When thou wouldst not accept these from me,
O son of Broadshielded Scannlan,
what sentence dost thou pass—it is of great moment—
on me from thyself alone, if so be thou wilt not accept my offers ?

These will I accept from thee if thou wilt ;
give me thy good son,
thy hand from off thee, and thy good wife,
thy daughter and thy very blue eye.

I will not give thee but spear for spear ;
I will be thy surrounding fire ;
the terrific black javelin shall wound thee :
a demon is entitled to no forgiveness.

Thou art singular beyond every king,
planning my misfortune from country to country,
notwithstanding that I reared thee
from the day thy mother bore thee.'

§ 16, p. 21. **great was the mulct for one egg**. See the first stanza in the preceding note ; according to the account given in the *Banquet of Dun na nGedh*, one of Congal's grievances was that, on the occasion of a banquet given by Domnall, son of Aedh, whereas a goose-egg was placed on a silver dish before every king at the board except Congal, a hen-egg on a wooden dish was given him. This incident is given at tedious length in the *Banquet of Dun na nGedh*, see pp. 15-39; see also *Battle of Magh Rath*, pp. 111, 129-131.

§ 16, p. 21. **yet I have befriended thee.** Congal was given in fosterage to Domnall; see *Banquet of Dun na nGedh*, p. 35.

§ 17, p. 23. **Glenn Bolcáin.** This place, which I cannot identify, figures prominently in our story. Hogan, *Onomasticon*, quoting H. 4. 21, fo. 47a, has: 'Tanaic Conall go hAth Muilt, alias Athfhirdiadh 7 a nGleann Mór, alias Gleann mBolcan,' and adds 'near Ardee.' Under Glenn Mór, quoting the same authority, he has 'alias G. mBolcan ag Athfhirdiadh.' The only Glenn Mór that I can trace in Co. Louth or the vicinity is Glanmore in the parish of Carlingford, in the ancient district of Cuailgne. This, however, can scarcely be the place referred to in our text, for at § 31 we have 'Glen Bolcain, which is called Glen Chiach to-day, in the plain of Cinel Ainmirech.' Hogan (*Onomasticon*) has Cenél Ainmire 'in Armagh or adjoining regions.' It seems to me, however, that it is more likely to be in N. Antrim; see Reeves, *Eccl. Antiq.*, p. 324. Reeves, *ib.* p. 90, states that there is a ridge called Dunbolcain (or Drumbolcain) about a furlong N. of Rasharkin. He adds that the place derives its name from St. Olcan, 'who is called Bolcan by some writers and in vulgar parlance.' We should possibly look to the same district for Glen Bolcáin: cf. p. 31, l. 3, 'Suibhne of Ros Earcain (Rasharkin) is my name.'

The only other reference that I can find to Glen Bolcáin is in the *Battle of Ventry*, ed. K. Meyer, p. 18. The king of France, literally flying before Oscar, 'went with the wind, and with madness before the eyes of the hosts of the world, and did not stop in his mad flight till he came to Glen Bolcain in the east of that territory.' It is not clear what territory is intended, though it seems likely that it was in Kerry. Perhaps we have here some confusion between Gleann na nGealt in Kerry and Glenn Bolcáin. There is a Glenn Bolg; see Táin, ed. Windisch, p. 457.

§ 19, p. 24. The metre of this poem is *lethrannaigecht mór*.

§ 21, p. 28. The metre of this poem is *rannaigecht bec*. (In the ninth stanza the words *laa*, *noa*, and *cua* are disyllables.)

§ 19, p. 28. **lía ar mairbh naid ar mbí**; cf. Fled Bricrend, ed. Windisch, § 5, ni ragam ar bit lia ar mairb oldáte ar mbí.

§ 19, p. 29. **on Tuesday was the rout**; see also p. 45, l. 5. The romantic accounts of the battle agree that the conflict was decided on a Tuesday; see *Battle of Magh Rath*, p. 111, and *Ériu* v, p. 247.

§ 20, p. 29. **The erenach of the church was Faibhlen.** It will be seen that the erenach (*airchinnech*) is almost invariably referred to—and his name given—whenever Suibhne comes to a church; see, for example, pp. 51 and 83. It was the erenach who dispensed alms and hospitality, and Suibhne's business as a mendicant would be with him. An interesting late account of the office of erenach is given in a letter from Sir John Davies to Robert, Earl of Salisbury, on the state of Monaghan, Fermanagh, and Cavan, 1607.

'. . . For the herinach there are few parishes of any compass in extent
where there is not an herinach, which, being an officer of the church, took
beginning in this manner : when any lord' or gentleman had a direction to
build a church, he did first dedicate some good portion of land to some saint or
other whom he chose to be his patron ; then he founded the church, and called
it by the name of that saint, and then gave the land to some clerk not being in
orders and to his heirs forever with this intent, that he should keep the church
clean and well repaired, keep hospitality, and give alms to the poor for the
soul's health of the founder. This man and his heirs had the name of errenagh.
The errenagh was also to make a weekly commemoration of the founder of the
church. He had always *primam tonsuram*, but took no orders ; he had a voice
in the chapter, when they consulted about their revenues and paid a certain
yearly rent to the Bishop. Besides a fine upon marriage of every one of his
daughters, which they call a loughhimpy, he gave a subsidy to the Bishop at his
first entrance into his bishopric.'

§ 21, p. 30. **Nidom fois**, ' I rest not,' lit. ' I am not of rest ' ; note the use
of the gen. here ; also *chois* for *chos* in the next line, giving the necessary internal
rhyme. Note also *nidom ncirt*, p. 28, l. 26.

§ 21, p. 31. **the bonds of terror come upon me** ; or should we render, ' the
bird-flocks of terror &c.,' associating the birds with his madness, and with
Ronán's curses ? See p. 43, ' thou hast leave to go with the birds.' See also
pp. 75, 87, 133.

§ 21, p. 32. **Beg mo chuid o thig laa, ni thæt ar scath la noa.** If the text
is sound—and both MSS. agree in this reading—the phrase *ar scath la noa* is
obscure to me.

§ 21, p. 32. **An gen fil ag Ros Ercach**, ' He who is at Ros Earcach ' ; who
is meant I cannot say: perhaps we should read *An gcéin* (*gein* K), and translate
' As long as he is at R. E.'

§ 22, p. 32. **clog an esparta** ; *esparta* here g. s. ; cf. ó tráth espurta, *Ériu*, II,
p. 194, l. 10 ; see also p. 142, supra, ll. 5 and 12.

§ 22, p. 33. **Snamh dha En on the Shannon, which is now called Cluain
Boirenn.** Cluain Boirenn is Cloonburren, in the parish of Moore, Co. Roscommon,
opposite Clonmacnois. Snámh dá Én would seem accordingly to have been
applied to a territory on right bank of the Shannon opposite Clonmacnois ; cf.
Book of Armagh, 11b 1 : Venit ergo Patricius sanctus per alueum fluminis
Sinnae per Vadum Duorum Auium (*Snám Dá Én*) in Campum Ai. For a poem
on the place see *Ériu* V, p. 221.

§ 23, p. 32. The metre of this poem is *rannaigecht bec*, except the second
and third stanzas, which are *dian airseng* (see Meyer's *Primer of Irish Metrics*,
p. 21).

§ 23, p. 33. **Though my talons to-night are feeble.** I can only conjecture
the meaning of this stanza. For *ingne* of B, K has *adhbha*, ' joints ' (?) ;
cf., however, the whole of the first and second stanzas in K ; the last line, too,
should have an internal rhyme for *cille*. It is probable that the stanza is corrupt.

§ 23, p. 34. **Siodhmhuine Glinne**; perhaps not a proper name at all, but 'the peaceful brake of the glen.'

§ 24, p. 35. **Cell Derfile**; St. Dervilla's church in the W. of Erris, Co. Mayo; *v.* Hogan *Onom.*, s.v. Cell Dairbhile; now Kildervila or Termon Dervila, *vide* F.M. 1248.

§ 25, p. 34. The metre of this poem is *debide*.

§ 25, p. 36. **Muichnidhe mh' aghaidh anocht,** 'gloomy is my night to-night'; or perhaps we should render, 'gloomy is my face to-night'; similarly in the third line of the same stanza; cf., however, the opening line of the poem, § 25, p. 34.

§ 25, p. 36. **Mairg romfuirgedh risin dáil**; cf. p. 86, l. 4. The 'tryst' was probably the battle of Magh Rath.

§ 25, p. 36. **Faolchú**. According to the *Chron. Scotorum* Faolchu, son of Airmeadhach, king of Meath, fell in the battle of Magh Rath together with Congal and many other nobles. But see *Battle of Magh Rath*, p. 305, where a Faelchu, son of Congal, is mentioned.

§ 26, p. 37. **and he found the track of his feet**; lit. the track of the points of his feet '; cf. *barrchos*, ' the toes and instep.'

§ 27, p. 38. The metre of this poem is as follows: stanzas 1, 4, 5, 6, 7, 8, 10 *debide*; 2 *debide gairit*; 3, 12 *rannaigecht mór*: 9, 11 *rannaigecht gairit*. The metre of the last stanza is doubtful. The 9th stanza of this poem is not in K.

§ 27, p. 38. **mhaonar dhamh a mbarr eidhin**; cf. *barr edin*, which occurs over the words *Tuaim Inbir* (or are they meant to be the title of the poem?) in the poem attributed to Suibhne Geilt, quoted in the Introduction. See Thurneysen's *Handbuch des Alt-Irischen*, II, p. 39.

§ 27, p. 39. **The man by the wall**. The place of the serf was by the wall, that is, farthest away from the fire.

§ 27, p. 40. **mo chollan i n-eidhnechaibh**. My translation rests on the very doubtful conjecture that *collan* is intended for *colainn* 'body'; K has clearly *collan*, but in B there seems to be a faint mark of length over the *a*.

§ 27, p. 40. **imma ngairid geilte glinne**. It is possible that *geilt glinne* is meant for some bird or animal; see that curious poem, or extract from a poem—enumerating various birds and animals—in Vol. VII of the Proceedings of the R.I.A., p. 190; *Dí gheilt glinne Ghleanna Smóil*.

§ 29, p. 42. The metre of this poem is *debide*.

§ 29, p. 44. **nochar úallcha neach anu**. I take *anu* to be for *indu* (O.I. *oldáu*), ' than I am.' The context would seem to require this rather than the *aniu*, ' to-day,' of K

§ 31, p. 45. **Ettan Tairb**; cf. *Táin Bo Cúailnge*, YBL., 53 a, Dolluid do Etan Tairb, dobert a etan frisin tealaig oc Ath Da Ferta, is de ata Etan Tairb i Muig Muirthemni. This is probably Edenterriff in par. of Annagh, Co. Cavan; it must have been the western limit of the plain of Muirthemne.

§ 32, p. 46. The metre of this poem is *debide*.

NOTES 167

§ 32, p. 46. **te duit ar chluimh cholcaidh cain**; apparently the feathers (*clúmh*) were put into the *colcaid*; see p. 58 *ar chluimh 7 ar cholcaidh*.

§ 32, p. 46. **ní íarr sibh bhar senchara**, 'you seek not your old friend,' or rather, 'ye seek not yeer old friend,' as it would be expressed in some Anglo-Irish dialects.

§ 34, p. 50. The metre of this poem is *debide*.

§ 35, p. 51. **For he had three dwellings in his own country . . . viz. Teach Mic Ninnedha, Cluain Creamha, and Ros Earcain.** All three would therefore appear to have been in the territory of Dal Araidhe. As to Ros Earcain (Rasharkin, Co. Antrim), see notes to § 12 and § 17. I have not succeeded in identifying the other two places. Hogan (Onomasticon) gives references to a number of places bearing the name Cluain Crema, but none to the C. Crema of our tale.

§ 35, p. 52. **Domgaibh dom formadh on.** The meaning of this curious phrase seems to be that the news of his father's death struck him with horror. O'R. has *formadh*, 'fear, apprehension,' and in this sense it is perhaps intended here.

§ 35, p. 52. **as é sin an banna dobheir an fer co lar**; cf. the metrical version on p. 56 (fifth stanza) : *as e sin an banna . . . dobheir an fer co talmain*. For *banna (banne)*, 'a drop,' 'a tear,' see Meyer's Contributions. I have not met the phrase elsewhere : the meaning seems to be that the blow (his son's death) is a 'last straw.'

§ 36, p. 52. The metre of this poem is *debide*. The latter half of the 4th stanza is not in K.

§ 36, p. 54. **Tigedhus do bheith gan mnaoi.** With this line and the following one cf. *Vision of Mac Conglinne*, p. 73, ll. 17 and 20. The remainder of the stanza presents many difficulties. B has *cad* ∾ i.e. *cadach*, while K has *cad* ◡. In the absence of a word rhyming with *adúdh* in the next line—which does not appear to be absolutely essential—I have chosen to read *cadach*, 'tartan, a kind of cloth, a coat of spotted tartan, formerly steel, mail, greaves, defensive armour'; W., cadach, 'a rag, a clout,' Dictionary of Highland Society. Cf. Fer beg truag irrusc olla nobid dogres dia chadud ar a thruaigi, Anecdota from Irish MSS., I, p. 7. I take *adudh* (= *adúdh*) to be inf. of *adóim*, 'I kindle.' For *henoires* read *aenaires* of K, 'one fire'; *aires* 'a firebrand.'

§ 36, p. 54. **As dorn im dhíaidh**, cf. O'Dav, 1586, Tor .i. imat, ut est, is dorn im diaid tor mbriathar ; tor, i.e. 'plenty,' ut est, a fist around smoke is a multitude of words (RC. XXVII, p. 88); cf. also *King and Hermit*, p. 29, na seóid dochí as dorn im ceo, the wealth thou seest is like a hand round mist.

§ 36, p. 55. **There is another calamity there**, &c. The inference seems to be that if he had not been a prince but some serf, scarred and in rags—as Suibhne was—the loss would not be mourned.

§ 36, p. 56. **Seinbhriathar so, serb an snomh, &c.** See the variant readings as given in the footnotes ; the stanza is possibly defective. The alteration of *snomh* to *sniomh* is not altogether convincing. P. O'C. has snomh .i. soiniamh, *new, fresh, blooming, freshness,* &c. Cf. Tibigh grian da gach tir | dedl lim fri sil snom, *no* son, C III 2 (R. I. A.), fo. 10ᵃ. (This is given in Four Old Irish Songs, ed. Meyer, p. 26 : Tibid grían dar gach tír | dedlaid lim fri sil snon.) Cf. *snob,* SG. 64a10. The meaning would seem to be that the point of the proverb was bitter. The whole of the stanza, however, is vague.

§ 36, p. 56. **nochan fuilinghim thúas don beirt,** lit. ' I cannot endure to be up from the deed.' With *thuas* here, cf. the use of *suas* in a number of examples given by Mr. T. O'Rahilly in *Gadelica* I, p. 65.

§ 36, p. 57. **all thy folk are alive**; see also § 37, p. 59 : the dramatic account given by Loingseachan of the death of Suibhne's father, mother, &c. (pp. 53–57), was evidently a ruse, intended to move Suibhne to such an extent that he might recover his senses.

§ 36, p. 57. **Eochu Salbuidhe.** He was one of the early kings of Emania ; see Rawl. B. 502, p. 157, l. 3.

§ 37, p. 61. **The mill-hag was enjoined not to speak to him,** that is, lest he should talk about his madness and, by dwelling on it, lapse back into his old life.

§ 38, p. 60. The metre of this poem is *debide.*

§ 39, p. 63. **Oilill Cédach, king of the Ui Faeláin.** An Ailill appears in the Hui Faelain genealogies in Rawl. B 502, 117d, as son of Dunlaing and fifth in descent from Catháir Mór ; but he appears to have been slain in 495. In the Book of Rights (p. 200) Ailill Cédach is called son of Cathair. Neither record fits in with our tale. See *Battle of Magh Rath,* p. 245, ' By Suibhne the populous in strife Ailill Cedach was slain.'

§ 40, p. 62. The metre of this poem is *cró cummaisc etir casbairdne agus lethrannaigecht,* except the last stanza, the metre of which is doubtful.

The stanzas not found in K are : 22, 30, 31, 43, 46, 48, 61.

§ 40, p. 65. **Thou oak, bushy, leafy,** &c. With this stanza and the ten stanzas that follow cf. the poem at p. 245 of *Silva Gadelica* I (translation at p. 278, Vol. II), which contains some curious lore concerning trees.

§ 40, p. 68. **Rob é guth gach aenduine** ; cf. *Battle of Magh Rath,* p. 234.

Ba h-e guth cach aen duine
do'n t-sluag détla daith,
na teit uaibh fa'n cael-muine,
fear in inair maith.

It was the saying of every one
of the valiant, beauteous host,
permit not to go from you to the dense shrubbery
the man of the goodly tunic.

§ 40, p. 68. **Ag dula dar eidhneachuibh**; with this stanza cf. *Battle of Magh Rath*, p. 236.

> Rop é sin mo céd rith-sa,
> ro pa luath an rith,
> d'eag urchar na gothnaidhe
> dam-sa res in cith.

> This was my first run—
> rapid was the flight—
> the shot of the javelin expired
> for me with the shower.

§ 40, p. 72. **Do mhuilenn an mheanmaráin domheilte do thúaith.** My rendering of this half-stanza is most doubtful ; as to *meanmarán*, see the gl. ; *domheilte* (the aspiration is curious), judging from the context, seems to be *melim*, 'I grind.' The stanza is not in K.

§ 40, p. 72. **demhan agat th' aidmilliudh,** 'a demon is ruining thee' ; here, as in many instances of the use of the word, *admilliud* seems to be used of persons 'bewitched,' 'possessed,' or under the influence of the evil eye ; cf. *Roboi admilliud furri i tossaig*, said of Mór of Munster ; see Proceed. of R.I.A., xxx., 1912 ; see also Cormac's Glossary, s.v. *milled*, i.e. *mí shilledh*, 'a mislook,' i.e. an evil eyeing, O'Cl. *droch amharc*. See also B. Da Derga 62, 71 ; Cóir Anm. § 54 ; Ac. Senórach (Stokes) 1638, 6355.

§ 40, p. 78. **damh dá fhiched benn,** 'the stag of twice twenty peaks' ; or better, perhaps, 'twice twenty antler-points,' as in the last stanza on the same page. Note the constant use of *benn* in most of the stanzas that follow ; there is evidently a play intended on the word. I find it difficult to grasp the significance of many of the stanzas between p. 74 and p. 80 ; no doubt some curious folk-lore is embedded in them.

§ 40, p. 81. **at puissant Toidiu in the south.** In the Latin and Irish Lives of St. Moling Tóidiu (also Táiden) is mentioned as the watercourse which the saint made to his monastery. 'In digging the Táiden great tribulation had he from devils and packs of wolves and evil men crossing him ' ; Félire of Aengus, June 17 (notes). For an account of the work see the Latin Life of St. Moling in Plummer's *Vitae Sanctorum Hiberniae*, II, p. 193. There are frequent references to it in the Moling poems in *Anecdota from Irish MSS.*, II, p. 20. The Tóidiu is said to have possessed many virtues for those who went into it or who drank of it ; see *Birth and Life of Moling*, ed. Stokes, p. 55.

§ 40, p. 81. **pleasant is the place for seats on the top of thy antler-points.** A stock miracle in Irish hagiology is that of making a living stag's antlers serve as a bookstand ; see *Lismore Lives*, pp. 268, 274, and 357. As to stags being yoked to draw loads see also *Lismore Lives*, p. 223 ; for other instances see Plummer's *Vitae Sanctorum Hiberniae*, vol. I, p. cxliii.

§ 43, p. 84. The metre of this poem is as follows : *ae freslige*, stanzas 5, 6, 7, 8, 9, 17 ; *ae freslige*, but with the third line ending in a monosyllable, 2, 3, 4 ; *rannaigecht bec*, stanzas 11, 12, 13, 14, 15, 16, 18, 19, 20, 21, 22, 23. The metre of stanzas 1 and 10 is doubtful.

Stanzas 5, 6, 7, 12, 14, 15, 17, 19 are not in K.

§ 43, p. 84. **seach ni fhagaidh cuibhdhe neich, &c.** It is difficult to translate *cuibhdhe* here ; the usual meaning is ' harmony,' ' concord ' ; in this half-stanza it seems to mean ' companionship.'

§ 43, p. 86. **Diamsat eolach, a fionnghág.** This stanza (which is not in K) is obscure to me as it stands.

§ 43, p. 88. **At uara dotachuisin,** ' it is cold they are,' lit. ' they are cold which exist.' For *docuisin* see Glossary to the Laws ; also Wb. 17b10, 21a3, Ml. 108d14.

§ 43, p. 90. **Creach na nGall ngorm dot gabháil,** ' may a raid of the blue(-coated) Norsemen take thee.' Or should we render ' swarthy Norsemen '? Cf. Tugas di gallcochal gorm, ' I gave her a blue Norse hood '; Bergin in Miscellany to Kuno Meyer ; Halle, 1912, p. 364, l. 10.

§ 44, p. 91. **Donnán of Eig.** He was an Irishman and a disciple of St. Columba ; he founded a monastery in the island of Eig. He and his community of fifty-one persons were put to death by a band of pirates in 617 ; see Reeves, *Adamnan*, pp. 223 and 303–309. His martyrdom is mentioned in the Félire of Aengus at 17 April.

§ 45, p. 90. The metre of this poem is *blogbairdne* (see Meyer's *Primer of Irish Metrics*, p. 16).

Stanzas 2 (latter half), 9, 10, 12, 14, 17, 20, 22, 24, 26, 27, 30, 31, 32 are not in K.

§ 45, p. 92. **mbláthmBoirne** ; as the rhyme here is faulty (gargOighle), perhaps we should read blatt ' strong.' The stanza does not occur in K.

§ 45, p. 93. **Dún Rodairce.** Is this intended for Dun Rudraige at Dundrum, Co. Down ?

§ 45, p. 96. **cloc na cruthailde.** My translation here is a mere guess ; unfortunately the stanza is not in K. Both *cloc* and *cruthailde* present difficulties. Can *cloc* here be used in the sense of ' a blister, a bubble, or blob in the water,' as given by P. O'C. ? On the other hand, it may stand for *cloc-thech*, ' a bell-tower, belfry, round tower.' As to *cruthailde*, see Meyer's Contributions, s.v. *alt* and *ailt* ' a house.' I have not succeeded in identifying Carraic Alastair.

§ 45, p. 97. **a rock of holiness.** The reference seems to be to Carraic Alastair ; but why ' a rock of holiness ' I cannot say, unless it was associated with St. Donnán of Eig.

§ 45, p. 96. **mar cuing n-imeachtair,** ' like an outer yoke ' ; Mr. Plummer suggests that it may mean the yoke of the outside ox ; cf. remithir cuing n-imechtraid (v.l. imechtair) a crand fil indi ' as thick as an outer yoke is the shaft that is in it,' Togail Bruidne dá Derga, p. 87. In the Félire of Aengus

(p. 72) Stokes renders imechtraid 'outer ox,' quoting (in the gl.) O'Cl. .i. dam imil na seisrighe. I take it that 'outer yoke' here stands for 'outer ox,' but what that actually signified I cannot say; it seems clear, however, that the 'outer ox' had to bear the brunt of the work and of the blows. For other instances of the use of the phrase see Acallamh na Senórach (Stokes), 1300, 5943.

§ 45, p. 96. **re nguin mh' échta-sa;** lit. 'before the blow (causing) my destruction.'

§ 45, p. 100. **tír conúachtus-sa,** lit. 'the land I have sewn together'; I take conúachtus to be the pret. of conúaigim 'I sew together'; see Meyer's Contributions (Addenda).

§ 47, p. 100. The metre of this poem is *sétrad ngarit*.

§ 47, p. 102. **Suibhne . . . ó Bhuais bhil.** Suibhne was of Dal Araidhe ; but it is probable that the river Bush was the dividing line between Dal Araidhe and Dal Riada.

§ 48, p. 103. **Eochaidh Aincheas, son of Guaire.** A king of the Britons named Eochaidh Aingces is mentioned in the *Battle of Magh Rath*, ed. O'Donovan ; see pp. 44, 45, 64, 65. O'Donovan regards him as a fictitious personage. As to Guaire, Sir John Rhys has suggested to me that he may be the Goreus whose name is found inscribed on a stone at Yealmpton, S. Devon ; see Hübner's Christian Inscriptions of Britain, No. 23. This stone is situated in the district where ogams of the Déssi occur in S. Devon. It would be interesting to know whether the Goreus stone has an ogam.

§ 50, p. 105. **Eas Dubhthaigh.** From the context one would expect this place to be in Britain, but Hogan (*Onomasticon*) gives Es Dubhthaigh— which is certainly in Ireland (the reference is to Gwynn's Dinnsh. VIII, 42)—but does not identify it.

§ 52, p. 106. The metre of this poem is *debide*. Stanzas 6 and 7 are not in K.

Ba talach(?)ar thairisi. This is quite obscure to me. O'R. has *talach*, 'dispraise, reproach,' &c.

§ 54, p. 108. The metre of this poem is *debide*. Stanzas 4 and 6 are not in K.

§ 54, p. 108. **Ni minic bhíos cumann trír gan duine fo fhodhord dibh.** Cf. ní gnáth comann comáentadach la triur iter, 'rare is accordant union with a trio,' *Cath Catharda*, p. 10.

§ 54, p, 108. **Ar mian o thigid cadhain gusan mbealltine ar samhuin,** '. . . when the wild ducks come' : cf. gigraind, cadhoin, gair re samuin. King and Hermit, ed. Meyer, p. 18.

§ 56, p. 112. The metre of this poem is *debide*. Stanzas 6 and 7 are not in K.

§ 56, p. 112. **Allata, fergach an fer,** 'Wild and angry the man'; *allata* is usually rendered 'famous,' from *allud* 'fame,' but it seems doubtful if the epithet is appropriate here. Should we not rather render ' wild,' ' unbridled,' regarding it as a parallel form to *allaidh* ?   See the many examples of the word in the gl. to *Cath Catharda*.

§ 58, p. 114.   The metre of this poem is *debide*.   Stanzas 3, 8, 10 are not in K.

§ 58, p. 116.   **Meisi i ferann ghlas nach glenn**, &c.   Suibhne can endure the wild and lonely glens, but is afraid of the fertile and populous plains.   He is cold in glens, but he would be cold also in the plains.

§ 61, p. 118.   The metre of this poem is *rannaigecht mór*.   Stanzas 10 and 11 are not in K.

§ 60, p. 119.   **from the time my feathers have grown**, i.e. since, through Rónán's curses, he became as a bird; see Introduction, p. xxxiv, footnote 2; see also pp. 33 and 49.   Cf. *Lismore Lives*, pp. 260 and 354, where a holy man is described as being ' without any human raiment, but all his body was full of bright white feathers like a dove or sea-mew.'   See also *Acallam na Senórach*, ed. Stokes, p. 325 (note to lines 6017 and 6018), *tuignech fírclúime*, ' dress of veritable feathers.'

§ 61, p. 121.   **Rathmor** ; in Magh Line.   It is situated about two miles to the N.E. of the town of Antrim.   It seems to have been the principal seat of the kings of Dal Araidhe down to the sixth or seventh century.   For a number of references to it see Reeves' *Eccles. Antiq.*, pp. 69 and 280.

§ 61, p. 122.   **dosgarus rem chruth gan clodh** : *clodh* here appears to go with *cruth*, ' my unsurpassed shape.'

§ 64, p. 123.   **Spectres on Sliabh Fuaid**.   Is this weird episode an echo of the tale of Orestes and the Furies ?

§ 67, p. 124.   The metre of this poem is *debide*.   Stanzas 4, 7, 8, 10, 14, 18 (latter half), 19 are not in K.

§ 69, p. 130.   The metre is *rannaigecht bec*.

§ 71, p. 134.   The metre is *ae freslige*.

§ 72, p. 134.   **All Fharannáin**.   See *Tribes and Customs of Hy Fiachrach*. The place referred to is Alternan, close to Skreen (Scrin Adhamnain) in the diocese of Killala, barony of Tireragh, Co. Sligo.   It is associated with Colum Cille, Farannan, and Adhamnan.   See also Betha Farannain in *Anecdota from Irish MSS.*, III, pp. 4 and 7.

§ 73, p. 136.   The metre is *rannaigecht mór*.

§ 73, 136.   **is édan rionntanach róin** ; rionntanach (rionntánach ?) is quite unknown to me.   The variant roinnteach is to be noted.   P. O'C. has róinteach ' of or belonging to sea-hogs'; cf., however, ' ag eistecht le riontach na rón 7 le fogar na ffaoilenn,' Betha Farannáin, *Anecdota*, III, p. 5, l. 4.   It is somewhat curious that the poem in which the above line occurs is one describing Farannán's Cliff.

§ 75, p. 136.   The metre of this poem is *cró cummaisc etir casbairdne* 7 *lethrannaigecht*.   Stanzas 3, 5, 7, 8, 13 are not in K.

§ 77, p. 143.   The description of the meal which the cook prepared for Suibhne is a strangely primitive touch.   If it has any special significance, I do not know what it is.

§ 78, p. 144. **gur gabh urrainn trid ar mbrisedh a droma ar dhó ann,** My rendering of this curious expression is but a conjecture. L has simply: tuc sathadth don lethgha fair as a láimh gur cuir trid.

§ 78, p. 145. **The herd made a thrust of the spear, &c.** In the *Birth and Life of St. Moling*, ed. Stokes, it is stated (p. 57) that a cowherd killed Suibhne.

§ 79, p. 145. **Énna mac Bracáin.** According to the Brussels version he was a member of Moling's community.

§ 80, p. 144. The metre is *debide.*

§ 80, p. 144. **biad do chorp inn-ethannaidh.** See the footnote in the text; it is strange to find that the half-stanza is in K but not in B; *ethannaidh*, if it be the word intended, is obscure to me. Should we read *etarnaidh* 'ambuscade,' 'lying in wait'?

§ 83, p. 146. The metre is *debide.*

Stanzas 4, 5, 6, 7, 8, 9, 10, 19, 20, 22, 24 are not in K.

§ 83, p. 152. **bheith icc luthmhairecht im linn.** The construction is peculiar; perhaps we should read *beich*, 'bees,' for *bheith*, and translate: 'bees buzzing about a pool and the cooing of the turtle-dove.'

§ 83, p. 153. **more melodious to me is the glorious chant, &c.** Suibhne contrasts the *ceileabrad* ('service,' or should we say 'mass'?) of the hounds with the *comhradh* of the students. See also p. 141, where he contrasts a leaf of the yew-tree with a leaf of St. Kevin's psalter.

§ 83, p. 154. **Romgon an cruadhmhucaidhe corr.** It may be that *cruadh* is a subs. here, and that *corr* goes with it, 'the pointed steel, or spear.'

§ 84, p. 155. **each man placed a stone on Suibhne's tomb.** As to this custom see Plummer's *Vitae Sanctorum Hiberniae*, vol. I, p. cix (note 7).

§ 85, p. 156. The metre is *debide.*

§ 85, p. 156. **Tucc dhamh, a chridhe, do lamh,** 'give me, O heart, thy hand,' but cf. cride láime, 'palm of the hand'; see Meyer's *Contributions*, s.v. cride.

§ 85, p. 157. **On me was imposed his preparation, &c.** See § 76 (p. 143), where Moling says that it was destined that Suibhne would come to Tech Moling, and ultimately die there.

BRUSSELS MS. 3410

FO. 59a TO 61b

DE S. RONANO MAC BERUIGH AS ECHTRA ŚUIBHNE

[Cap. I.]

Naomh uasal oirdnidhe robaoi sunn a ttír nEirenn .i. Ronán Fionn mhac Beraigh mhic Criomhtainn mhic Coluim Cúile mic Eirc Logha mic Laoghaire mhic Neill Naoighiallaigh. Fer chomhaillte tiomna 7 congmhala cuinge an Choimdedh 7 fuilngthi inghrema 7 treabhlaide ar gradh Dé. Ba mogh naoimhdhiles da anmain 7 ba crochaidh a chuirp 7 ba scciath dídin ría drochaimsibh diabail an fer min moronórach sin. Ro tórainnedh ceall lais feacht n-áon .i. ceall Lainni a nDail Araidhe a ccoiccedh Uladh. As aicce robaoi ferannus 7 forlamhus Dháil Araidhe .i. ag Suibhne mhac Colmáin Chuair mhic Cobthaigh. Rochuala sein guth cluig Ronáin aít a raibhe ag tórainn a chille 7 rofiarfaigh dia muinntir ciodh adchúaladar. Ronán Fionn mhac Beraigh atá ag tóruinn a chille ad chrích-si 7 at ferann. As e guth a chluig adchluini-si anosa. (As follus de sin nar chedaigh an naomh do Śuibhne an ecclas do thionnsgana.)[1] Et rolonnaigedh 7 ro fergaighedh go mór imón rígh 7 ro éirigh go dían deinmnedach do díchur an chleirigh on chill. Roglac a bhen .i. Eórann ingen Chuinn Chíannachta err an bhruit robhaoi uime 7 rotriall a fosdadh gur sgeinn fon teach an tsibhall (.i. dealg) argaitt robaoi isin brut 7 fágbhais a bhrat agan rioghain 7 dochuaidh lomnocht do dhíochur an chleirigh on chill go riacht airm (.i. áit) a raibhe ina réim roretha go ffarnaic (.i. go bfuair) antí Ronán ar a chionn. Is amhlaidh robaoi an cléirech ag moladh Rí nimhe et talman 7 ag solasghabháil a śalm 7 a śaltair líneach lánálainn ina fiadhnaisi. Tuargaibh (.i. do thógaibh) Suibhne an tsaltair 7 teilgis uadha í a bfúdomhain ina locha lindfuair robáoi ina bfiadhnaisi gur baidhedh an tsaltair ann. Gabhais láimh Ronáin íaromh 7 tairrngis na dhiaigh tar an ccill amach é et nir léicc lamh an chléirigh fón uaidh go ccúala an t-éighemh. As é dorinne an t-eighemh sin giolla Chonghail Claoin mhic Sccannláin rí Uladh arna thoideacht ar cenn Suibhne o Chongal Claon do cath Muighe Rath.

---

1 in brackets in MS.

[Cap. II.]

Doruacht an giolla go Suibhne 7 adfed (.i. roinnis) sccela dhó o thús go deiredh. Téid Suibhne lais 7 fagbais Ronán go dubhach dobrónach ar mbáthadh a saltrach 7 ar ndénamh a dhímigne 7 a easonóra. Día mbói ló go n-oidche iarsin doriacht dobharchú asin loch go Rónán 7 a saltair lais gan milledh líne nó litre innte. Doroine Rónan altugadh buidhe do Dhia do chenn na míorbuile sin 7 mallaighis Suibhne iarsin. Mo ched-sa for ced an Choimdhe chumhachtaigh ar sé amhail tainic Suibhne dom dhíochur-sa 7 sé lomnocht gurab amhlaidh bhias doghrés (.i. do ghnáth) lomnocht ar fáoindel 7 ar foluamhain seachnóin an domhain 7 gurab bás do rinn bhéras fo dhéoigh 7 mo mallacht fair 7 mo bennacht for Eórainn rothríall a fasdadh 7 an la adcífet clanna Colmain an tsaltair robáidhedh gurab díth 7 dílgenn dóibh 7 dorinne an laoidh :

Suibhne mac Colmain romcráidh,
romtarraing leis ar lethláimh,
d'fágbháil Cille Lainne lais,
dom beith athaigh na heccmais. 7 rl.

Dochúaidh Ronán iaramh go Magh Rath do dhénamh síthe idir Dhomhnall mhac Aodha mhic Ainmireach .i. rí Erenn et Congal Claon mhac Sccannláin rí Uladh 7 nir fét a siodhughud. Dobeirti immorro an cleirech a ccomairce ettorra gach laoi go nách marbhthaoi neach ettorra on uair rotoirmesgtha an cathughud no go ngabhtha doridhisi. Ticcedh thrá Suibhne tar lamha an chleirigh gacha trátha oir gach sídh 7 gach osadh doníod Ronan idir fiora Erenn gach n-oidhce nomhilledh Suibhne ria ttráth éirghe gach laoi oir no marbhadh fer ria ttráth an chomhlainn gach laoi 7 fer eile ar sccur an chomhlainn gach n-oidhche. An lá immorro rocinnedh an cath mór do thabairt tainicc Suibhne re ccách dochum an catha 7 tarla Rónan dó 7 ocht sailmchedlaigh dia muinntir ina farradh 7 iad ag cur uisge coisrectha tar na sluaghaibh 7 rochuirset tar Suibhne a ccuma cháich. Dar laisiumh bá dá fochuidbhed rocuiredh an t-uisge fair 7 dorad a mher a súainemh na sleighe robháoi ina laimh 7 rodiubhraic do sailmceadlaidh diobh go romarbh. Dorad an t-urchar tanaisi do chum an cleirigh féin gur bhen isin clocc báoi for a ucht go roscceind a chrann as a n-airde isin aiér. Gonadh ann adbert an cleirech : Guidim-si an Choimdhe, ar sé, i n-airde dochoidh an crann isin aiér 7 a nellaibh nimhe go ndechair-si ar gealtacht amhail gach n-eathaid 7 an bás roimris for mo dalta-sa, ar se, gurab edh nosbérai-se fa deoigh .i. bas do rinn 7 mo mallacht fort 7 mo bhennacht for Eórainn 7 Furadhrán 7 Teille uaim n aghaidh do síola uile 7 chloinne Colmáin cúair, 7 dorinne an laoidh :

Mo mhallacht for Suibhne, 7 rl.

[Cap. III.]

Ciodh trá acht ó rochomraicsiot na catha fochedóir robhúirsett 7 rogairset na sluaigh da gach leith ; ódchuala Suibhne na gáire mora sin 7 a bfreccartha 7 a bfuaim 7 a macalla a néllaibh nimhe 7 a bfroighthibh na firminnte rofech súas 7 rolíon némhain 7 dásacht 7 fáindeal 7 fualang 7 foluamhain é 7 miosgais gach ionaidh a mbiodh 7 serc gach ionaidh nogo roichedh. Romheirbhlighsett a mheóir 7 rochrithnaighset a chosa, roluathadh a chridhe, roclaochlá a chédfadha, rosáobadh a radharc, rothuitset a airm as a lamhaibh go ndeachaidh la breithir Rónain ar gealtacht amhail gach n-eathaid 7 gach n-én bfoluaimhneach 7 antan ráinic as in cath amach ba hainminic notaidhledh a chosa an talamh ara lúas tainicc 7 an trath dotaidhledh an chos an talamh as conntabairt go mbenfadh a dhrucht don fhér ar a ettroma 7 ar a aierdacht an cheime rocingedh 7 nir fhan don reim roretha sin gu nar fhagaibh magh no machaire nó coill nó moin no mothar i nEirinn gan taisteal an lá sin 7 rochaith a aois 7 a aimsir ar gealtacht i nEirinn 7 a mBretain an ccein romair, gan furtacht gan fóiridhin gan taobh do tabairt le dáoinibh amhail dherbhas an leabhar sgriobhthar air fein darab ainm Buile Suibhne. Oir a n-aon uair tainicc taom ceille chuicce 7 dosanntaigh taobh do tabairt le dáoinibh tre mhed gach bochtachta da bfúair an fedh dobaoi ar gealtacht 7 docuaidh roimhe d' ionnsuidhe a tire ; dochuaidh ar an aithgealtacht doridhisi oir dofoillsighedh do Ronán táomh ceille do techt cuige 7 a bheith ag dol d'ionnsuidhi a thíre dúthaighe 7 d'fanamhain aca 7 adubhairt Ronán : Aitchim-si (.i. guidhim-si) an ri uasal uilecumhachtach nár léiccther an t-ingreinntigh 7 an sgriostoir sin na hecclai si da hingreim no da sgríos doridhisi amhail dorinne (.i. dotriall) roimhe. Et an tinneachadh tuccadh fair na raibhe furtacht na fóiridhin dó dhe nogo scara a ainm re a chorp. Roeist Dia an itche sin Ronain óir antan tainicc Suibhne go medhon Sleibhe Fúaid tarfás taidbsi iongantach dó a medhonoidhce .i. méidheadha maoilderga 7 cinn gan colla 7 síad ag síangal 7 ag gréchaigh imón slighidh anonn 7 anall et antan rainic-siumh ettorra a medhón atcualaidh ag comhradh iad dar lais 7 asedh roraidhsett : Geilt é, ar ar céidchenn ; geilt Ultach, ar an dara cenn; a lenmhain, ar an tres cenn ; gurab fada an lenmain, ar an cetramhadh cenn ; nógo ría an fhairrge, ar an cúiccedh cenn. Rofhersat an guth a n-aoinfeacht chuige uile. Rothóguibh rompa da gach muine for a chéile 7 gerbó mor an glenn nothegmadh fris ni siubhladh-somh é acht nolingedh do bheinn na tolcha for a céile. Acht ata ní cena rocaith-siumh a aimser an ccein romhair ar buile 7 ar gealtacht tré easgaoine Ronain, 7 fuair bás do rinn (amhail innises a stair féin)[1] amail dosir Ronán ar Dhía gonadh é sin adhbar bhuile Suibhne tre easonoir an chléirigh.

---

1 in margin.

[Cap. IV.]

As amhlaidh so fuair Suibhne bás do rinn. Feacht n-aon dia ndeachaidh Suibhne 7 sé for a gealtacht gonicce an áit a bfuil Tech Moling mar a raibhe Moling. Is annsin robhaoi Moling ag teccuscc luchta an léighinn 7 tainicc an gheilt for srath na tioprad 7 robaoi ag ithe bioruir. As mochlongadh sin, a ghealtacáin, ar Moling, 7 doronsatt an láoidh :

> Moling cc. : Mochtráth sin a ghealtacáin
> ré cceileabhradh cóir.
> Suibhne : cidh moch lat-sa a chleirecáin
> táinicc teirt ag Roimh. 7 rl.

Et doraidh Moling ris:[1] Ca fios duitsi cá cuin (.i. uair no aimser) tig teirt ag Roimh. Fios dogeibhim om tigerna, ar se, gacha maidne 7 gacha nóin. Innis duinn sgela do Día, ar Moling. Ata fios aguibh fein, a Moling, ar sé. Cred fodera duitsi mh'aithne? ar Moling. As meinic me ar an bfaithche-si, ar Suibne, 7 ni deinim comnaidhe i n-áonáit. Cionnus eile, ar Moling, a bfuighe tú trocaire? Dogébh, ar Suibhne, óir ni thabhair pein form acht beith gan fos nó comhnaidhe. Dia ttegthá asteach dogebtha proinn aguinn. As doilghe lem a bheith gan brat, ar eisiumh. Dogebhair-si mo chochall-sa nó mo bhrat, ar Moling, madh áil let. Doronsat tres iomagallmha 7 chainnte re ceile mar sin 7 dofhiarfaidh Moling de : cáit a ttig do saoghal? ar se. Aodhaire dod muinntir-si marbhus mé, ar Suibhne.[2] As fochen do thoidheacht, ar Moling, óir atá a ndán duit bheith annso 7 do sgela 7 th' imtheachta d'fagbáil ann, 7 th' adhnacal a reilicc fíreoin 7 cid mór sirfi-si (.i. do siubhal) gach láoi, ar se, tair gach easparta chuccam-sa go sgriobhthar do sgéla lem. Robaoi Suibhne ré bliadhna fon samhla sin 7 gibe haird d'áirdibh na hErenn a ttéigedh gach laoi nobíodh um easpurta gacha nóna ag Moling.

Roordaigh Moling don bhanreachtaire proinn bhecc do thabairt dó risin ré sin 7 as amhlaidh doniodh an bhanairgheach, dosáitedh a cos a mbualtrach do leith imeal na búailedh 7 dodhoirtedh bainne a n-ionaidh a coise 7 dothigedh Suibhne dia caithemh sin go faiteach fuireachair, go ttárla lá airithi íarsin iomcháined.ı idir mhnaoi an bhuachalla 7 ben eile go roraidh an bhen eile fria-si gu·ab olc an gniomh doghniadh narbh annsa le a fer féin iná an gheilt dobaoi ∃ga tahaidhe risan mbliadhain sin. Co rochuala siur an bhuachalla sin roinnis dó amhail adchuala 7 san laithe arnamarach táinic Suibhne amhail dognathaigedh 7 baoi ag ól bainne 7 innisidh a siur don bhuachaill anní cedna amhail roinnis roimhe et tig an buachaill amach 7 lethgha lais 7 fuair Suibhne ina luighe 7 sé ag caithemh a phroinne 7 tucc sathadh don lethgha fair as a láimh

---

1-2 This is a close paraphrase of the metrical version, see p. 138 supra.

gur cuir trid. Adchonnairc cleirech do muinntir Moling dobi ag búain cluig primhe anni sin 7 dorinne an laoidh :

> Truagh sin a mhucaidh Moling
> dorignis gniomh talcair tinn
> mairg do marbh a los a neirt
> an rí, an naomh, an naomhgeilt. 7 rl.

Dochuaidh an cléirech mar a raibhe Moling 7 roinnis dó amhail rogonadh Suibhne. Tainicc Moling guna chleirchibh gus an ait a raibhe Suibhne 7 rohongadh leo é 7 tuccadh corp Christ dó 7 roaltaigh-siumh a caithemh. Tainicc an buachaill cuca 7 adubairt Suibne fris gurab olc an gniomh dorinne a marbadh gan adbar. Da ffesainn-si go madh tu nobheith ann ní ghonfainn tú, ar an buachaill. Mallacht Chriost ort, ar Moling ris an mbuachaill, as olc an gniomh doronais 7 gairde saoghail duit 7 ifrenn fa deoigh. Ni fhuil tarbha damsa dhe sin, ar Suibhne. Dogebhair-si éraic mhait, ar Moling .i. beith i nimh maille frimm-sa duit. Tainicc nell do Suibhne iarsin 7 rotoccbadh a leacht le Moling 7 leis na cléircibh. Eirgis Suibhne as a nell 7 rogabh Moling a lámh ina laimh 7 rangattar rompa go dorus na cille 7 tucc Suibne a guala re dorus na cille 7 roleicc osna mór as 7 dochuaidh a ainim dochum nimhe 7 rohadhlaicedh a chorp go n-onóir 7 go n-airmhidin ag Moling, gurab amlaidh sin fuair bás do rinn tre mallacht Rónáin.

GLOSSARY OF THE RARER WORDS

[The references are to the pages]

abairt *a feat*, n. pl. abarta 2.

ablachóg dim. of ablach, *belonging to the apple-tree* 64.

adhbha *habitation* 50.

adhbronn *ankle* 142.

adíu *hence* 14.

adúas *has been eaten* 94; see Wind. Wörterb. s.v. dúad.

adúdh 54; see Notes, p.

áeghaire *a herdsman* 140.

áenoires? 54; see Notes, p. 167.

áerdha *aereal* 50, 52.

aiccept *instruction, a lesson*; g.s. aiccepta 136.

aicill *preparation, lying in wait* 156.

aidhbhle *vastness* 98.

aidmilliudh 72, v.n. of admillim *I destroy*; see Notes, p. 169.

aigh *ice* 114.

aimhles *disadvantage, hurt* 146, 148.

ainriocht (anricht) *evil plight* 42.

airchinnech 28, 50, 82; see Notes, p. 164.

airchissechú, see oirchissecht.

airdhena *signs, tokens* 2.

aire *herd, attention* 84.

airfidiudh *music, minstrelsy* 56.

airide *high seat, dais*; g.s. airidhni 62.

airittiu *reception*, airittin 146.

airiugudh *perception* 50.

airlech *slaughter*, inf. of air-sligim oirlech 130, airligidh 68.

áirne *a sloe* 110, n. pl. airnidhe 22.

áirnechán *little sloe-tree* 64.

aisseola for ois-seola? *deer-tracks* 90; cf. oisbherna 92.

aitchim *I entreat* 122, 156.

áith *sharp, keen* 114.

áithétrom *keen and light (footed), very light* 16.

aithféghadh 124 v.n. of ath-fégaim *I regard*.

aithgein *counterpart, equivalent* 122, 132.

aithghealtacht *re-madness* 122.

aithigidh *act of visiting* 42, v.n. of aithigim.

aithmire *re-madness* 128.

aitten *furze*, g.s. aitin 120.

alchuing *a rack or shelf for arms* 142.

allata 112; see Notes, p. 171.

allmurdha *foreign* 52, 104.

ammus *an attempt* 42.

án *splendid* 6, 152.

anaithnid (anaichnid) *unknown* 108.

anall *hither* 14.

anba *huge, terrible* 6.

anforbthe *imperfect* 114.

anforus *unsteadiness, restlessness* 46.

anmaoin .i. mioscais *hatred, pique* P. Ó'C. 56.

N 2

ansádhal *unsettled, uncertain* 110 ;
ansádhaile 132.

ansochair *unquiet*, comp. ansochra 132.

ansódh *unhappiness*, g.s. ansóidh 28.

antuicceseach *not understanding* 74,
from tuigse *understanding*.

anú 44 ; see Notes, p. 166.

aobh *beauty, form* 58.

aonaidhe ? 70, P. O'C., citing this tale,
has aonaidhe .i. aonar *one person,
alone.*

arberim bith *I partake of, I use*,
airbhirinn b. 38, roairbir b. 36.

argain *plundering, reaving*, n. pl.
airgni 24.

arim for ar mo 42.

asglann *a load borne on the shoulder* 24.

astadh v.n. of adsuidim *I hold fast, I
bind* 8.

athach gáeithe *a blast of wind* 104.

athaigh *a space of time* 6.

atchar *expulsion* 6 ; v.n. of atcuirim.

athghlasán *very green one?* 64 ; see
foot-note, p. 65.

athlam *active*, n. pl. athlumha 18.

athtuirseach *very weary* 34.

athtuirsi *great weariness* 34.

atrochair *he fell* 58 ; cf. dorochair,
used as perf. of dotuitim *I fall.*

báeghal *danger, hazard*; ata b. aonmhna
sunna agad *there is but one woman
here before you* 50; cf. baegul échta,
gl. ío Acallamh na Senórach, ed.
Stokes.

báeithgeltacht *furious madness* 84.

báethbenn *a wild mountain-peak,*
baithbendaib 86.

báethréim *a wild course*, baeithrei-
mennaibh 130.

báigh *contention* 60.

báire *a goal* 30.

balc *strong* 70.

banchoig *a woman-cook* 142.

banchuire *a band of women* 16.

bandál *a tryst with a woman, an
assembly of women* 16.

banna *a drop* 52, 56; see Notes,
p. 167.

bantracht *a band of women* 110.

barclán *quite full, crowded* 30 ; barc
.i. iomad O'Cl., see also gl. to Cath
Catharda.

barrchas *curly-haired* 100.

bathais *the crown of the head* 24.

béiceadhán *little screaming one* 62, 82,
from bécim *I roar.*

beittid 20, 3 pl. 1 fut. of subs. verb; for
instances of this form see Strachan's
Subs. Verb, p. 61.

benaccán 50, 84 *a calf* (Contributions),
here apparently used as a dim. *of ben*
a woman.

benáil *act of cutting* 90.

bendachad *a benediction* 134 ; here *a
blessed site*, i.e. a place that has been
blessed through a saint dwelling
there.

benghág *a wrinkled, haggard woman?*
86.

benn *a peak, antler-point* 78 ; see
Notes, p. 169.

bennachtach *blessed?* 66.

bennán *a young buck, a calf* 62, 82.

bennín *a little peak or point*, n. pl.
beinníni 80.

bern *a gap* 64.

bert *effort, deed* 56.

bertín *a little bundle* 88.

bethe *the birch-tree* 66, 70.

bíatach *a victualler*, biatachaibh 52.

bíathadh *act of feeding* 60.

bil *good, blessed* 40, 102, 120.

bine *crime, sin?* 34.

biororán dim. of bioror *watercress* 116.

biorragán? *a plant name* 22; Cameron (Gaelic Names of Plants) has *biorrag*, equisetum hiemale, dutch rush or shave-grass.

bioth in phr. tar gach mb. *everywhere* 30; cf. tria bithu and tria bithu sír.

blicht *milk*, g.s. blechta 114.

bloisgbéim *a resounding blow* 124.

borr *vast, mighty* g.s. buirr 70.

borrfadach *swollen, elated, proud* 66.

bothleaptha *a hut-couch?* 92.

breac-bán *speckled-white*; see Notes, p. 161.

breacegair *variegated* 52, from breac *speckled* and eagar *arrangement* 52.

breacsról *variegated silk* 104, 106.

brecbhern *a gap with many tints* 92.

brégairecht *barking, yelping* 76.

brétaim *I break up*, 3 pl. perf. ind. robhretait 118.

brugaid *a land-holder, a hospitaller* 52, 102.

bruiden *a hostel* g.s. bruighniu 62.

búabhall *a buffalo, wild ox* 52.

búabhallda *made of buffalo horn* 10.

búaidre *deafness, confusion* 30.

búaile *a milking yard, cattle fold* 142.

búain *act of reaping* 60.

búaltrach *cowdung* 142, 144.

búar *kine* 82, 86.

buile *frenzy, ecstasy, madness, vision*, 2.

builidh *flourishing, joyous* 104.

buinne *a torrent, a wave* 124.

búiredhach *roaring, bellowing* 110.

búiredhán *little bellowing one* 62, 82.

búrim *I roar*; 3 pl. perf. ind. robhúirset 14, v.n. búriudh 62.

cabhán *a cavity, a hollow* 14.

cacht (1) *bondage, constraint*, (2) *a fast, hunger* 20, 48.

cadadh 54; see Notes, p. 167.

cadhan *barnacle goose, wild goose* 108.

cádus *veneration*, g.s. cadhasa 96.

cáeirechán dim. of cáerech *consisting of berries* 64.

cáelmhuine *narrow copse, shrubbery*, 68.

cáera *a sheep* 76, 116.

cáerthann *rowan-tree* 64.

cáidh *revered, holy* 26, 140.

cair *a fault* 8.

calg-dét *a tusk-hilted sword* 104.

caoilsnáithaide *slender-threaded* 10.

carrmhogal *carbuncle* 10.

casnad *a particle*; n.pl. casnaidhe *shavings, chips* 18.

ceirteach *a ragged garment* 30.

cennach *buying, a bargain* 88.

cennacht *headship* 88.

ceólán *a little bell* 134.

cerc-fráech *a grouse* 152.

cert *a rag* 38, dim. certín 88.

cethern *kerne, foot-soldiers* 112.

cíamhair *gloom, sadness* 24.

cíar *brown, dark* 66, 108.

cích *a pap, a teat* d.pl. cigibh 58.

cith-ainbthenach *a shower with storm* 100.

cladh *a ditch, rampart* 56, 98.

clannaim *I plant*, 3 s. perf. with infix. pron. of 1 s. romchlann 40.

class *a hollow*; do chlais chúil *to the hollow of the poll*, i.e. *nape of neck* 124, cf. im chlaiss a chúlaid, Contributions s.v. class.

clithar *shelter*, cliuthar 110.

clithardhlúith *a close shelter* 14, 82.

clithmharán dim. of clithmar *sheltered, snug* 66.

clíu *the left, left side* 10.

cloc 96; see Notes, p. 170.

clochadart *a stone pillow* 92.

clochánechta *hail* 92.

clúmh *down, plumage* 18, 46, 48, 118.

cnaipe *a button,* cnaipidhibh 10.

cness *skin, surface* 136.

cnú *a nut* n. pl. cná 110, 116.

cnúas *nuts* 136.

cochlán *a little hood* 138.

cóemhna *protection* 38.

coill in phr. dul fon ch. *to go as an outlaw* 150; see Contributions s.v. caill.

colbha *a post, pillar, doorpost, bedpost, bedside* 62.

colcaid 46, 58; see Notes, p. 167.

coll *hazeltree, hazelnut,* call 136, dim. collán 64.

collan 40, ? for colainn *body* ; see Notes, p. 166.

comha *a condition* 12, n. pl. comhada 18.

comairce *protection* 8.

comhaitte (comfhaide) *equal length* 146, 150.

comól *a drinking together* 152.

comramach *combative, triumphant* 112.

comthocht *companionship* 24.

congab *state, condition,* acc. s. congaib 132.

congna *horn, antler* 144.

conmír *a dog's meal* 126.

conúachtus 100 ; see Notes, p. 171.

corbaim *I defile, maim,* romchoirb 108.

cornairecht *horn-blowing* 78.

corr (1) *a heron* g.s. cuirre 86, 102; n. pl. corra 76; g. pl. corr 96; d. pl. corraibh 40; (2) *pointed, round,* n. pl. corra 84, 154.

corracht *unsteadiness* 12.

corrchennach ? 72.

corrghaire *the cry of a heron* 76.

corthar *a fringe,* cortharaibh 66.

cortharach *fringed* 4.

crádim *I torment,* romchráidh 6.

cráesfhairsing *jaws wide open* 100.

crannacht *decrepitude* 12.

creabhar *a woodcock* 74, 102.

creamh *wild garlic* 22.

creamhlus *wild garlic* 116.

creamthanán dim. of cremthann *a fox* 74.

creg *a rock* 96.

creic *a selling* 26.

creim *a gnawing* 74.

críonach *dry sticks, faggots* 104.

criothugud *trembling* 66.

criss *a girdle,* g.s. creasa 30 (but see Dinneen s.v. creas), n. pl. creasa *loins* 94.

crithach *the aspen-tree* 66.

critheólach *trembling?* 98 ; cf. crith-ánach and crithoman, gl. to Cath Catharda.

crocairecht (crochairecht?) *the cry of the badger?* 78.

crochbán *deathly pallor?* 138 ; the MS. has cróchban, but the metre requires crochbán ; see cróch and cróchderg, Contributions.

cróderg *blood-red* 130.

crónán *a humming* 58.

cronnghlachán *a round little handful* 94.

crúadhchomaidh *hard company?* 96.

crúadhlom *hard and bare* 82.

crúadhluirgnech *hard-shanked* 96.

crúadhmhucaidhe 154 ; see Notes, p. 173.

crúaidhghuilbnech *having a hard beak* 96.

crúaidhleadhbach *hard and ragged* 96.

crúaidhleidhb *a hard slattern* 128, ledb *an untidy person.*

crúaidhrinn *a hard point* 10.

crúandatha *saffron colour* 130.

cruthailde 96 ; see Notes, p. 170.

cúach *a bowl, a cup* 52.

cúairt f. *a circuit*, g.s. cúarta 98.

cúan *a pack of wolves* 110, cuanaibh 40.

cúartugudh *wandering round, searching* 134.

cubar *a bird of prey*, n. pl. cuifir 20.

cúchairecht *cooing* 152.

cuchtach *shapely* 30.

cufir see cubar.

cúi *a cuckoo* 32.

cuibhdhe *agreement, sympathy, companionship* 84, 112 ; see Notes, p. 170.

cúicherán P. O'C. has *singing of cuckoos, cooing of doves, lowing of kine,* &c. 62.

cuilenn *holly* 66, 110.

cuin *when?* .i. úair no aimser L, 138.

cuing *a yoke* 2, 96, cuing n-imeachtair, see Notes, p. 170.

cuirm *ale* 62.

cumaim *I form*, dochum 150.

cumair *brief*, here *a summary* 62.

cumann *companionship* 108.

cumma for cumbe *cutting* 64, *shape, fashion* 18.

cumus *power, control* 82.

custul *next to, close to* 10.

daiger *a blast of fire, a furnace* 114.

daith *swift, eager* 68.

damghaire *a herd of stags?* 58.

damhghairecht *the belling of stags* 78.

damim *I grant, I yield* 2 s. pres. ind. dámha 64.

damhradh *stags* 14, coll. of dam.

dé *smoke*, acc. s. díaidh 54, see Notes, p. 167.

deacar *hardship*, deacraibh 62.

dédla *bold, valiant* 68.

deinmneadach *hasty* 4.

deithidin *care, anxiety* 36.

dercon *an acorn*, n. pl. dercoin 110, 116, 130.

dergnámha *an implacable foe* 74.

derthan *a shower, a storm* 114.

dídine in phr. dia na haoine d. 32, 34, g.s. of díden *last.*

dífreagra *unanswerable* 112.

digeann *outcome, end?* 144 ; see Magh Rath, p. 216 and Laws Gl. s.v. dicend.

dílghenn *extinction* 6.

dímhíad *dishonour*, g.s. dímhíadha 122.

dímigin *contempt, reproach* 122, g.s. dímigni 4.

dingim *I force, I crush*, nodhingedh 142.

dioghainn *protruding, defensive* 24 ; cf. tres in ndeirg ndruimnig, Battle of Magh Rath, p. 152 ; see gl. to Cath Catharda, *copious, abundant.*

dioghair *fervent, zealous* 18, .i. dían P. O'C.

díol *disposal* 24.

díth *destruction, ruin* 6.

díthreb *a desert* 34.

diubhracaim (díbairgim) *I cast, I throw*, rosdiubhraic 10.

diule (diliu) comp. of dil *dear, beloved* 42.

dligtheachán dim. of dligtheach *lawful* 80.

dobhar *darkness, gloom* 14.

dobrán *an otter* 8.

dochnáidh? 132 ; cnáidh I take to be from cnáim, *I gnaw, fret, pine,* Contributions.

docomhul *a difficulty* 118.

-dom for -dam, for O.I. -ta or -da, 1 s. pres. ind. (neg.) of the copula nidom 28, 30, 40; cf. nidat 2 s. 64, nidot 3 pl. 48.

domacht 12, P. O'C. quoting the stanza in which it occurs here has *scarcity. fewness, my curse on Suibhne a full reward.*

dománuig 3 s. pret. and perf. of do -icc *comes*, with infix. pron. of 1 s.

domeccad 30 ; this seems to be 3 pl. pres. ind. of do-icc *comes*, with infix. pron. of 1 s., do-m-eccad.

domelim *I eat*, 2 s. pres. subj. tormalla 138, notoimledh 154.

domheilte 72 ?

donálach *yelping* 152.

dord *belling* 34, dordán 152.

doroidnacht 3 s. perf. ind. of doindnacim *I bestow* 8.

dos *froth, scum* O'R. 138 ; O'Dav. has dos .i. doinnim *unfortunate.*

dotachuisin 88, see Notes, p. 170.

dreachsolus *with bright face* 104.

dreann *a fight* 102.

dréim *an attempt* 92.

dremhan *fierce, angry* 20.

dreollán *a wren* 132, 134.

dris *a bramble, a briar*, n. pl. dreasa 30, 110, drisi 108, driseóg 64.

drochammus *a wicked attack*, drochaimsibh 2.

droigen *blackthorn*, n. pl. droigni 108 ; droighnéin 64.

druimnechóg 64 dim. of druimnech *arched, curved, undulating* (or perhaps *with knots or knobs*), see 3. na Rann, 4516, 5388 ; see also Gael. Journal 1909, p. 169.

dualaig *vice, sin*, doalcibh 2.

dúarcus *sternness* 100.

dubhlén *black (intense) woe* 92.

dúil *an element* 132.

dúnárus *a dwelling* 36 n. pl. dúnáruis 50.

dursan (dirsan) *sorrowful, alas!* 34.

eadarbhúas *hovering* 42.

eadarnaigh (etarnaid) *an ambuscade, a lying in wait* 156 ; ethannaidh for etarnaidh ? 144 ; see Notes, p. 173.

eala *a swan*, ealaib 34.

earrchaidhe *vernal* 98.

eatarfhásach *an interspace* 142 ; for other instances of the word see gl. to Cath Catharda.

éc *death*, éccuibh 30.

écalma *feeble* 100.

éccaointeach *mournful, plaintive* 124.

écht *heroic exploit, murder* 144, g.s. échta 96.

écert *injustice* 38.

écomhnart *unequal strength, feebleness* 48.

égemh *an outcry, an alarm* 4, 6.

eidhinn *ivy* 66.

eidhneachán dim. of eidneach *full of ivy* 66.

éimh⌣ ? 40.

eing (eng) *track, footstep* 126.

eire (ere) *a burden* 86.

eite *a wing*, e. an bhrait 4.

eitil *flight* 134.

ell *advantage, opportunity* ; with gabaim ; gabhaid uile a eill 68, cidh 'mongeibhe mh'e. 72, luath nogheibhedh m'e. 74 ; cf. cona ragbat demhnu m'ell, Birth and Life of Moling, ed. Stokes, p. 52 ; Imraidi iarum Cuirrech modh nodgabad eill for Find, Rennes Dinds. p. 49.

ellteóg *a small hind or young doe*, P. O'C. 68 ; from eilit.

enechrus see oinechtreas.

énlaith coll. *birds* (énꜰlaith) 110.

eól *home* 16, 24.

eólach *knowing* 86.

eólchaire a *longing for home, home sickness* 64 ; see Voyage of Bran, I, p. 41.

érgna *noble, famous* 18.

éric a *fine, satisfaction, blood fine* 146, 150.

érlumh a *patron* 2.

esparta *vesper-time* ; see Notes, p. 165.

étach *clothes*, ettaighibh 52.

ethaid a *bird* 10, 52 ; P. O'C., citing the present tale, has a *wild beast or fowl*.

ethannaidh ; see eadarnaigh.

étrom *light of weight*, compar. ettromó 44.

faitech *cautious* 142.

fál a *wall, fence, hedge* 142.

fán-glenn a *sloping valley* 62.

fáoinnel (fóindel) a *straying* 4, 14, 28, 102, 124.

faón *supine* 20.

feadóg a *plover* g.s. feadóige 104.

fedghaire a *shrill cry* 104.

feithemh *watching* 140.

femar *some kind of waterplant* 116.

ferán-eidhinn a *turtle-dove* 74, féránn-e. 152.

fern *the alder tree* 64.

fían *warrior bands* 24, 94.

finndlochtán a *fair little bunch* 94.

fionnghág *fair and wrinkled* ? 86.

fionnmhuir *white sea* 92.

firmaimint *firmament*, g.s. firmaminnte 14, firmaiminti 22.

fochann *cause* 2.

fochraic a *reward*, fochraicciu 2.

fochuidmedh *mocking, flouting* 10.

fodhord a *murmuring, conspiracy* 108.

fogha a *short spear* 10, 12.

fogharán dim. of foghur *sound* 80.

folach *concealed* 154.

folúamain *flight* 2, 4, 14, 102, 124 ; folúaimhnech 2.

foradhán dim. of foradh *shelf, seat* 80.

forbrechtrad *variegation* 10.

fordorus *lintel, outer door* 44, 110.

fordul *error* 112.

forfaire *watching* 80.

forlés a *skylight* 42, 62.

formadh ? 52 ; see Notes, p. 167.

fosaidh *steadfast* 20.

fotha a *foundation* 30.

fothlocht *some kind of waterplant, perhaps brooklime* 22, 24, 70, 116 ; see *Stories from the Táin*, ed. Strachan, s.v. fochlocht.

fraisnéll a *showery cloud* 22.

fraissíne a *storm with rain* 90 ; from frass a *shower* and sín *storm*.

freislighe a *lying down with* 78.

fritháilim *I attend, I wait on*; perf. ind. 1 s. rofriothálus 70, 3 s. romfrithái 56.

fúaim *noise* n. pl. fuamanna 14.

fúalang *frenzy, giddiness* ? 2, 14 ; P. O'C. citing the Buile Suibhne has *distraction, derangement, madness* ; see also Fled Bricrind (Windisch), p. 263, l. 18, and Battle of Magh Rath, 230, 232.

fúathróg a *girdle* 10, 104, 106 ; see gl. to *Táin*, ed. Windisch.

fuilech *bloody* 52.

fuirgim (fuirigim) *I delay*; romfuirgedh 36, 86.

fuit *cold* 40.

fuithir *land* 62.

furechair *watchful* 142.

gainemh *sand* 156.

gáisidech *hairy* 122.

gamhnach darach ? 66.

gaoinemh ? 56 ; cf. gáine = gaoine *a prank*, Duanaire Finn, p. 25 ; also gáine .i. maith, O'Cl.

gaoithánechta *wind-driven snow* 90.

gealtagán dim. from gealt 108, 134, 136.

gealtóg dim. from gealt 108.

géc *a branch, a bough*, g.s. géicce 30, n. pl. géga 30.

géibenn *a gyve* 60.

geilt f. *a madman* 26, 30, 40, &c. ; the word seems to have been applied specially to a crazy person living in woods, a 'wild man of the woods' ; also endowed with the power of fly- ing; see Introduction, p. xxxiv, foot- note 2. Cf. volatiles .i. gealta, Chron. Scotorum, p. 122; see also Macbain's Dictionary, geilt .i. folúamhain.

geilt glinne ; see Notes, p. 166.

géire *sharpness, harshness* 116.

geis *a prohibition* 110; acc. pl. gesa 102.

gen *a smile* 40.

genidecht *goblin-like* 14, from genit *a goblin, a sprite.*

gerc *a cormorant*, g.s. gaircce 104.

gioghrann *the barnacle duck* 86.

gláedh *a shout, call* 102 ; see Saltair na Rann 1290, 6554, 6794.

glaismhín *green-mead* 90.

glaisreódha *shining with frost* 90.

glansrotach *abounding in clear streams* 130.

glas *green, grey, the sheen of reflected light, as applied to a sword*, &c., 22, 30.

glasán see foot-note, p. 65.

glédenn *bright-coloured* 58.

gleórán *cuckoo-flower* 32.

gleórdha *luminous, bright* 88.

golfortach *lamentation* 124, cf. golfa- dach, *Lis. Lives*, torannfadach, Ériu II, pp. 157, 161.

gonim *I wound*, 3 s. perf. ind. with infix. pron. of 1 s. romgett 70.

gorm *blue, swarthy* 90 ; see Notes, p. 170.

gort *a field* 86.

gothnaide from gothnat *a little dart* 68.

graigh *a herd, a stud*, g.s. groidhi 78.

greann *gravel* 88.

grechach *screams* 144.

greim, fuaras do gh. *I was able to catch thee* 68.

grinne *a crowd of people* 58.

guirt *bitter* 68.

guiseóg *a stalk, a straw* 74.

íall (1) *a flock, a herd*, (2) *a thong, a bond*; n. pl. íalla 30; see Notes, p. 165.

iardraighe *remnants, vestiges, after effects* 52 ; also iardaige, see gl. to Lismore Lives.

iarmerge *nocturn* 152.

imchumang (1) *very narrow* 16, (2) *close confinement* 110; see Cath Catharda 5154.

imeachtair *outer* 96 ; cuing n-i. ; see Notes, p. 170.

imrall (imroll) *mistake, error* 60.

imśniomh *great trouble* 62.

imthacmang *act of surrounding* 16.

ind *end, point* 114.

lugu *a talon, nail*, n. pl. ingne 32, ingni 94.

ingreim *persecution* 122, ingreama 2.

ingrintidh *a persecutor* 122.

inmhe *position, rank* 134.

inne *sensus* 112.

inneachadh *vengeance* 122.

inníreach *angrily* 142.

iodhnaidhe *awaiting, enduring* 70.

iomarchrúas *great rigour* 38.

iomargho *deceit* 112.

iomcháineadh *a disputing* 142.

iomchumang see imchumang.

iomlán *very full, numerous* 110.

iomram *a rowing* 54.

ionfhúar *cool, refreshing* 80, 110.

ionnailt *a handmaid* 106.

iosgad *the hough or hollow at the back
of the knee* 124.

ith *corn*, g.s. eatha 114.

iubrachán dim. of iubar *yew* 66.

iubraidhe *of the nature of yew?* 70;
but see iubrach in gl. to Acallamh
na Senórach (Stokes).

laghad *smallness* 104.

lámhaim *I handle, I touch*, romlamh-
aigh 94.

laoi *steering oar, rudder* 54.

láthar *vigour, influence* 132.

leacht *tomb*, 154, leachtán 156.

learg *a slope, a plain* 92.

leathgha lit. *half-spear* 144, but cf.
líathga *Táin*, ed. Windisch 5930.

legairecht for ledairecht (?) *rending*
76.

léige go l. *in the meantime*; O. I.
colléice, colléic 28, 30.

léimnech *act of jumping* 122.

lenamhnach *persevering, stubborn,
obstinate* 42, from lenamhain *to
pursue.*

lenn *a mantle, a cloak, coat of an
animal*, 78, lennín 80.

lennán *a lover* 46.

leptach *bedding* 22.

lesrach *the thighs* 124.

less *a fold, an enclosure*, acc. s. léis 76.

less *a thigh*, n. pl. leasa 94.

leth in phr. i l. re *by the side of,
helping?* 44.

lí *splendour, colour, beauty* 64.

líach *sad, piteous* 28.

líneach *lined* 4.

linnghlas *grey (shining) water* 102.

linnúaine *green-watered* 102.

liosda *importunate, irksome* 42.

lomlán *quite full*, lomnán 20, 26.

lomnocht *stark-naked* 8.

lon *a blackbird*, g.s. luin 64, 76.

lonn *strong, fierce* 120.

los *herds, produce generally?* see Gl.
to Laws, n. pl. lois 64.

los a l. *owing to, by dint of* 122, 144.

lúaidhim *I mention* 150.

lúamgheilt *leading madman?* 102;
lúam *a pilot.*

luirgnechóg *little long-legged one?* 68.

lus bian? 22, 116 ; P. O'C., citing the
Buile Suibhne, has *herbage, herb
viands.*

lúth *vigour, strength*, g. s. lúith 122.

lúthmhairecht 152, from lúthmar *active,
vigorous.*

ma 38, for mad *good* in composition
with following verb; see *Stories from
the Táin* s.v. mad.

mac tíre *a wolf* 76.

máelderg *bare and red*, n. pl. maoilderga 122.

máethainder *a tender maiden* 48, from
máeth *soft, tender* and ainder *a young
woman.*

máethéttrocht *tender and bright* 48.

máethnatoin 116 *some kind of plant?*
cf. maothán *a twig, an osier, a bud*
O'R.

mairgnech *sorrowful* 100.

mál *noble* n. pl. málla 52.

malloghadh *cursing* 130.

mana *a presage, an omen* 62.

mannraim *I destroy*, 3 s. perf. ind. with infix. pron. of 2 s. rodmannair 100.

marthain *remaining, existence, life* 54, 58.

mas (mass) *beautiful, elegant* 20.

meabhail *treachery*, g. s. meabhla 112.

meanmarán 72 *little floury one?*, men *meal, flour*,. but cf. menmar cach cáinte, *Instructions of Cormac*, ed. Meyer, p. 22.

meathach *a weakling* 142.

méide *neck, trunk*, n, pl. méidhedha 122.

meigeallaigh *bleating (of a goat)* 152.

méiligh *bleating (of a sheep)* 152.

meirbhnéll from meirb *weak* and néll *a swoon* 92.

melle (melde) *atriplex, golden herb* 22, 116.

menic *often*, compar. meince 84.

mennat *a little dwelling*, mennataibh 118.

mennatán dim. of mennat 64, 134.

mennchrot *a lute, a lyre* 58.

mes *acorns, fruit* 132, 136.

mether *clothes* 108.

mín *gentle* 54 ; tre míne *gently* 54.

minchomairt *a broken mass* 82, comairt *pounding, a mash*.

mínén? 64; the name of some plant, m. muire occurs in the Metr. Gl. (Archiv für C. P., I) and in Hogan's Luibhleabhrán as *parsley piert, meadow saxifrage.*

míodh *mead* 82, 86.

miodhbhun 22 *a plant-name?*, see Dinneen s.v. miodhbhán.

miodlaochda *effeminate, timid* 142.

míol muighe *a hare* 134, 136.

mionbhrúar *little bits* 82.

mír *a bit*, n. pl. mírenna 42.

mochlongadh *early eating* 136.

mochthráth *dawn, early hour* 136.

móirédrocht *very bright* 118.

mónann *a whortleberry, cranberry* 116.

mónarán *a bogberry*, O'R. 94.

monúarán *woe is me!* 84.

mórmhonorach *greatly toiling* 2, monar *work.*

mothar *a woody swamp* 14.

mothar-mhuine *a dense thicket* 24.

múaidh *noble, glorious* 44.

múich *sadness* 119, 120, 122.

múichneachus *gloominess, misery* 118.

múichnidhe *gloomy* 36.

muincinn *a strait, a pass* 44.

muinterrdha *friendly, familiar* 2.

muirn *clamour* 22.

naid (nait) for ináid *than are* 28, O. Ir. indáte, oldáte.

náimhdidhe *hostile* 64.

nár *noble, modest* 156.

neamhfann *not weak* 26.

néll *a faint, a swoon* 158.

nemhain 14, P. O'C., citing the Buile Suibhne, has .i. dasacht no mire *frenzy, madness, distraction*; see *Táin*, ed. Windisch, p. 339.

nía *a champion* 40.

nochatfia for nachatb[h]ia 62, here fia (bia) 3 s. fut. of subs. verb.

nothaidhledh 3 s. imperf. ind. of do-aidlim (to-ad-ella) *I visit* 14, taid-lenn 30.

nothaigtais for O. I. notéigtis, 3 pl. imperf. ind. of tíagu *I go* 22.

núallan *a wail* 30.

odhar *dun colour*, but here *the nipple of the breast* 144; cf. odar cíche, Acall. na Senórach (Stokes), 3314.

óg *young, fresh*, n. pl. úagha 110.

oighreadh *ice* 18 ; see aigh.

oigreata *icy, frozen* 90.

oil *reproach* 148.

oinech *honour, mercy, generosity* 66.

oinechtreas apparently for enechrus *safeguard* 84.

oirchill *lying in wait* 20.

oirchissecht *compassion* 54, 76, 82, 84.

oireamh *a ploughman*, g.s. oiremhan 78.

oisbhern *a deer-pass?* 92.

ong *a groan, lament* 40.

orc (? **orca**) *the calf of the leg*, oircnibh 124.

ord *ordo, sacred office* 32, g.s. uird 106.

os *a deer*, n. pl. ois 64 ; ois allta *wild deer* 134.

osair *a bed, a litter* 80.

osgur *ignorant* 74.

osnadach *sighing* 100.

prab *sudden* 46.

prímh *the canonical hour of prime*, g. s. prímhi 144.

ráe *a field, plain* 120.

raithnech *a fern* 80.

ráitsech *words, speech* 138.

ráthaighthe *guaranteed* 140.

rathmar *fortunate, gracious* 18.

rathonn *a great wave* 92.

realtánach *starry* 76.

reb *sport*, g. s. reabha 90.

rébaim *I tear*, 3 pl. perf. ind. rorébsat 30, v.n. rébad 30, 48.

renga *the reins of the back, the loins*, reandaibh 88.

reód *hoar-frost*, g. s. reóidh 30, 76, 118, 126.

rinnglas *blue-starred* 20.

riocht *shape* 38, 132.

rionntanach 136 ; see Notes, p. 172.

riothugud *racing* 66.

rod *violent, fierce* 38.

roga *choice*, roignibh 22.

romhac *great son* 18.

rón *a seal* 134.

rorer 38 ; this seems to be intended for 1 s. perf. ind. of renim *I sell*.

rúathar *onrush* 24.

ruire *a prince, chieftain* 36.

sádhal *comfortable, easy* 46, 110, 134.

sádhudh *a thrust* 144.

sáeirchendaidh *a noble leader?* 86.

sál *heel* 142.

samhad *wood-sorrel* 22, 116.

samhlaim *I liken* ; rosamhlaidhedh a righe fris 60.

sanusláidh *a secret song?* 96.

scáth ar s. *for the sake of* 2, 32 (?).

scé *hawthorn* 28, g.s. sgíach 22.

sceanbaidhe *prickly, thorny*, from scenb a thorn 64.

scenbhgér *prickly and sharp* 116.

scendim *I spring*, rosging, 4, 10.

sceo *and* 64.

scíamdha *beautiful* 140.

seach in phr. ma s. = fa s. *in turn* 66.

sead *a nest* acc. s. seit 126; see Dinneen s.v.

seghais *a wood* 120.

ségda *stately* 102.

ségonn *an accomplished person, a champion* 58.

séimh *thin, smooth* 18.

seimnech *riveted* 10.

seisbhéimnech *resounding blow* 124.

seisi *a mate, companion* 106.

seisreach *a plough-team* 78.

sén *hap, chance, luck* 66.

seng *slender, emaciated* 50, g.s. singi 88.

sengbhlén *slender groin* 92.

sesc *sedgy land* 38; see Laws IV, p. 144, 7.

sescenn *a moor, fen, morass* 38.

sésdán *a shout, din, clatter* 22, 124.

séselbe *a tumult* 124.

sét *wealth, a treasure* 26, n. pl. seóide 118.

sgailp *a cleft* 22.

sgal *cry, shriek* 74, cf. léicid fead no scal as, Oss. Soc. V, p. 30. See also Dinneen s.v. scal and scol.

sgáthaighthe *shunned, dreaded* 140.

sgeachóir *a haw*, n. pl. sgeachóra 116.

sgeile *pitiful, grievous* 86.

síangal *hootings, croakings* 122, 124.

sibheanradh 76 *mirth, laughter, jollity*, P. O'C.; see Ann. Four Mast. 1638.

sioball *fibula, pin* 4; in L it is glossed dealg.

sioc *ice* 126.

siomsán *wood-sorrel* 22, 116.

sionnach *a fox* 76.

síor-éighemh *a prolonged cry* 124.

siorsan *fortunate* 70.

siregdha *made of silk or serge*, from siric *silk, serge* 52.

sirtheachán dim. of sirthech *begging?* (see gl. to Lismore Lives) 80.

síst *a while* 106, 122, 126.

slinnén *a shoulderblade* slinnenibh 124.

slinnlethan *with broad blade* 10.

smech *a chin* 62.

smér *a blackberry* 110.

snáth *a thread* 30.

snáthad *a needle* 52, 56.

snige *trickling* 136.

snímche *grief, sorrow* 34.

snomh 56 ; see Notes, p. 167.

snúadhamail *having colour, beautiful* 18.

socht *silence*, 112.

soclán *full of prows*, from soc *a prow* 30.

soil (sail) *the willow* 70.

soinmech *prosperous* 132.

solusghabáil *blithely chanting* 4.

so-mblas *sweet-tasting* 52.

so-óla *good to drink* 52.

soraidh *happy, successful* 72.

srann *a snore* 38.

srath *a brink* 28, 82, 136.

sreabnaidhe *filmy, membranaceous* 10.

sreithegar 10, from sreth *row, rank*, and egar *order, array*.

sriobhúaine *green-streamed*, from srib *a stream* and úaine *green* 118, 134.

srólda *consisting of satin* 52.

sruthfhairrge *the main, the sea* 96.

stocairecht *trumpeting* 78.

stúagaim *I bend* 24.

stúaglúb *a bow-loop* 110.

súairreach *trivial, mean, weak* 76.

su-aithnidh *easily known* 46.

su-aithenta (súaichenta) *well known* 102.

súanach *sleepy* 46.

subh *a berry* 64, subha craobh *raspberries* 116.

surdlaigh *leaping wildly* 126; cf. nobid ic surdlaig ina fiadhnaise Rev. Celt. IX, 464.

tacha *scarcity* 108.

tadhall *visit, approach* 22, v.n. of to-ad-ellim.

táebh, with dobeir . . . fri *he trusts in* 16, 18, 42, 102, 110, 122.

táes 1 s. pres. subj. prototonic of dotíag *I come* 40.

táeth 3 s. pres. subj. used as pret. of tuitim *I fall* 144; táethus (taotus) 80 seems to be 1 s. fut. pres. of the same verb.

tafonn *act of hunting, chasing* 8, 42.

táimhnél *a faint, a swoon* 154.

tairber 2 s. impv. of tairbrim (do-air-berim) *I bring forth* 34.

táire *reproach* 126.

tairisi *trust, loyalty* 106.

tairnic 3 s. perf. ind. of tar-iccim *I end* 48.

tais *soft, easy* 120.

talach ? 106.

talchair *stubborn* 144, talchaire *self-will* 94.

taom *a particle, a scrap* 122.

targaid *he offered* 18, 3 s. imperf. of do-aircim.

tarrachtain *act of overtaking* 100.

tasci *come!* 58.

tásg *news, report* 56, 58.

táthad *union, addition* 56.

tearbaim *I sever*, romthearbadh 26.

tecómhnaccair *evenit* 2.

teibersin *spurting* 134.

tenn *strong* 78, 80; go teinne *stoutly* 12.

tenngharg *strong and fierce* 86.

terc *scarce*, n. pl. terctha for terca 48.

tesmholta *characteristics, habits* 62; see Passions and Hom. p. 29; note the variant testmolta.

tibim *I smile* 40.

tigedhus *housekeeping, husbandry* 54.

time *fear* 30.

tinnebradh *sleep* 38, 132.

tinnesnach *hasty* 124, 134, 136.

tiomghairim *I ask*, rothiomghair 156.

tiopra *a well*, g. s. tioprat 136, n. pl. tioprata 80.

tlás *weakness, cowardice* 118.

tochrádh *tormenting* 8, 44.

tocht *act of going* 144.

tocht *silence, stillness* 58.

toich *acceptable*, compar. tocha 46, 142.

toici *fortune* 52.

toichim *a course* 10.

toirnech *thunder*, toirneachaibh 40.

toirrchim *drowsiness* 132.

toisg *an errand, business* 52.

tolg *a bed* 60, 62.

toll *gaping, leaking* 40, 52, 54.

tollaim *I pierce*, romtholl 28, tolladh 22.

tórainn *act of marking out, measuring* 2.

torrchennach ? 72.

tothachtach *wealthy* 134.

trealmach *equipped, armed* 26, from trelam *military weapons, equipment*.

tregdaim *I pierce, I transfix*, rotreghd 118, treaghdadh 22.

tréntógraim *a close pursuit* 124.

treórach *strong* 86.

tríamhain *sad* 28.

troig *a foot*, n. pl. troighthiu 118.

tromthocht *heavy (oppressive) silence* 20.

túairgim *I beat* 34.

tucaitt *cause* 2.

tucc 156, used here as 2 s. imperv. from dobiur *I give*, cf. Wb. 10ᵃ30.

tuilledh or tuillemh, inf. of tuillim *I earn, deserve* 2.

tulmhong *the surface, top* 114, cf. co ndechaid i tulmuing in talman, *Magh Rath*, p. 152.

turrag *act of searching* 22, from túrim *I search*.

úallach *proud* 44.

úarán *a well, a pool* 80, n. pl. úaránna 22.

úarsioc *cold frost*, g.s. úairseaca 90.

úathbás *mortal terror* 124.

uchbhadach *groaning, sighing* 100.

udmhaille *unsteadiness, motion* 14.

uilléngér *having a sharp angle or point* 10.

uinnes *the ash-tree* 66.

uiseóg *a skylark* 74.

urbhadach *baleful* 66.

urbaid *bale* 54.

urradhus 18 *chieftainship, authority*; see Glossary to the Laws.

urrainn *a point* 144.

ursoinn *threshold* 158.

INDEX OF FIRST LINES OF POEMS

INDEX OF PLACES AND TRIBES

Dairbre 86. Three places of this name are mentioned by Hogan (Onomasticon).

Dál Araidhe 2, 14, etc.

Doire Choluim Chille 34, Derry.

Druim Cirb 38.

Druim Damh 36.

Druim Fraoch 36.

Druim Gess 136 ; there is a townland named Drumgesh in p. of Balteagh, Bar. of Keenaght, Co. L.derry. There is another townland of the same name in Co. Cavan.

Druim Iarainn 134, perhaps D. Iairn, Drumherlin in Kilkieran district, Co. Kilkenny ; see Hogan, Onom.

Druim Lorgan 106, probably Lurgan, Co. Armagh.

Dún Cermna 92, on the Old Head of Kinsale.

Dún Máil 80.

Dún Rodairce 92 ; see Notes, p. 170.

Dún Sobairce 82, 92, 128 ; Dunseverick, Co. Antrim.

Echtge 118 ; see Sliabh E.

Eig g. Eghae 90, an island off the west coast of Scotland.

Ella 78, Duhallow, Co. Cork.

Es Dubhthaigh 104 ; see Notes, p. 171.

Es Rúaidh 142, Assaroe, on the Erne at Ballyshannon.

Ettan Tairb 44 ; see Notes, p. 166.

Fiodh Gaibhle 62, 82, 130 ; Feegile, in p. of Cionsast, near Portarlington.

Gabhal 130 ; the river Feegile, which joins the Barrow near Monasterevan

Gáille; see Crích G, also Glas G.

Glais Chille Cró 140.

Glais Gháille 120.

Glanamhrach 116 ; cf. Glendamrach, Táin, ed. Windisch, p. 651.

Glenn Aighle 76, Glenelly nr. Strabane.

Glenn Bolcáin 22, 26 etc. ; see Notes, p. 164.

Glenn Chíach 44 ; see Notes on G. Bolcain, p. 164.

Glenn Earcain 14, 16 ; see Notes, p. 162.

Glenn na nEachtach in Fiodh Gaibhle,' q.v. 62.

Íle 30, Islay.

Imlech Iobhair 86, Emly, Co. Tipperary.

Innis Bó Finni 142 ; Innisboffin off the coast of Mayo.

Innis Muredhaigh 90, Innismurray W. of Sligo.

Lagin 114.

Latharna 78, Larne.

Lethed Láin 80 ; perhaps Layd, Lr. Glenarm, Co. Antrim ; cf. Reeves, Eccl. Ant., p. 83 ; cf. Four Mast., A.D. 622.

Life 120 ; see Magh L.

Líne 76 ; see Magh L.

Loch Cúan 98, Strangford Lough.

Loch Diolair 34 ; Hogan, Onom. has Druim Dilair, at Belleek.

Loch Éirne 92, Lough Erne.

Loch Léin 78, Lakes of Killarney.

Loch Ribh 118, Lough Ree.

Lúachair Deadhaidh 132 ; Slieve Lougher, near Castleisland, Co. Kerry.

INDEX OF PERSONS

IRISH TEXTS SOCIETY

Cumann na Scríbheann nGaedhilge

1995

OBJECTS • SUBSCRIPTION
OFFICERS AND COUNCIL
LIST OF PUBLICATIONS

IRISH TEXTS SOCIETY,
c/o THE ROYAL BANK OF SCOTLAND PLC,
DRUMMONDS BRANCH, 49 CHARING CROSS,
ADMIRALTY ARCH, LONDON SW1A 2DX

IRISH TEXTS SOCIETY

The Irish Texts Society, founded in 1898, is established to advance public education by promoting the study of Irish literature, and as ancillary thereto to publish texts in the Irish language, accompanied by such introductions, English translations, glossaries and notes as may be deemed desirable.

MEMBERSHIP

Membership is open to individuals and libraries.

The Annual Subscription is payable on the 1st January.

INDIVIDUAL MEMBERSHIP:

*Annual subscription £9 stg., IR£9, US$15.
*Benefits: – Entitled to all new publications at a special price (approximately 50% of retail price).
– Any two back volumes at half price plus postage in any one year.
– Volumes supplied in response to orders.

LIBRARY MEMBERSHIP (two options:)

Option 1: Full Library Membership
(directly or through agents)

*Annual subscription £9 stg., IR£9, US$15.
*Benefits: – Entitled to all new publications at a special price (approximately 50% of retail price).
– Any two back volumes at half price plus postage in any one year.
– Volumes supplied in response to orders.

Option 2: Library Circulation Membership
(directly or through agents)

*No annual subscription
*Benefits: – All new publications automatically sent directly to library. Payment against invoice.
– Full retail price to apply. Society to bear the cost of postage.
– All existing publications available on request at full retail price. Society to bear the cost of postage. Payment against invoice.

Non-members can obtain he Society's publications by placing an order with their usual bookseller.

In case of difficulty, they should contact the Honorary Secretary of the Society or
ÁIS (Book Distribution Centre), 31 Fenian Street, Dublin 2, Ireland.

PRICES OF VOLUMES

(for currencies not quoted please use the sterling equivalent)

Volumes 5, 10, 12, 19, 20, 21, 24, 26, 27, 29, 29a, 38, 46, 47, 50, 53, 54, 55
£16 stg., IR£16, US $30

Volumes 11, 13, 17, 18, 22, 23, 25, 37, 40, 51, 52
£18 stg., IR£18, US $34

Volumes 3a, 4, 7, 8, 9, 15, 28, 30, 31, 32, 33, 34, 35, 39, 41, 42, 43, 44, 45, 48
£20 stg., IR£20, US $38

Volume 16
£24 stg., IR£24, US $44

Volume 6
£30 stg., IR£30, US $54

Volume 36, 56
£32 stg., IR£32, US $60

Volume 2, 14, 57
£34 stg., IR£34, US $64

Dinneen's IRISH-ENGLISH DICTIONARY
£20 stg., IR£20, US $38

Father Dinneen – His Dictionary and the Gaelic Revival
£2 stg., IR£2, US $5 (incl. postage)

SUBSIDIARY PUBLICATIONS SERIES
Nos. 1, 2 & 3
£3.50 stg., IR£3.50, US $7 (incl. postage)

SPECIALLY BOXED SETS
FORAS FEASA AR ÉIRINN (volumes 4, 8, 9, 15)
£120 stg., IR£120, US $225 (members – £60 stg., IR£60, US $115)

CINN-LAE AMHLAOIBH UÍ SHÚILEABHÁIN (volumes 30, 31, 32, 33)
£150 stg., IR£150, US $280 (members – £90 stg., IR£90, US $170)

POSTAGE PER VOLUME
Britain & Ireland: £2 stg., IR£2. Surface Mail U.S.A.: $6
All other countries: £3 stg. or equivalent

All communications should be addressed to the
Honorary Secretary, Irish Texts Society,
c/o The Royal Bank of Scotland plc, Drummonds Branch,
49 Charing Cross, Admiralty Arch, London SW1A 2DX.

LIST OF IRISH TEXTS SOCIETY'S
PUBLICATIONS

Out of Print   *Issued*

1* **Giolla an Fhiugha.** (The Lad of the Ferrule.)
   Eachtra Cloinne Rígh na h-Ioruaidhe.
   (Adventures of the Children of the King of Norway.)
   Edited by Professor Douglas Hyde, LL.D., D.Litt., M.R.I.A.
   ISBN 1 870 16601 9   1899

2 **Fled Bricrend.** (The Feast of Bricriu.)
   From Leabhar na h-Uidhre.
   Edited by George Henderson, M.A., Ph.D.
   ISBN 1 870 16602 7   1899

3* **Dánta Aodhagáin Uí Rathaille.**
   (The Poems of Egan O'Rahilly.) (See Volume 3a New Edition)
   Edited, chiefly from MSS. in Maynooth College by
   The Rev. P. S. Dinneen, D.Litt.   1900

3a **Dánta Aodhagáin Uí Rathaille.**
   (New Edition of the Poems of Egan O'Rahilly.) (See Vol. 3)
   Revised by Professor Tadgh Ó Donnchadha and
   The Rev. P. S. Dinneen, D.Litt.
   ISBN 1 870 16603 5   1911

4 **Foras Feasa ar Éirinn.** (History of Ireland.) Part I
   By Geoffrey Keating. (See Vols. 8, 9 and 15.)
   Edited by David Comyn, M.R.I.A.
   This volume contains Professor Breandán Ó Buachalla's
   new introduction (1987)
   ISBN 1 870 16604 3   1901

5* **Caithréim Conghail Chláiringhnigh**
   (The Martial Career of Conghal Clairinghneach.)
   Edited by The Rev. P. M. MacSweeney, M.A.
   ISBN 1 870 16605 1   1904

6 **Imtheachta Aeniasa: The Irish Aeneid.**
   The Irish Version, from the Book of Ballymote.
   Edited by The Rev. George Calder, B.D., D.Litt.
   This volume contains Dr. Erich Poppe's
   new introduction (1995)
   ISBN 1 870 16606 X   1907

THE SOCIETY'S IRISH-ENGLISH DICTIONARY
Edited by THE REV. P. S. DINNEEN, D.Litt.
(1340 pp.) ISBN 1 870 16600 0

Father Dinneen – His Dictionary and the Gaelic Revival
Text of a Lecture by Noel O'Connell

SUBSIDIARY PUBLICATIONS SERIES

1. **A New Introduction to Lebor Gabála Érenn,**
The Book of the Taking of Ireland,
Edited and Translated by R. A. Stewart Macalister, D.Litt.
by John Carey

2. **The Contention of the Bards (Iomarbhágh na bhFileadh)**
and its Place in Irish Political and Literary History
by Joep Leerssen
Professor of European Studies, University of Amsterdam

3. **The Irish Aeneid: Imtheachta Aeniasa**
– the Classical Epic from an Irish Perspective
by Erich Poppe

NEW VOLUMES AND REPRINTS

Volume 2: Fled Bricrend

Based on two separate motifs, the 'Hero's Portion' and the 'Champion's Bargain', the story of Bricriu's Feast links the Celts of Ireland with those of Western Europe who, according to the Greek writer Posidonius, also told these tales. Henderson's volume in this series remains the standard edition of this work.

Volume 6: Imtheachta Aeniasa: The Irish Aeneid

This is the only edition of the full text of the Irish version of the *Aeneid*. The Irish were among the first to provide vernacular translations of Latin classical texts, adapting them to local taste and displaying in the process a "proud confidence in the Irish techniques of story-telling". This adaptation was made in the fourteenth century. Originally edited by Rev. Dr. George Calder, a new introduction by Dr. Erich Poppe has been added to this reprint.

Volume 14: An Irish Astronomical Tract

This is the first, and only edition of a text adapted into Irish from a Latin translation made in the thirteenth century of an originally Arabic text. The Irish adaptation was probably made in the fourteenth or fifteenth century, a period in which the level of learning in Ireland was very high. This adaptation of a scientific text is an excellent example of its kind. Edited by Maura Power, the Volume was originally published by the Society in 1914.

Volume 56: Oidheadh Chloinne hUisneach – The Tragic Death of the Children of Uisneach

This is the Early Modern Irish version of what is sometimes referred to as 'The Deirdre Story'. It is one of the most popular of the late medieval Gaelic Romances, forming one of a group known as 'The Three Sorrows of Storytelling'. The editor, Dr. Caoimhín Mac Giolla Léith of University College, Dublin, has provided a lengthy introduction exploring the relationship between this text and other versions of the Deirdre story.

Volume 57: St. Finbarr of Cork: The Complete Life

'Where Finbarr taught, let Munster learn'. The Society's new volume for 1993, which is edited by Professor Pádraig Ó Riain of University College, Cork, will contain the most comprehensive edition ever attempted of an Irish saint's life. In his introduction, Professor Ó Riain, who has written extensively on the subject, traces the origins and development of Finbarr's recorded legend, including the story of his school.

INTRODUCING THE SOCIETY'S
SUBSIDIARY PUBLICATIONS SERIES

In the case of all publications in this series, the intention is to introduce the relevant text to a non-specialist readership in a way calculated to make the content more accessible and also to convey an application of its status and significance within its particular *genre*, literary, historical, etc. Additionally, in the case of texts already published by the Society, the intention of the Subsidiary Series (published in conjunction with the main series of texts) it to take the opportunity of a reprint to update the original introduction by noting the main developments in the field since the original publication. In such circumstances, these publications are included as additional introductory material. They are also published independently as moderately priced booklets with a view to making them available to interested readers who may not necessarily wish to acquire the reprint of the relevant text.

---

1. **A New Introduction to Lebor Gabála Érenn, The Book of the Taking of Ireland, Edited and Translated by R. A. Stewart Macalister, D.Litt.** by John Carey, formed the new introduction to the reprint of the Society's edition of the eleventh century text, originally published between 1939 and 1956. It provides a brief overview of the tradition of pseudohistory on which the text drew, and which it came to dominate; and it outlines the development of *LGÉ* scholarship down to the present day, placing Macalister's edition within this perspective.

---

2. **The Contention of the Bards (Iomarbhágh na bhFileadh) and its Place in Irish Political and Literary History** by Joep Leerssen, presents a reinterpretation of this compilation of early seventeenth century texts (forming volumes 20 and 21 in the Society's series), examining the political and literary context and themes of what he considers to be "a unique registration of an ancient literary tradition trying to come to terms with the drastic disintegration of both its social *raison d'être* and its cultural *Weltanschauung*".

---

3. **The Irish Aeneid (Imtheachta Aeniasa): the Classical Epic from an Irish Perspective** by Erich Poppe, considers this text as exemplifying an important aspect of medieval Irish literary culture. He explores such related aspects of the mentality of the literati as their attitudes towards foreign literary and historical works and their adaptation into the vernacular. He outlines some of the more important changes involved in the adaptation of this text and presents a new hypothesis about its function: that it was perceived as an historical narrative rather than as a literary epic or mere entertainment.

Cumann na Scríbheann nGaedhilge
IRISH TEXTS SOCIETY

IRISH TEXTS SOCIETY,
c/o THE ROYAL BANK OF SCOTLAND PLC,
DRUMMONDS BRANCH, 49 CHARING CROSS,
ADMIRALTY ARCH, LONDON SW1A 2DX

APPLICATION FOR LIBRARY MEMBERSHIP

To: The Honorary Secretary   **Date:** _____

I wish to apply for Full*/Circulation* Membership of the Irish Texts Society.
(*delete as appropriate)

Name of Library: _____
(BLOCK CAPITALS)
Address: _____

_____

Authorised by: _____

Title: _____

Date: _____

_____

Payment of Full Membership Subscription and Order for Volumes

Volume numbers _____

Amount for Volumes   £_____

Postage & Packing   £_____

Subscription   £_____

Total Amount   £_____

(Only complete the following if different from information given above
or if you are an existing member).

Name: _____

Address: _____

_____

Cumann na Scríbheann nGaedhilge
IRISH TEXTS SOCIETY

IRISH TEXTS SOCIETY,
c/o THE ROYAL BANK OF SCOTLAND PLC,
DRUMMONDS BRANCH, 49 CHARING CROSS,
ADMIRALTY ARCH, LONDON SW1A 2DX

APPLICATION FOR INDIVIDUAL MEMBERSHIP

To: The Honorary Secretary   **Date:** _____

I wish to apply for Individual Membership of the Irish Texts Society.

Name: _____
(BLOCK CAPITALS)
Address: _____

_____

Occupation: _____

Signature: _____

_____

Payment of Subscription and Order for Volumes

Volume numbers _____

Amount for Volumes   £_____

Postage & Packing   £_____

Subscription   £_____

Total Amount   £_____

(Only complete the following if different from information given above
or if you are an existing member).

Name: _____

Address: _____

_____

PRINTED BY ELO PRESS LTD., DUBLIN 8, IRELAND.